A Medieval Life

THE MIDDLE AGES SERIES

Ruth Mazo Karras, Series Editor
Edward Peters, Founding Editor

A complete list of books in the series
is available from the publisher.

A MEDIEVAL LIFE

Cecilia Penifader
and the World of English Peasants
Before the Plague

Judith M. Bennett

PENN

UNIVERSITY OF PENNSYLVANIA PRESS

PHILADELPHIA

The current work is a revised edition
of the book first published in 1998 as
A Medieval Life: Cecilia Penifader of Brigstock, c. 1295–1344.

Published by
University of Pennsylvania Press
Philadelphia, Pennsylvania 19104-4112
www.upenn.edu/pennpress

Printed in the United States of America on acid-free paper
1 3 5 7 9 10 8 6 4 2

A catalogue record for this book is available from the
Library of Congress
ISBN 978-0-8122-2469-6

CONTENTS

PREFACE

I am fortunate in this book: it was fun to write in its original form, and it has now been fun to revise. For this new edition, I have taken advantage of digitized editing to correct errors, add substantive comments, and smooth phrasing. But I have not changed the core of the book, and its chapters remain much as they were. The most extensive additions are in Chapter 1, where I have tried to prepare readers better for a book that is as much an introduction to medieval peasants as a life of one peasant woman (the slightly changed title works to the same purpose). Because we now live in a world where accusations of fake news can quickly morph into accusations of fake history, I have also included in Chapter 1 a brief discussion of historical methods and historiography, and I have added to each chapter a sidebar on how historians know what we know. I hope these examples—on subjects like puberty, climate change, and DNA—will bring into better focus the methods, interpretations, and collegial arguments that lie behind the "received wisdom" provided here.

The illustrations have been entirely reworked so that most medieval images are from a single source: the famous Luttrell Psalter, created not far from Cecilia and during her lifetime. The Luttrell Psalter provides a coherent visual program, and because many of its images are available online in full color, readers can easily investigate them further. A simple search under "luttrell psalter" will turn up a plethora of online images, but a good place to start is the British Library's own treatment of the volume, found at https://www.bl.uk /collection-items/the-luttrell-psalter. The images are reproduced here by kind permission of the British Library, © British Library, Add Ms 42130, with the folio citations given under each image.

Suggestions for further reading have been fully updated.

CHAPTER I

Ordinary People

Crusaders marching off to reclaim the Holy Land; kings besieging castles with archers and men-at-arms; bishops celebrating Masses in new cathedrals; merchants haggling for bargains at fairs and markets. These are the people whose stories are told in most histories of the Middle Ages—and these people were, to be sure, important movers-and-shakers in their time. But they were also atypical. Most medieval people were not knights, kings, churchmen, or merchants. Most (more than nine out of ten) were peasants who eked out hard livings from the land. Yet even our modern dramas of medieval-like worlds almost forget this vast peasant population. The *small-folk* of the Seven Kingdoms in *Game of Thrones* are mere background, mentioned passingly as dirty, dull, and mildly dangerous; even the free, unsettled, and foreign *wildlings* get more respect. In *Lord of the Rings, halflings* are cleaner, smarter, and more benevolent, but they are hobbits, not humans. Ignored in elite histories and dehumanized in dramatic fantasies, medieval peasants have mostly disappeared from our imagination. This book seeks to right the balance by telling the story of the English peasantry through the life of one very real, very human, and very medieval peasant: Cecilia Penifader who lived in the English midlands in the decades just before the Black Death (1347–1349).

Why should we care about peasants? The simple fact that we have turned medieval peasants into filthy smallfolk and hobbits with hairy feet suggests we had better take a second look. *Peasant* is not a word that we usually apply today to people who cultivate crops in first-world countries—instead, we call these people *farmers* and *farm laborers*. We use *peasant* to describe cultivators— small cultivators—in less developed economies. In Europe, peasants are understood to have disappeared with modernization, a process that, in the phrasing of one famous book on the subject, made nineteenth-century peasants into modern Frenchmen. In North America, European colonists are deemed to have been transformed—by virtue of their migration and resettlement—from peasants into farmers. In China, where perhaps 50 percent of the population were peasants c. 1950, economists now argue about whether there are any peasants left at all. Yet societies of small, subsistence cultivators persist and even thrive today, especially in Central and South America, in sub-Saharan Africa, and in south Asia. To put this another way, peasants and peasant economies are part of our present as well as our past. If we think of today's peasants as smallfolk or halflings, we risk profoundly misunderstanding our contemporary global economy.

For historians of medieval Europe, the importance of peasants derives from two particular ideas about humans and human society. First, ordinary people have mattered in the making of history. U.S. History provides a good example. Any general history of the twentieth-century U.S. rightly talks about extraordinary individuals like Henry Ford, Al Capone, Eleanor Roosevelt, Billy Graham, Rosa Parks, and Bill Gates, but it also describes how the lives of ordinary people changed between 1900 and 2000—better housing and diets, more education, changing sexual mores, and the like. And it also considers how ordinary people changed the course of history, sometimes through collective protest (as with the Vietnam War and civil rights) and sometimes through everyday, private decisions (as with diminished birthrates). Ordinary people make history too—and as we shall see, this was as true of medieval peasants as of modern citizens.

Second, historians understand that history is richer when seen from the margins. It is easy to forget about medieval peasants (the margin) if you start in royal courts and wealthy monasteries (the center). But it is hard to overlook monarchs and monks if you start from peasant cottages. This might sound abstract, but it is concrete and real. For a modern example, consider professional sports. Team owners and players stand at the center of this industry, but if we think about sports only from their perspective (worries about revenues, salaries, and advertising contracts), we can almost lose sight of the fans without whom there would be no revenue-producing leagues and championships. If we flip the perspective and look at professional sports from the viewpoint of the fans (exciting games and charismatic athletes), we never risk forgetting the owners and players, who are simply too rich and famous to ignore. Fans might be on the margins of the sports business, but adopting their perspective helps us remember that professional sports are fundamentally about entertainment.

Cecilia Penifader

By looking at medieval peasants, then, we can see both their rural world and the broader medieval society of which they were a critical part. We stand on the muddy margins with peasants and, looking upward and inward, we can better understand not only poor peasants but also prosperous churchmen, knights, and merchants, all of whom relied on peasant labor. Cecilia Penifader, who will be our guide to the medieval countryside, stood—as a woman and an unmarried one at that—on the edges of her own community. We know a lot more about Cecilia than most other peasants, but a lot less than we would like. Unlike persons featured in modern biographies, Cecilia has left no diaries we can read, no houses we can walk through, no friends or family to be interviewed. Yet the few dozen extant details of her life—each a remarkable and precious survival from a society long past—make her particular story a gateway into the world in which she lived. When paid guides take tourists by foot or bus around cities like London, Paris, or Berlin, they always personalize their spiels by throwing in a few tidbits about themselves (hometown, favorite beer, and the like), both to amuse their audiences and also to make the big city more human and real. Cecilia Penifader will be this sort of guide for us; we will learn the known facts of her particular life, but we will also walk with her through the broader world of medieval villagers and **villages**.

Cecilia Penifader was born at the end of the thirteenth century; 1297 seems the most likely year. At that time, peasants were just beginning to pass surnames from one generation to the next. Cecilia's derives from *Pennyfather*, and it suggests that Cecilia's paternal grandfather or great-grandfather was known for his miserly habits. Perhaps the penny-pinching of her ancestors explains, in part, the prosperity of her family. Compared to knights and ladies, Cecilia's parents were poor peasants, but compared to other peasants, her parents numbered among the well-off. As a result, Cecilia grew up in a better-built cottage and with a better diet than many of her poorer neighbors. She also grew up with more siblings than most: three brothers and four sisters. When she was about twenty years old, Cecilia acquired her first bit of land in Brigstock, and for the next twenty-seven years, the records of Brigstock tell a great deal about how she acquired and used her various meadows and fields. They also reveal that she was known to her family and friends as Cissa (a name that the clerks sometimes used instead of the Latinized Cecilia). These same rolls also report that Cecilia sometimes stole grain from her neighbors, sometimes argued with others, and sometimes owned animals that went astray. She never married, but she lived for about a decade next door to one brother, and she later shared a household for about five years with another brother. When she was about forty-five years old, Cecilia fell ill, and after more than a year of poor health, she died in 1344. Just before her death, she tried to give her landholdings to three young people (including one nephew and one niece), but after long and acrimonious arguments, her sister Christina inherited her properties. This is the bare outline of Cecilia's life, but the medieval archives of Brigstock tell much more.

Like other medieval peasants, Cecilia Penifader left no diaries, letters, or other personal writings. Occasionally a bright and lucky peasant learned to read and write, but most peasants were illiterate. Of the few who gained literacy, almost all were men. The most famous was Robert Grosseteste, born of poor parents about 1168, who escaped his background so thoroughly that he taught at Oxford University and rose to become bishop of Lincoln. Yet Robert Grosseteste was exceptional. He was so intelligent, some sources say, that his surname began as a nickname—"large head"—for a precociously clever boy. Still, his cleverness might have come to nothing. If his parents had needed him at home or if his **bailiff** had opposed his education, he might never have left the place of his birth. So the educational success of Robert Grosseteste is the exception that proves the rule. Peasants, usually unable to read or write, have left no direct testimonies about their hopes, their fears, their delights, or their disappointments. Even Robert Grosseteste—who wrote a great deal about matters both philosophical and practical—never thought it worth his while to describe the world of his humble youth.

As a result, we know about peasants and their lives indirectly—from the writings of their social superiors. In the tripartite view of society that was popular by the High Middle Ages, peasants rested at the bottom of **three orders**. As "those who work" (in Latin, *laboratores*), peasants supported people more privileged—"those who pray" (*oratores*) and "those who fight" (*pugnatores*). Each of these three orders ideally helped the other, with clergy contributing prayers and knights providing protection, but the mutuality of the system was more ideal than real. Also, the three groups were not equal. A peasant might have benefited from the prayers of a nun or from the protection offered by a knight, but a peasant was deemed to do work of lesser value and to be a less worthy person (see Figure 1). Born into this unexalted state, a peasant's lot was to

Figure 1. Lords and Peasants. The mutual support of the "Three Orders" was a nice idea, but this image offers a different view. The two hooded peasants on the left are angry—one crossing his arms, and the other holding a tool (a yoke?) and brandishing a glove as a sign of challenge. The object of their discontent looks to be a bailiff or other manorial official (he wears no humble hood), and he is pointing (in justification? or in blame-shifting?) toward a fourth person who approaches with something (a document?) in hand. Some images in the Luttrell Psalter are easy to decipher, but others are, as here, hard to nail down. The bleeding through of images from the other side of the page (here, a fantastical creature with a dog's head and huge beak) does not help. Yet the Psalter's depictions of rural life are lively and beautiful—and well worth looking at, again and again. (British Library, Luttrell Psalter, folio 197v.)

labor for the benefit of others. This was unfortunate for peasants, but fortunate for historians. Because peasants were important economic assets, both "those who pray" and "those who fight" kept careful records of peasant doings. Today, we can use these records to reconstruct the life of an ordinary woman who was born more than seven hundred years ago—and also to learn about the world in which she grew up, matured, and died.

How Do We Know What We Think We Know?

Before we consider the documents in which we find Cecilia Penifader and her world, let us consider history and what it can and cannot claim. History and historians once embraced a noble dream, a dream that historians told the truth about the past. Like a god sitting on high, a historian looked back at dead people and wrote The Truth about their lives. Today, truth seems a lot more elusive. Globalism and multiculturalism have taught us that perspective matters—that, say, the voyages of Columbus brought opportunity for Europeans and devastation for Native Americans. Postmodernism has taught us to doubt all truth claims. And social media have produced an epidemic of so-called fake news through which we wade every day, sometimes every hour. Instead of the certain truths of the twentieth century, we now seem to trust nothing and nobody.

The causes of our twenty-first-century skepticism are new, but skepticism is not. Medieval students, who loved music just as much as students today, sang this complaint,

> Bad faith and deception grow like weeds
> And blatant lying too,
> Which steals away the very seeds
> Of all that once was true.

Lies and fake news are serious worries, but they have one positive effect: they encourage skepticism which is almost always a good thing, especially among students and voters. Modern life demands that we ask all the time: How do we know what we think we know?

In history, what we know relies on the interplay between two different streams of knowledge: facts and interpretation. Every historian aspires to add new facts to what we know about the past, usually by finding new sources (a diary in an attic!), or using new technologies (DNA analysis!), or simply reading old sources with new questions. For example, when I was a graduate student, I looked at a well-known but little-studied payment required whenever a **serf** woman married—the payment was called **merchet**. I found a register that listed hundreds of merchets; I created a database from them; and my analysis allowed me to introduce a new fact to history—that is, that young brides often possessed enough cash to pay this fine themselves.

All historians are fact-finders, and students of history must, of course, get their facts right. Interpretation—the thinking and arguing side of history, where historians discuss what facts actually mean—is just as important. Since some brides paid their own merchets, does this mean that they worked and saved on their own before marriage (much like many women do today)? Were they therefore the economic equals of their husbands? Is merchet-payment a sign of women's power (they had the cash to pay their own obligations) or a sign of their oppression (merchets were not required of bridegrooms)? Historians thrive on debate—it makes us think harder, read our sources better, and produce new facts. So we almost never agree on a single interpretation for very long. But this does not mean that interpretation is mere bias or opinion. Interpretation must be reasonable, logical, and fact-based. We can argue about what bride-paid merchets meant, but we cannot deny the evidence, and we cannot use the evidence to claim what it cannot prove. It would be poor thinking, for example, to argue that because brides sometimes paid their own merchets, medieval marriages were love matches.

Some historians miss the old noble dream of a god-like history. I do not. By abandoning claims that History = Truth, professors today are, oddly enough, more truthful about what we can and cannot know. Uncertainty can be scary and it can also be abusively deployed, but humility in the face of the world's marvels simply makes sense. It discourages dogmatism, encourages wisdom, and is steadied by the *received wisdom* (or common knowledge) on which all historians agree, at least for a time.

This book, like all history books and especially history textbooks, relies on the received wisdom of history—that is, it relies on the knowledge of medieval peasant life that has been forged by generations of fact-finding and interpretive debate. In this regard, *English* rural history has a huge advantage. Every nation in Europe has its own traditions of rural history. For example, French historians have focused on the oppressive powers of local lords and their castles; Spanish historians have studied the technologies of "dry farming" (mostly Christian) and irrigated farming (mostly Muslim); Polish historians have tackled differences between German settler communities and established Slavic communities; and Italian historians have dwelt on relations between the great city-states of the peninsula and their rural hinterlands. Peasants are present in all these inquiries, but passively so; peasants appear as mere background to histories of feudal power, technology, migration, and urbanism. Not so in English history where, since the publication in 1942 of George Homans' *English Villagers of the Thirteenth Century*, peasant lives have been intensively studied. Historians since have studied how English peasants farmed, how they were housed, what they ate, how they organized their families, their land, their communities . . . and a host of other topics that we will take up in this book. The stark facts of Cecilia Penifader's life have much fuller meaning, in other words, because we can place her within a common narrative about the medieval peasantry that is especially deep and rich for England.

Received wisdom is the starting point for all students of history (and their textbooks), but the dynamic workings of history—the new facts and new debates—are the very heartbeat of the discipline. I cannot send each of you into

the archives to discover the fun of deciphering old documents or send you to
conferences to watch historians battle over opposing interpretations. But I have
provided glimpses of the fact-finding and fact-interpreting pleasures of history
in a brief sidebar in each chapter. These let you see historians at work—digging
up new sources, offering new interpretations, and sometimes stumbling into
epic failures. I hope you enjoy them.

Manors and Manorial Records

So. How do we know what we think we know about medieval peasants? Clues
about how privileged people in the Middle Ages regarded peasants can be found
in their courtly songs, sarcastic proverbs, nasty jokes, and pious sermons.
Knights and ladies were fond of songs known as *pastourelles* that told, among
other things, about how easy it was for knights to have sex with peasant women
or, failing that, to rape them; monks and students enjoyed jokes that portrayed
peasants as ludicrously dumb and foolish; and priests, **friars**, and bishops
preached sermons that depicted "those who work" as objects of pity, charity,
and disgust. Even *Piers Plowman*, a sympathetic portrayal of rural life written a
few decades after Cecilia Penifader's death, portrayed the peasant's lot as hard
and pitiable. These literary texts are useful for understanding the often astound-
ingly negative attitudes of elites toward peasants, but they tell little about the
peasants themselves. For information about the daily lives of peasants, the most
abundant and most useful sources are legal and economic documents that report on the administration of **manors**.

    Manorialism was the economic system whereby peasants supported the
landowning elite. On manors, in other words, the working lives of peasants in-
tersected with the financial needs of their social superiors. Manors consisted of
land and tenants, and they were common in regions with fertile soils that rewarded intensive cultivation: southeast and central England, northern France,
western Germany, and certain regions of southern Europe, such as the Rhone and
Po valleys. The land of the manor belonged to a landowner, the lord (*dominus*)
or lady (*domina*) of the manor. (Roughly 10 percent of manors were held by
women, mostly widows.) Some manorial land, called the **demesne**, was reserved for direct use of the landowner; most was held by peasants who owed
various rents and dues for their holdings.

    Manorialism first developed in the Early Middle Ages, and manors were
originally worked mostly by slaves and other dependent tenants. Some were de-

scendants of the *coloni* who had once worked the villas of the Roman Empire; others had been forced into a dependent state by violence and war; and still others had surrendered themselves into bondage in return for protection. By the eleventh and twelfth centuries, slavery was disappearing in most of Europe, thanks to a combination of Church policies, opposition from peasants, and practical concessions on the part of the landowning elite. By Cecilia's time, most manors were worked by **free peasants** and **serfs** (in England, **villeins**). Freedom or serfdom was determined at birth; if born of parents who were serfs, a boy or girl was bound to serfdom. Serfs were not slaves; they could not be bought and sold at will, and they were protected by custom (that is, they were obliged to serve their manor as their parents had served—and no more). But because serfs were obliged not only to stay put but also to supply labor services, they provided landowners with an unusually exploitable work force for the cultivation of the demesne. In England in 1300, about half of all peasants were serfs and the other half were free.

As manors developed, they grew more economically complex. In the Early Middle Ages, manors generated profit directly: the crops peasants cultivated in the fields; the goods they produced in manorial workshops; and the rents they paid for the plots they tilled on their own. By 1300, lords and ladies profited from manors in additional ways. First, they took the produce off the demesne and either consumed or sold it. The demesne, once cultivated by slaves, was by then usually cultivated by serfs and wage-laborers. Second, they collected rents from peasants who held plots of land from the manor. Tenants paid rent in cash, in kind (perhaps a chicken at Christmas and a few eggs at Easter), and, if serfs, in labor (under the direction of the manorial officers, serfs sowed, weeded, and harvested the demesne). Third, lords and ladies profited from legal rights that had accrued to manors over the course of centuries. Tenants had to attend manorial courts, where their small fines and fees produced valuable income; they were often obliged to pay for the use of manorial mills, ovens, winepresses, and other such facilities; and they had to pay a variety of small charges when they married, when they traveled, and even when they died.

Free peasants and serfs endured the burdens of manorialism because they had little choice. The economic privileges of "those who pray" and "those who fight" were buttressed by considerable military, political, and social powers. In this regard, manorialism was complemented by the culture and power of the military elite. Between the ninth and eleventh centuries, a cohort of warriors had emerged in Europe distinguished by their skill in fighting on horseback, their close ties to one another, their hereditary claims to knightly status, and their control of the land. Historians have since coined the term **feudalism** to describe the culture, relationships, and rules by which these warriors lived, but this word often generates more confusion than clarity. *Feudalism* is a modern word (a medieval person would probably have talked about *vassalage*), and the term implies more order, system, and standardization than was the case. Worse yet, feudalism has two distinctive and confusing meanings today. Some scholars use it to describe the general economy of the Middle Ages; to them, feudalism is a stage of economic development in which serfs on manors were forced to labor on behalf of a warrior class. This stage was seen by Karl Marx as falling between slavery and capitalism. Many students encounter this definition of feudalism in economics and sociology courses. Yet most medievalists use feudalism in the more limited sense employed in this book; that is, to describe the customs and relationships of an elite who governed ordinary people by virtue of their military, political, and social power. In the England into which Cecilia was born at the end of the thirteenth century, this small feudal elite, headed by a king, ruled the land. They waged war and negotiated peace; they judged and punished wrongdoers; they decided who could pass through their territories. In short, they governed by virtue of their wealth, aristocratic birth, and military might. Peasants were taught to respect the authority of the feudal elite as natural and good, but respectful demeanor was a practical matter too. Faced with a powerful and arrogant knight, Cecilia—or any other peasant—knew that deference and obedience were the safest behaviors.

To profit from manors, lords and ladies needed not only to wield power effectively but also to manage their manors efficiently. In the late eighth century, Charlemagne, king of the Franks, had sought to compile detailed lists of royal manors, and in the ninth century, registers of lands, tenants, and income were kept for some ecclesiastical estates. But it was in England in the thirteenth century that systems of manorial record-keeping more fully developed. There, an array of stewards, bailiffs, **reeves**, clerks, and other manorial officers supervised manors, and they kept copious records to prove that they were conscientious and honest administrators (and, in some cases, to hide their cheating). These records tell a great deal about the peasants with whom manorial officers dealt on a regular basis. *Custumals* detailed the customs of a manor. In Brigstock, for example, a custumal specified that a sick person who gave away land had to be strong enough to leave his or her house after the gift; if the grantor died without so doing, the transfer was invalid. This rule ensured that no dying persons could be pressured to preempt, on their deathbeds, the claims of heirs. *Surveys* and *rentals* listed the tenants of the manor, telling what lands they held and, in the case of rentals, what rents (in cash, kind, or labor) they owed. No such records survive for Brigstock in Cecilia's day, but a rental from 1416—about seventy years after her death—suggests that her family fortunes had plummeted; not a single Penifader was listed among the tenants of the manor. *Account rolls* noted the expenses and profits of a manor, usually for a year starting at Michaelmas (29 September), the traditional end of the harvest season. No complete accounts survive for medieval Brigstock, but, if they did, they might tell about the stipends given to manorial servants or the wages paid to workers hired on a daybasis to do specific tasks. *Court rolls* describe the proceedings of manorial courts, which dealt with a wide variety of contracts, disputes, and petty crimes. These courts usually met either twice a year or, as in Brigstock, every three weeks. After clerks finished writing down all the court business, they rolled the parchment up for easy transport and storage—hence, "court rolls" (see Figure 2). When court rolls survive in abundance—as they do for Brigstock in the late thirteenth and early fourteenth centuries—they offer unparalleled information about crime, controversy, and commerce among medieval peasants.

During Cecilia Penifader's lifetime, almost all members of the feudal and ecclesiastical elite in England relied on manors and peasants for some of their support. When kings, queens, barons, ladies, bishops, monks, and nuns sat down to supper, they ate food produced by the labor of serfs on manorial demesnes. When they purchased fine silks from the East, built new houses in stone, or arranged to have wine shipped from Gascony, they spent money accumulated from the rents, fees, and fines of their manorial tenants, free and serf. Yet the manor was not the only point of fiscal intersection between peasants and their social superiors. Monarchs held manors of their own, but they also claimed some authority over all peasants within their realms—even those who lived on manors owned by others. In England, the king could tax all peasants, could compel male peasants to join his armies, and could even force peasants to sell him animals or food at set prices. Cecilia Penifader was unfortunate to live in a time of particularly harsh royal exactions, a time when the three Edwards—Edward I (1272–1307), his son Edward II (1307–1327), and his grandson Edward III (1327–1377)—turned repeatedly to ordinary peasants to find money, men, and food for their wars in Wales, Scotland, and France.

Bishops, monks, and nuns were also supported by manors, and like monarchs, they had further interests in the peasants who lived outside their episcopal

Figure 2. A Court Roll. This court roll for Brigstock in 1314–1315 is composed of sixteen parchment membranes stitched end to end, and it is more than nineteen feet in length. It is open to show the records of a single court. The entries are in highly abbreviated Latin, and the notes in the left margin mostly track income generated by court business. Fifty-five rolls (containing more than five hundred court sessions) survive for Brigstock manor between 1287 and 1348. (Northamptonshire Record Office, Box X364A, roll 26.)

palaces and monastic walls. In common with all medieval Christians, peasants were compelled to **tithe**, which meant that each year one-tenth of their harvested grain, new lambs, and other produce was given to the Church. (Peasant tenants on Church manors were not cut any slack—they paid both rent and tithe.) Peasants were also subject to Church law, and, if brought into an ecclesiastical court for fornication, slander, bigamy, or other offenses that fell under Church supervision, they could face fines and physical punishments. Some peasants so angered Church officers that they even endured excommunication, that is, they were cut off from participation in the sacraments and community of the Church. In January 1299, for example, the bishop of Lincoln ordered the excommunication of everyone in Brigstock who had participated in a robbery the week before. The thieves had secretly entered the chamber of Hugh Wade, a lodger in the house of a local widow, and stolen money and goods out of his strongbox. (The bishop probably responded so strongly to this theft because Hugh Wade was in his service.)

It was in the interest of monarchs and ecclesiastics to keep good records of these additional dealings with peasants. Wherever tax lists, military requisitions, ecclesiastical court books, or bishops' registers survive, they provide further information about the lives of ordinary people in the medieval countryside. As with manorial documentation, so too with these other types of records: they are especially full and abundant for England in the thirteenth and fourteenth centuries.

To sum up, we can study medieval peasants because their labor was so important in supporting the Church, the monarchy, and the landed elite. And we can especially study peasants *in England* because the archives there are especially full. In some cases, the superiority of English archives stems from the more careful record-keeping of its administrators, but, in most cases, it has been a matter of survival through the centuries. Thanks to a strong legal system, a relatively stable social order, and a hefty dose of luck, England's medieval archives have survived especially well. In France, for example, many medieval archives were destroyed during the French Revolution, and in Scotland, untold thousands of state documents were lost when a ship carrying them sank in 1661. History is built on evidence, and if there is little evidence, historians have much less to study and much less to say. Fortunately, the extant English archives allow us to say a great deal indeed about English peasants, and from that foundation, we can sometimes see enough in other archives to know how the English peasantry matched or differed from the peasantries of France, Scotland, Spain, Germany, Italy, and elsewhere.

Although all records pertaining to manors and peasants are useful, the most useful are manorial court rolls. Peasants brought most of their legal business to these courts. Although free peasants could take some complaints to county or royal courts and serious crimes (such as murder and rape) often had to be judged in higher courts, it was to manorial courts that most rural disputes, crimes, inheritances, and contracts were reported. The court records for the manor of Brigstock survive in exceptional number for the time of Cecilia Penifader: 549 courts held between 1287 and 1348.

It is important to recognize, at the outset, that manorial courts were different from modern courts. Today, most of us go to court only when forced by special crisis or summons; in the fourteenth century, Cecilia Penifader and other tenants in Brigstock attended court every three weeks, accepting its meetings as an ordinary and expected obligation. Today, we usually go to court for unpleasant reasons, especially to resolve conflicts or crimes; Cecilia and her neighbors certainly raised such difficulties in their court, but they also registered agreements, exchanged land, and agreed on ordinances. Today, courts are dominated by professional lawyers without whom almost nothing can be done; the peasants of Brigstock were so fully conversant with the rules of their courts that they seldom needed specialists to help them. The meeting of a manorial court was so ordinary a part of life in Brigstock that most people probably felt as comfortable in court as they did in church or in the lanes in front of their houses. Since there were no purpose-built court buildings, peasants gathered, on court day, at their local church, in the lane, on the green, or at some other familiar location.

In its origins, a manorial court was an instrument of seignorial power, a way for the lord or lady to control the manor's tenants and to extract income from them. In actual practice, especially by Cecilia's day, peasants used manorial courts for their own purposes, and the courts reflected local customs as well as the landowner's interests. In a sense, the manor was the institution that convened the courts and kept records of the proceedings, but another institution, the peasant community, helped to determine what actually happened at any meeting. If jurors did not want to tell the court that a young woman had broken into the manorial sheepfold, then she could get away unpunished. If local custom determined that youngest sons inherited their fathers' lands instead of oldest sons, then no lord or lady could go against that tradition in court. If tenants were unhappy about an action taken by a manorial officer, they would not hesitate to complain in court and even seek redress. So when Cecilia Penifader and her neighbors gathered every three weeks for the meeting of the Brigstock court, they were unlikely to be awed or alienated by the proceedings. Some peasants were more active and powerful in the court than others, but most probably saw it as a necessary burden and a useful forum; through it, they resolved conflicts, punished assaults and crimes, registered inheritances and transfers of land, checked that brewers and bakers did not cheat their customers, recorded loans and other contracts, and otherwise managed the day-to-day life of their community.

Brigstock and Cecilia Penifader

In the early fourteenth century, there were thousands of rural communities scattered across the landscape of Europe. Neighboring villages could be quite different from each other, and differences between the regions of Europe were even more striking. As a result, Brigstock, the community in which Cecilia Penifader lived for almost fifty years, certainly does not represent the Medieval Manor. In Italy, for example, settlement was more continuous with Roman traditions than was the case in England; manorialism relied less on labor services and more on cash rents; and drier soils required different tools, different crop rotations, and different crops. In the Holy Roman Empire, for another example, as German lords sought to colonize lands east of the Elbe in the eleventh and twelfth centuries, they offered special privileges to attract settlers; as a result, peasants in these newly colonized areas enjoyed extensive freedoms and low rents that would have been the envy of their counterparts elsewhere. Brigstock does not even represent English communities, for to the north of Brigstock lay areas where hamlets were more common than villages and manorial authority was lightly felt; to the east lay East Anglia, renowned for its intensive and sophisticated techniques of farming; and in Devon and Cornwall to the southwest, there were few communities that closely resembled Brigstock in either manorial structure or economy.

In much the same way, Cecilia cannot represent the Medieval Peasant. Many peasants were poorer than she; many were male, rather than female; and most married, but she never did. No one village or person can be typical of such European-wide diversity, but Brigstock and Cecilia were, at least, not wildly atypical. Brigstock, located in the heart of the most manorialized part of England (see Map 1), provides an especially fine example of the intersection of manor, village, and **parish**, and Cecilia's life, supplemented by the lives of her married brothers and sisters, offers an unusually clear view of the opportunities

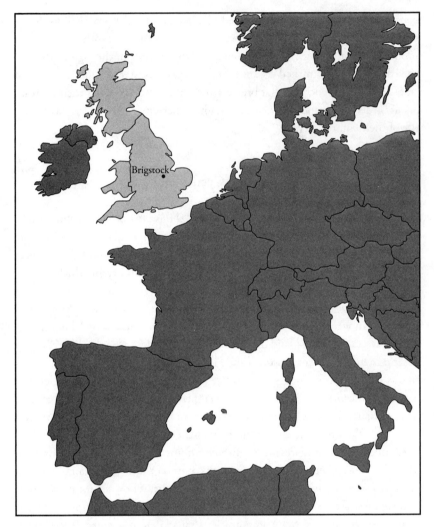

Map 1 The Location of Brigstock in Europe.

and choices that women and men faced in rural communities. Moreover, Brigstock and Cecilia are exceptionally well documented, a fact of no small importance when studying humble people who lived many centuries ago. Still,
Cecilia's life is best read as a case study, not a universal example. In some ways, she
was quite common, average, and perhaps even representative; in other ways, her
story was uniquely her own. Sometimes typical and sometimes not, Cecilia's life

allows us to approach, in an intimate way, the ordinary lives and communities of medieval peasants.

Brigstock is located in the English midlands, about seventy-five miles north of London. Today, Brigstock lies in open country, but in the Middle Ages, it rested in the heart of Rockingham Forest, a royal preserve for hunting. For Cecilia, this meant that near her house stood not only fields and pastures but also a royal hunting lodge, woodlands, and parks maintained by the king's foresters. These officers allowed the people of Brigstock to use the woods and parks in some agreed-upon ways, such as collecting fallen wood for fuel and feeding their pigs in the woods. Yet the king's foresters also stood ready to arrest any peasant who tried to hunt game in Rockingham Forest or attempted to clear bits of the forest to bring new lands under the plow. In 1255, for example, the foresters searched for Hugh Swartgar and Henry Tulke of Brigstock, suspected of placing nets in the forest for catching hares; both men were eventually caught, judged guilty, and imprisoned. The economies of most forest communities were diverse and flexible, and Brigstock's economy was no exception. Cecilia's neighbors supported themselves primarily by farming and animal husbandry, but they also profited from poaching, charcoal-making, and fishing. Some also worked in trades such as carpentry, thatching, and brewing, and a few seem to have taken on industrial work, such as making pots, weaving yarn into cloth, and quarrying stone.

In Cecilia's day, Brigstock consisted of three overlapping institutions: village, manor, and parish. The village of Brigstock was the oldest of the three, for long before there were manors or parishes, the peasants of Europe had settled themselves on the land. There is some evidence of Roman activity in Brigstock, but it was probably during the period of Germanic settlement in the fifth and sixth centuries that people first came to the area, settled in a cluster of houses, and began to clear the surrounding fields. When these first settlers built their houses huddled together in a central location in Brigstock, they formed one common sort of rural community in the Middle Ages—a *nucleated village*. Elsewhere, peasants established different types of settlements. Some lived on farmsteads scattered through the countryside, each settled on its own plot of land, and some lived in small hamlets, with a few households in a single location. These alternative forms of settlement were common in England and Europe, especially in regions of difficult terrain or poor soil. Brigstock's nucleated village was typical of settlement in the English midlands, and it was found in other parts of northern Europe where soils were rich enough to support many families at once.

The manor of Brigstock was much bigger than the village itself. It was also an ancient manor, more than two hundred years old by Cecilia's time, for it was described in the **Domesday Book,** a realm-wide survey of manors, landowners, and tenants completed in 1086 for William the Conqueror. Brigstock manor then comprised almost all of the village of Brigstock and parts of three other settlements—much of Stanion to the northwest, and small parts of Geddington to the southwest and Islip to the southeast. Stanion was particularly important, for it had been created, sometime before 1086, when men and women from Brigstock decided to carve out new lands deeper in the forest. In Cecilia Penifader's time, Stanion and Brigstock remained closely tied. Her parents held lands in both villages, as did almost all of their children once they grew up.

Brigstock was also part of a parish, and like Brigstock manor, the parish was bigger than Brigstock village. A church dedicated to St. Andrew stood at the center of Brigstock, and it was an important focal point for the community. People worshiped in the church of St. Andrew not only on Sunday but also on holy days. Their faith was mixed with pre-Christian customs and practices, and it was profound and heartfelt; there were no atheists in medieval Brigstock, nor in any other medieval villages or towns. Moreover, as the biggest and sturdiest building in Brigstock, the church of St. Andrew was a place of work and play, as well as a place of worship. People held meetings in its **nave**, stored grain in its driest corners, and sold goods in its churchyard. The priest assigned to the church of St. Andrew had numerous and important duties, but he also had a second set of responsibilities: the church of St. Peter in Stanion was designated as a dependent chapel within the parish of Brigstock. In other words, the parish of Brigstock embraced two villages, Brigstock and Stanion, and two churches, St. Andrew's and St. Peter's. For most purposes, the people of Stanion worshiped in their own church, but on major feast days such as Christmas, Easter, and the feast of St. Andrew, they probably walked the few miles to Brigstock to celebrate in St. Andrew's, the main church of the parish.

For Cecilia Penifader, these institutions—village, manor, and parish—were very real. She agreed with other villagers on when to plant and when to harvest; she paid fines and fees at the manorial court; she rendered her tithe to the parish. It might often have seemed to her as if village, manor, and parish blended one into another. Parish funds could be used to repair a village bridge; manorial courts met on rainy days in the nave of St. Andrew's church; villagers worked together to meet manorial obligations. But the three entities did not neatly coincide, and, with its messily overlapping boundaries of manor, parish, and village, Brigstock was typical of many rural communities, in England and elsewhere. As economic and ecclesiastical districts overlaid upon the already settled patterns of villages, the boundaries of manors and parishes were drawn according to their own logic. In a world where villages had been settled by peasants, manors created to support the landed elite, and parishes drawn to care for Christian souls, boundaries of the three were sometimes coterminous, but often not.

The Plan of the Book

Most of the illustrations in the book come from drawings in the margins of the Luttrell Psalter, a devotional book created during Cecilia's lifetime for Sir Geoffrey Luttrell, lord of the manor of Irnham in Lincolnshire, located about thirty miles north of Brigstock. The Luttrell Psalter (a "psalter" is a copy of the biblical book of Psalms) is justly famed for its depictions of rural life (including precise renditions of plows, carts, and windmills), and full-color versions are readily available for you to examine online. These drawings offer unparalleled glimpses of ordinary people doing ordinary things, but they sometimes depict peasants fancifully (showing peasants' clothes as brightly dyed) and rudely (depicting peasants with rough features and unkempt hair). Some of the images were meant simply to entertain, but many were created as commentaries on the text (for example, shepherds shown alongside the story of the Nativity). The Luttrell images are, in other words, just like any historical document—they are revealing, but not transparently so. I hope you will look hard at the images in the book, examine at the originals online (try the British Library's special site at https://www.bl.uk/collection-items/the-luttrell-psalter or simply search with keywords such as "luttrell psalter shepherds"), and familiarize yourselves with this extraordinary psalter and its interpretive challenges. The sidebar in Chapter 10 addresses the particular challenges of using creative works—and especially the Luttrell Psalter—in writing history.

The chapters that follow begin with Cecilia's childhood and end with her death, but they are organized topically rather than chronologically. We begin with three chapters that examine the main institutions of Cecilia's life: the homes, lanes, and fields of her native place; the manor under whose authority she was born and lived; and the parish that nurtured her faith through the years. In laying a critical foundation, these chapters allow us to understand

WHAT CAN WE KNOW FROM MANOR COURT ROLLS?

The history in this book derives from my own archival work on Brigstock and the Penifaders ("original research") and also from the writings of many other historians who have conducted their own original research on medieval peasants ("historiography"). My research was based on 549 manor courts held in Brigstock between 1287 and 1348. I learned a lot simply by pondering the court proceedings, and I also undertook a "family reconstitution" of Brigstock—that is, I recorded every mention of every person, and then sorted those people into families. This was a long, slogging process: the records are written in Latin, they are hard to read, they use lots of legal jargon, and most of all, I had to make many difficult analytical decisions. For example, I had to decide whether "Cissa" Penifader mentioned in some entries was the same person as "Cecilia" Penifader mentioned in others (she was). The summary here of a Brigstock court session gives you a taste of this sort of source and its challenges. Once you have read it through and have a general sense of what was going on, try your hand at historical work. You might study what this court can tell you about peasant surnames; or differences between women and men; or family dynamics; or the legal practice of *pledging*. The court was held in the midst of the Great Famine (1315–1322) when Cecilia was about twenty-two years old. Her sister and father appear in the court, but she does not.

Legal terms are italicized at first use and explained at the end. There were 12 pennies (or pence) in a shilling; wages were about 1½ pennies a day for a man and about 1 penny for a woman.

The Court of Lady Margaret Queen of England held in Brigstock on the Thursday next after the feast of St. Matthias the Apostle, in the tenth year of the reign of King Edward II (3 March 1317)

ATTENDANCE

These people are excused from *common suit*:

    Christina Penifader excused by Robert Penifader senior.

    William son of John Tailor excused by Adam Reeve.

    Walter Tulke excused by Henry Tulke.

    Richard son of Walter at Lake excused by Simon Swetman.

    Henry Kyde excused by William Pikard.

    Bartholomew of Bekeswelle excused by Richard son of Hugh at Lake.

    Henry son of Ralph Tulke excused by William son of Geoffrey Forester.

    William Clerk, vicar and defendant in a debt case with Hugh of Felde,

is excused by Richard son of John Chaplain.

William Kykhok, complainant against Emma of the Hilde in a debt case, is excused by Robert Pidenton.

BUSINESS FOR THE NEXT COURT SESSION

Thomas Dandelion complains against Robert Moke in a case of broken contract, and Robert is to be *distrained* to answer him in the next court.

Robert Pidenton, attorney for Anthony of Sudborough, complains in a case of debt. The defendant (unnamed) has not come to court, and he is to be distrained to answer in the next court.

William Mirre complains in a case of trespass against William Pikerel, who is to be distrained to answer in the next court.

As before, it is ordered to distrain Ralph son of Richard at Hall of Stanion to answer for a trespass made against his mother.

It is ordered to distrain those who stood pledge for a mare suspected of having been stolen, so that they will bring the said mare to the next court.

OFFENSES AGAINST THE MANOR

John Dogge failed to *wage his law* successfully against the steward to prove that he did not draw customers away from Brigstock's mill and to Stanion's mill. He has not come to this court. Therefore, he and his pledge are fined 2 shillings. Pledge, Henry Helkok.

Henry son of Emma the Shepherd likewise. Therefore, he and his pledge are fined 2 shillings. Pledge, Simon Coleman.

DISPUTES

Robert son of William son of Richard senior complains in a plea of debt against Henry Bonenfaud of Rothwell who does not come. Therefore Henry and his pledges Richard the Boys and Richard Gerveys are fined 6 pence. And Henry is to be better distrained.

Walter Balribbe of Stanion gives 12 pence for the court to compel William Rote to give him nineteen bushels of barley. William and his pledges are ordered to come to the next court to settle the dispute.

Richard Katelin complains against Henry Pidenton and William his brother in a plea of trespass because they plowed and seeded land which Richard had formerly cultivated and for which he had paid two years' rent to our lady the Queen. And Henry comes and says that they are not required to respond in this jurisdiction. It is ordered to distrain them.

John Hirdman (his pledges are Henry Kroyl and William of Werketon) complains against Robert Penifader senior (his pledges are Adam at Solar and Simon Coleman) for trespass and defamation. Six men are sworn as jurors; they discuss the matter and report that Robert Penifader senior wrongfully and maliciously defamed John Hirdman and the *tithingman* on the day of the *View of Frankpledge*. Therefore Robert is fined 2 shillings. His pledges for the damages as well as the payment to the court are Adam at Solar and Simon Coleman. And the damages are assessed at 6 shillings and 8 pence.

LAND TRANSFERS

Henry son of Mabel Tulke returns to the steward a parcel of land in Woderodehill for himself and his heirs. Robert son of Henry Kroyl comes and takes possession of this land for himself and his heirs. His payment is excused. Pledge, the said Henry Kroyl.

Emma Scharp returns to the steward her rights in a small house, both for herself and for her heirs. Strangia and Alice daughters of Peter Anice receive it for themselves and their heirs. Their payment is 6 pence. Pledge, Alice wife of the said Peter.

Adam Swargere asks for the court to determine whether Hugh of Felde can claim by *tally* three narrow strips of land in his croft. This will be determined in the next meeting of the court.

Henry son of Mabel Tulke returns to the steward a quarter-acre of land in Brimberne for himself and his heirs. Henry Kuit takes the quarter-acre for himself and his heirs and he gives nothing for possession. Pledge, Adam Kyde.

Adam the Turner returns to the steward a quarter-acre of land in Aywenig for himself and his heirs. Geoffrey the Turner takes the quarter-acre for himself and his heirs and gives 6 pence for possession. Pledge, Adam the Turner.

Maud widow of Robert son of Maurice of Stanion returns to the steward a half share of a house (14 feet in length and 36 feet in width) that lies on the highway between the house of Richard at Cross and the house that William son of Reginald bought from Richard at Cross. John son of William son of Reginald takes this half share for himself and his heirs, and he pays 2 shillings. Pledge, John in Cemetery.

The said Maud returns to the steward the second share of the said house for herself and her heirs. Robert her son takes this half of the house for himself and his heirs, and he will have full possession after Maud's death. He pays 6 pence. Pledge, John son of William son of Reginald.

The *aletaster* for Stanion is Alan Koyk.

The aletasters for Brigstock are Adam Kyde and William of Werketon.

They present that the following are fined for brewing against the *assize of ale*: the wife of William Golle, 4 pence; the wife of Henry Helkok, 4 pence; the daughter of Adam Swargere, 4 pence; the wife of John Coleman, 4 pence; the wife of Henry son of Henry, 4 pence; the wife of Walter son of Henry, fine excused; the wife of Robert Pikerel, 4 pence; Emma the Shepherd, fine excused.

CONCLUSION

Affeerors: Adam Kyde, Simon Coleman, Gilbert son of Simon.

Sum of court receipts: 13 shillings and 3 pence.

Legal Terms

affeerors: men responsible for setting the amount of court fines.

aletasters: men responsible for supervising the sale of ale.

assize of ale: requirement that ale had to be of good quality, measured fairly, and sold at proper prices.

common suit: the obligation to attend all meetings of the court.

distrain: to seize a person's property in order to compel a response.

steward: an officer who manages an estate of multiple manors.

pledging: by pledging, a person ("the pledge") took responsibility for another person or object.

tally: receipt made by notching a wooden stick.

tithingman: the head of a tithing (a group of men legally responsible for each others' misbehaviors).

View of Frankpledge: a special court session, held twice a year, that checked tithings and punished petty crimes.

wage law: to defend oneself in court.

FOR MORE ON how I worked with the Brigstock records, see my "Note on Method" in *Women in the Medieval English Countryside: Gender and Household in Brigstock Before the Plague* (1987), pp. 199–231. For more manorial courts in translation, see Ray Lock, ed., *The Court Rolls of Walsham-le-Willows*, in two volumes: *1303–1350* (1998) and *1351–99* (2002). Or see the printed series for Wakefield Manor accessible online through the Yorkshire Archaeological and Historical Society at https://archive.org/details/yorks hirearchaeologicalandhistoricalsociety?sort=titleSorter&and[]%20=firstTitle:W.

Cecilia in the context of village, manor, and parish. In Chapter 5, we will turn to what was probably the most traumatic experience of Cecilia's life, a famine that afflicted Brigstock and most of northern Europe between 1315 and 1322. In the years when Cecilia was coming of age, she saw many of her neighbors and probably also her father and mother suffer from hunger, sicken, and die. But Cecilia herself survived the Great Famine and, as we shall see, even profited from the greater distress of her neighbors. In subsequent chapters, we will explore further aspects of her story: how her relations with parents, siblings, and kin evolved over the course of her life; how she supported herself through labor, land, and trade; how she stood in relation to her neighbors and fellow tenants; and finally, how her female gender did and did not shape her experiences. We will end by assessing what Cecilia Penifader's life can tell us about the medieval world in which she lived and the modern world from which we observe her history.

Suggestions for Further Reading

For the German states, see Werner Rösener, *The Peasantry of Europe* (1994), much stronger on Germany than elsewhere; for England, Edward Miller and John Hatcher, *Medieval England: Rural Society and Economic Change 1086–1348* (1978); and Phillipp R. Schofield, *Peasant and Community in Medieval England, 1200–1500* (2003); and for France, chapter 2 in Graeme Small, *Late Medieval France* (2009), pp. 53–94. For lively microhistories, see Richard Wunderli, *Peasant Fires: The Drummer of Niklashausen* (1992); Robert Bartlett, *The Hanged Man: A Story of Miracle, Memory, and Colonialism in the Middle Ages* (2006); Thomas N. Bisson, *Tormented Voices: Power, Crisis, and Humanity in Rural Catalonia, 1140–1200* (1998); and Emmanuel Le Roy Ladurie, *Montaillou: The Promised Land of Error* (1978). For medieval stereotypes of peasants, see Paul Freedman, *Images of the Medieval Peasant* (1999).

For different national historiographies, see Isabel Alfonso, ed., *The Rural History of Medieval European Societies: Trends and Perspectives* (2007). For debates among English historians, see Phillipp R. Schofield, *Peasants and Historians: Debating the Medieval English Peasantry* (2016); and John Hatcher and Mark Bailey, *Modelling the Middle Ages: The History and Theory of England's Economic Development* (2001).

For an introduction to English manorial archives, see Mark Bailey, ed., *The English Manor, c. 1200–1500* (2002).

For a full-scale reproduction of the Luttrell Psalter, see Michelle P. Brown, ed., *The Luttrell Psalter: A Facsimile* (2006). For interpretation, see Michael Camille, *Mirror in Parchment: The Luttrell Psalter and the Making of Medieval England* (1998).

CHAPTER 2

The World Around Her

August 1316, Brigstock Court: Cecilia Penifader first appeared in the manor court when she was a teenager, still living at home under the authority of her father Robert. A neighbor named Richard Everard complained that Cecilia and her father had gone into his part of the Northmeadow, ignored his boundary stones, and taken hay from his land. Robert Penifader denied these charges, and he promised to prove his innocence. The dispute is not recorded in later courts, so Richard and Robert likely settled their differences out of court.

Cecilia Penifader was born into a sizable and prosperous family in Brigstock village, or more likely, the adjacent village of Stanion, then part of Brigstock manor. (Brigstock and Stanion were tied so closely together——for example, Cecilia and her parents held lands in both—that I shall treat the two settlements as the single community of Brigstock.) Her parents, Robert and Alice, had a large number of children, at least three sons and five daughters (see Figure 3). Two children, Emma and Alice, seem to have died young, and only one child, Christina, lived long enough to witness the horrors of the Black Death when it arrived in Brigstock in 1349. Although it is impossible to reconstruct precise patterns of birth and infant mortality from medieval records, it is clear that the Penifaders were fecund and fortunate. If Cecilia's mother married her father at the usual age of about twenty, she would have had twenty fertile years to produce her family (medieval women rarely bore children in their forties). Bearing eight children in two decades, she followed a biologically predictable pattern; if a peasant wife used no effective birth control and nursed her infants (an activity

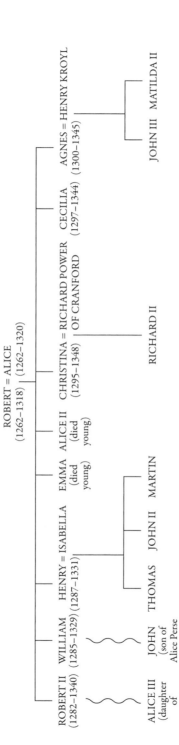

THE PENIFADERS

ROBERT = ALICE
(1262–1318) (1262–1320)

ROBERT II   WILLIAM   HENRY = ISABELLA   EMMA   ALICE II   CHRISTINA = RICHARD POWER   CECILIA   AGNES = HENRY KROYL
(1282–1340)   (1285–1329) (1287–1331)   (died   (died   (1295–1348) OF CRANFORD   (1297–1344) (1300–1345)
                                                 young)   young)

ALICE III   JOHN   THOMAS   JOHN II   MARTIN   RICHARD II   JOHN III   MATILDA II
(daughter   (son of
of   Alice Perse
Joan de   of
Lowyk)   Kingsthorpe)

Except for the death dates of Robert Penifader and his daughter Cecilia, all dates are approximate reconstructions. Information about, the third generation of the family (that is, the nieces and nephews of Cecilia Penifader) is too sparse to justify estimated years of birth and death. As indicated by wavy lines, the children of Robert II and William were illegitimate.

Figure 3.   The Penifaders.

that delayed the resumption of menstruation), she usually gave birth at intervals of about 2½ years. Aristocratic women, who not only married at younger ages but also employed wet nurses (women paid to breastfeed the infants of others), usually produced larger numbers of children. Eleanor of Castile, who married Edward I when she was about ten years old, bore fifteen (or possibly sixteen) children; Philippa of Hainault, who married Edward III at the age of fourteen years, gave birth to twelve children.

Bearing eight children in twenty years, Alice Penifader made the most of her fertility as a nursing mother, and she seems never to have tried to prevent or terminate a pregnancy. This was not through lack of knowledge. Medieval women knew about a wide variety of plants that could discourage conception or sometimes induce early abortion. Their concoctions were not as effective as methods used today, but they sometimes worked. Artemisia, which inhibits ovulation, and rue, which causes uterine contractions, were among the plants readily available to women in Brigstock. Alice seems never to have resorted to such measures, but many women did. Alice and her husband Robert were also lucky enough to beat the odds of infant and child mortality. In most medieval villages, almost half of all children died before reaching adulthood, but most of the children of Alice and Robert grew to full age. All in all, the Penifader household was atypically large. Most of their neighbors in Brigstock, like most peasant couples, produced only three children who survived them.

House and Farmyard

Cecilia was the seventh of eight children, born into a house filled with three brothers and three sisters. Their house was comfortable by Brigstock standards but humble by the standards of our day. Like all the houses in Brigstock, it was dark. Some houses had no windows, but the Penifaders, as well-off tenants, might have cut a window or two into their walls. If so, the windows had no glass, and only shutters kept out the wind and cold. Like all the houses in Brigstock, the Penifader house was filled with smoke. A fire was essential for warmth and cooking, but, as chimneys were unknown among peasants, smoke was vented through a hole in the roof. Perhaps the Penifaders, like others who could afford it, built an especially high roof to draw up smoke to the hole in its apex and ease the smokiness. Finally, like all the houses in Brigstock, the house in which Cecilia grew up was small. Peasant houses were usually twice as wide as they were deep, and a prosperous family like the Penifaders probably lived in a house about 30 feet by 15 feet. Dark, smoky, and cramped, peasant houses were not welcoming places. It was no wonder people preferred, weather permitting, to sit outside on benches set against the walls of their homes.

Until recently, a stone house that dated back to Cecilia's day stood in Brigstock. Its walls were built of rubble, not stone blocks, but even this was fine by the standards of the early fourteenth century. Most medieval peasants used rubble only for a low foundation a foot or two off the ground; they then built the walls by placing posts every few feet and filling in the gaps with wattle and daub, that is, sticks and twigs woven together with the gaps filled by clay, straw, moss, and other such materials. (Sometimes these walls were so flimsy that robbers literally broke into a house by avoiding the locked door and forcing entry through the walls.) Set at a low point in the walls of the Brigstock house were crucks, long curved timbers, that rose up to brace the wall and hold the roof. The roof was straw thatch; this was cheap and easy for medieval peasants and prone to disastrous fire. A house like this was built with a combination of family labor and hired labor. If a family could afford it, they were especially likely to hire skilled workers to lay the foundation, erect the timber frame, and set the thatch.

The interior of the medieval house that until recently stood in Brigstock had a second floor, but this was a later addition. In Cecilia's house, there would have been one floor only, a packed dirt floor, possibly covered with straw (see Figure 4). Perhaps boards laid across braces of the crucks provided, at one end of the house, a loft for storage or extra sleeping. Furnishings were minimal: benches or stools for sitting; a trestle table that could be put away when not in use; a chest to hold bedding, towels, and other linens; a cupboard to hold jugs, bowls, and spoons. All these would have been pushed against the walls. When it was time to eat, the table would be unfolded, the bowls and spoons set out, the benches put in place.

The Penifaders' diet was simple. Parents and children ate bread and drank weak ale at every meal, and they also ate, whenever available, such other foods as bacon, cheeses, eggs, fish, onions, leeks, garlic, cabbages, apples, and pears. Meat, cooked by boiling, was a rare treat, and pottage—a stew or thick soup made of whatever ingredients were to hand—was common. When it was time to sleep, the tables and benches were set aside, and bedding (at best, a cloth bag stuffed with either straw or chaff from threshed oats) was laid out in their place. The one immovable feature of the interior was the hearth, set in the center of the house, with its pots and trivets; it was around the hearth that everyone sat, ate, and slept. Perhaps the Penifaders' house, like the main floor of the now demol-

Figure 4. Inside a Peasant House. With few windows and no chimneys,
peasant houses were dark and smoky. Windows were fully closed, as needed
for warmth or security, with wooden shutters, but they were not glazed.
Some were entirely open to the elements when not shuttered, and others
were covered by stretched cloth or animal hide. (Derived from a
reconstruction found in Maurice Beresford and John Hurst,
Wharram Percy: Deserted Medieval Village (1991), p. 40.)

ished Brigstock house, was partitioned to create a small room on one side. This
room was used for storage and sleeping; it offered a bit of privacy, but it was far
from the hearth in winter.

Cecilia, in other words, grew up in a house that provided the essentials of
life: a hearth for cooking and warmth; a shelter from wind, rain, and snow; a
place to eat and sleep. But her house was not a place to linger, and whenever she

could, Cecilia wandered into the farmyard around her house where her parents and siblings also spent much of their time. Sometimes houses stood together along a street, built with shared walls, and in such cases, farmyards ran behind the houses. More often, however, houses stood separately within their farmyards; in these cases, most of the farmyard ran behind the house, but some of it could also lie in front and along the sides. The farmyard was a large area, perhaps an acre or more, closed off by fences or ditches from street, lane, and neighbors. (An acre measures 43,560 square feet, roughly 75 percent of a football field in the United States.) In the Penifader farmyard, Cecilia sat with her family in the early evening, assisted her mother in many tasks, or watched over the safekeeping of some of the household animals. (In the winter, cows, pigs, chickens, and other animals were sometimes taken into the house to protect them from the elements and to add to the interior warmth. But in warmer weather, animals were usually kept in the farmyard, sometimes in a barn.)

The farmyard was a social place, especially in front of the house, where children like Cecilia found benches for sitting, fences for leaning, and a cobbled space for games (see Figure 5). The farmyard was also a place for storage: a barn for animals, a shed for tools or grain, a well or cistern for rainwater, a haystack or two, and certainly, at some distance from the house if possible, a dung heap where human and animal waste was carefully accumulated for spreading as fertilizer on the fields. Most importantly, the farmyard was a place of work, especially for women and children. Cecilia's mother brewed ale in the farmyard; she milked cows and made cheese; she took advantage of outdoor light to mend old clothes and stitch new ones; she tended a beehive; she collected eggs from her roosting hens; she fattened her pigs; she cared for a few apple and pear trees; she cultivated a garden that yielded such products as onions, turnips, peas, beans, leeks, garlic, cabbages, flax, hemp, and herbs. The farmyards of Brigstock, small, readily fertilized, easily worked on an intermittent basis, and free of any communal regulation, were the most intensely cultivated lands in the community. The products that came from farmyards were valued for the variety they brought to diets and for the cash generated by sales in local markets.

As Cecilia grew up in the house and farmyard of her parents, she followed hygienic practices that today can seem crude. Bathing was rare, not only because of fears of drowning but also because baths were considered unhealthy—liable to lead to colds, fevers, or worse. On occasion, she splashed herself with water and soap, but more often than not, cleanliness meant clean hands, clean face, and little more. She also had no toilet, and she either walked out to the dung heap in the farmyard or used a bucket. Like her parents and siblings, Cecilia

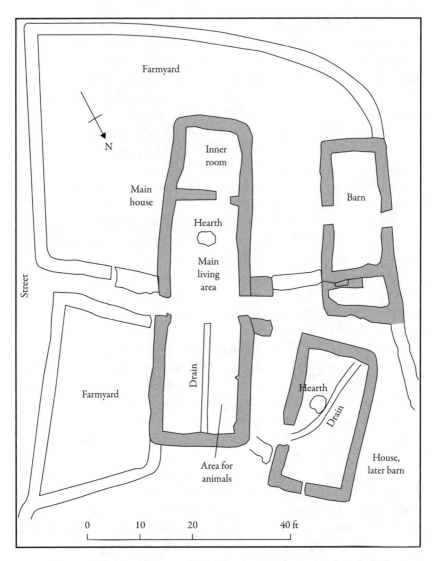

Farmyard

N

Inner
room

Main
house

Barn

Hearth

Main
living
area

Street

Drain

Hearth

Drain

Farmyard

House,
later barn

Area for
animals

0   10   20   40 ft

Figure 5. House and Farmyard. This is a drawing from an archaeological
dig, and at its center is a house much like the house whose interior is shown
in Figure 4. Farmyards were large and well-used, with space for gardening,
henhouses, storage, stables, and all sorts of domestic work. (Derived from an
excavation drawing in Guy Beresford, "Three Medieval Settlements on
Dartmoor," *Medieval Archaeology* 23 (1979): 98–158.)

wore simple clothes: stockings and leather shoes; gowns made of wool or flax (men's gowns stopped at the knee; women's were longer); and for warmth in the winter, coats or cloaks and hoods or caps. All clothing fitted loosely. This made it slightly easier for Alice Penifader to clothe her family by stitching a new cloak or altering an old one for a hand-me-down.

Arable, Pasture, Stream, and Forest

Outside the immediate house and farmyard of her family, Cecilia found a large and complex community. Brigstock lay in the heart of Rockingham Forest, a royal preserve for hunting. The Norman kings William II (1087–1100) and Henry I (1100–1135) hunted in the forest and maintained a lodge at Brigstock. Built of wood, it consisted of a hall, a chamber, and a stable. As far as we know, no kings visited the lodge after Henry I, but they kept it in good repair; Cecilia might have stared at these buildings and crept around them as a child. By the late fourteenth century, however, the lodge had fallen into ruin, and it was so thoroughly demolished that modern archaeologists have not yet succeeded in pinpointing its location. Local tradition holds that the manor house that now stands in Brigstock, an imposing structure of fine stone blocks built about 1500, rests on the site of the timber lodge of Cecilia's day.

Brigstock and Stanion today are thriving villages, clustered in a gently roll- ing landscape. Both settlements are nucleated, with all the houses gathered into a central location. In Cecilia's time, the Penifaders and their neighbors had al- ready settled along the same main streets of Brigstock and Stanion that can be seen today, but their lives were different and much less prosperous from the lives of those who now inhabit these villages. The peasants of fourteenth-century Brigstock relied on an economy of makeshifts, responding flexibly to any op- portunity that arose. They had to "make shift"—that is, to juggle many tasks and to manage with whatever materials, cash, and work they could find. Peas- ants often relied a bit on wages earned by working for others or on profits gained from selling ale, bread, wool, or other commodities, but they especially relied on what they could produce from the land. Two anchors kept this highly flexi- ble economy going—first, the arable fields on which peasants grew wheat, bar- ley, rye, oats, and other crops; and second, the meadows and pastures that fed their sheep, horses, and oxen.

Like many communities across northern Europe in the Middle Ages, Brig- stock had **open fields** that were plowed, sown, weeded, harvested, and left

fallow (that is, unplanted) according to common agreement. Brigstock had several such fields (each given a local name), and the Penifaders held bits of land in most of them—a half-acre here, a parcel there, another half-acre over there. (When Cecilia grew up she too would hold land scattered about the manor. In 1335, for example, she acquired an acre of arable that was distributed in three locations—"under the Sale," "in Stitches," and "between the Valkmill and the new dyke.") Every year, the Penifaders' use of each small bit of land, whether they planted it with wheat or rye in the autumn, or oats, barley, or beans in the spring, or left it fallow, was determined by the collective agreement of all tenants. Robert and Alice, in other words, were not able to sit on their front bench and plan what to plant where and when; instead, they had to use their land in ways agreed upon with their neighbors. This system of agriculture is different from the large blocks of land, farmed by single owners, that now dot the landscape of Europe. Yet it worked well at the time.

First, consider that many households held lands scattered throughout the fields of a manor, rather than compactly consolidated into one family farm. This arrangement is sometimes called *strip farming* because each field was divided into **strips** tended by different families. Scattering a family's lands had several advantages. It spread risk, for if crops in one field had a bad year, crops in another might do fine; it facilitated the sharing of plows and draft animals, for several households could pool their resources to plow a field containing their strips; and it encouraged parental generosity to children, for instead of a block of family land that had to be held together for a single heir, parents held many strips that could, if they wished and their bailiff allowed, be more easily dispersed among many children.

Second, consider that boundaries between strips were unfenced (hence the term *open field*). Instead of fences, stones or other low markers marked boundaries between strips (in the court case that opens this chapter, Richard Everard accused Cecilia and her father of ignoring these markers). Boundary stones could be moved as well as ignored, and this was a serious offense. If one household could thereby gain a foot or two of land, it gained a great deal, especially if stones were moved ever so slightly again and again. Despite such problems, boundary stones were preferred for one reason: fencing would have obstructed the movement of plows during planting and animals eating stubble after harvest. With boundary stones lying close to the ground, more of the land could be cultivated more easily.

Third, consider that tenants had to cooperate with each other over how a field containing the strips of many people might be used. This limited individual initiative, but it was essential. If the Penifaders had decided to plant oats in a field where everyone else had planted wheat the autumn before, they would have created havoc. In the early spring, when they would have needed to prepare their strip for sowing oats, they would have dragged their plow through the maturing wheat of their neighbors. This would have made the Penifaders few friends and many enemies. Cooperation was eased by custom. It was not as if everyone had to debate every year about the use of every field; there was a set pattern of rotation that everyone expected and therefore more easily observed.

By Cecilia's time, many open-field villages in England had adopted a three-field course of rotation. Peasants planted one field with a winter crop (wheat or rye) sown in the autumn, cultivated a spring crop (oats, barley, peas, or beans) on the second, and let the third field lie fallow. Every year they rotated the use of the fields; the winter field would then have a spring crop, the spring field lay fallow, and the fallow field was sown with wheat. The **three-field system** was an innovation of the High Middle Ages, and it improved on a variety of less efficient rotations, especially the **two-field system** (in which half the land was fallow at any one time). In the eleventh century, many villages in Northern Europe began to shift from a two-field rotation to one based on three fields. But the change was a slow one; in Cecilia's day, the three-field system was used in Brigstock but probably not in Stanion. Although Stanion did eventually adopt a three-field rotation, many others did not. In villages with poor soils and in Mediterranean villages, where summers were too hot for spring crops, the three-field rotation was not feasible. On the rich plains of the north (including the midlands of England), however, the three-field system helped peasants not only to minimize fallow but also to sow a valuable second crop in the spring.

Fourth, consider that peasants left large portions of arable land—usually one-third or one-half—untilled every year. Fallowing was common because animal and human waste was insufficient for fertilizing the land, and few other alternatives were available. Since fallow land naturally replenished itself, the Penifaders and their neighbors carefully left each field untilled every two or three years. Also, they made sure that sheep grazed the stubble from the harvest and that other animals were turned out onto the fallow. The droppings from these animals helped further to replenish the soil. In many communities, fallow fields and pastures were considered to be **common lands** available for the flocks and herds of everyone, and in such instances, villagers often carefully specified how many animals each household could place on these commons. This was so that no single tenant could, as the Brigstock custumal of 1391 stated, "overcharge the commons."

HOW DO WE KNOW ABOUT MEDIEVAL CLIMATE?

We have lots of weather reports from the Middle Ages, especially from chroniclers who complain about wet summers or bitterly cold winters. But for climate—that is, long-term trends in weather—we look to nature and science. Our main tools are tree rings and ice cores. Because trees have an annual cycle of growth and dormancy, each ring provides a proxy measure for that year's precipitation and temperature, whether by its thickness (a good climate for growth) or thinness (poor climate). Tree rings also supply—in their concentrations of radiocarbon—information about solar irradiance (or sun-power) and especially sunspot activity. Because building timbers as well as recently felled trees can be studied in these ways, tree ring analysis (or *dendrochronology*) can extend back thousands of years (current analyses go back as far as fourteen thousand years).

Ice cores extend even farther back in time, and they tell us even more. Like tree rings, the annual deposit of ice found on cores taken from Greenland and Antarctica varies in thickness depending on annual precipitation and temperature. They also contain tiny bubbles of air trapped by the pressure of accumulated ice; by releasing these bubbles, we can capture and measure air that is centuries old. Some cores also contain pollen that tell us what plants then flourished, and some even have ash left from volcanic eruptions.

Climate historians use more than just these two measures—they also, for example, look at sediments on lake or ocean beds and at the minerals in stalactites and stalagmites in caves. But the basic principle is always the same: analyze the extent and content of natural deposits, made over time. This might sound simple but it is devilishly complex. You cannot just chop down a two-hundred-year-old tree and discover the last two centuries of local climate. Different species of trees react to climate in different ways; tree growth can vary by individual tree and also by setting and soil; and although tree rings indicate years of good and poor growth, they do not report the relative contribution to growth of temperature, precipitation, sunlight, and wind. Large and selective samples help; so, too, does careful analysis; and we can be most confident of all when completely independent measures—written records, tree rings, ice cores, and stalactites—corroborate similar trends.

Climate history (or *paleoclimatology*) has used these methods to establish the main features of the European climate during the Middle Ages. A Medieval Warm Period (or MWP) prevailed from the ninth to the thirteenth centuries, with temperatures about 1°C higher than before or after. This might not seem like much, but this was enough warming to open the north Atlantic to commercial fishing and to allow Europeans to settle in Iceland, Greenland, and Newfoundland. By the 1260s, the MWP was winding down. Less solar heat was reaching the earth, partly because the sun went into a quiescent phase (known as the Wolf Solar Minimum) and partly because a series of volcanic eruptions from as far away as Ecuador blocked the sun's energy with ash and aerosols. Worse yet, the earth's atmosphere was perhaps further clogged in the 1290s by an onslaught of meteors, as reported by chroniclers from China to Ireland and as suggested by telltale chemicals, especially ammonium and nitrate, in ice cores. Waning sun-power meant, of course, global cooling, but it also reshaped weather patterns in ways that differed regionally—less rain in Asia, for example, and more in Europe. Most of all, though, the climate between about 1250 and 1350 was everywhere unstable and more extreme.

Paleoclimatology illustrates how historians, immersed as we are in past times, are also creatures of their own times. Historians once paid little attention to climate, but as the earth has warmed over the past few decades, climate history has attracted much more interest. Historians, who are citizens as well as scholars, rightly turn to the past to understand present-day dilemmas. Thus, for example, the MWP features in modern debates about climate change. Some argue that just as the earth was slightly warmer before 1250, so our current warming might also be part of a natural cycle we do not yet fully understand. Others point out that the MWP makes a poor precedent for modern warming, because its temperature change was relatively small. In such ways, history-writing is about both past and present. Historians rightly respond to the compelling issues of our own times and places—by asking ever-changing questions and producing from those questions ever-new research.

To LEARN MORE, see Richard C. Hoffmann, *An Environmental History of Medieval Europe* (2014), and Bruce M. S. Campbell, *The Great Transition: Climate, Disease, and Society in the Late-Medieval World* (2016).

The arable land of Brigstock was important and closely regulated, but it accounted for only one-fourth of the land of the manor. Most of the rest was given to the second anchor of Brigstock's economy: *pastures* in which animals grazed and grassy meadows used either as hayfields or for further grazing. These lands were also held in parcels scattered through many fields. Elsewhere in England and Europe, some peasants supported themselves almost exclusively with animal husbandry, particularly if they lived in mountainous regions or areas with poor soils. In Brigstock, where the landscape rolled only gently and the soil richly repaid cultivation, animals still contributed critically to the economy. Horses and oxen pulled wagons and carried burdens; sheep produced wool that could be marketed to local merchants; cows and goats gave milk that could be turned into cheese (people rarely drank milk); pigs were raised especially for their meat. These animals supported peasant families directly with their wool, milk, and meat, and indirectly through their contributions to arable husbandry; their waste fertilized the fields, and their pulling power enabled peasants to plow those fields. As a result, the rural economy of villages such as Brigstock and Stanion is best considered an economy of *mixed farming*. Peasants raised crops and animals, and the two activities supported each other. No animals meant infertile fields; infertile fields meant no stubble for animals to feed on.

When Cecilia walked around Brigstock and saw open fields given over to arable, pasture, and meadow, she saw something else as well, especially on the outskirts of the fields. She saw small parcels of land, enclosed by fences or ditches, each of which belonged entirely to one family. The Penifaders might have held several of these, and if so, they called them, as did everyone else in Brigstock, *newsets* or, more commonly, **assarts**. The first word gives an important clue about how these private enclosures were formed, for they were newly cultivated lands, created when a family or a group of families decided to fell trees, clear land, and put it to productive use. Sometimes this was done surreptitiously; Brigstock peasants sometimes cleared edges of Rockingham Forest, doubtless hoping, often correctly, that the king's foresters would either not notice or not care. Sometimes it was done with license, for holders of unproductive land were often delighted to see it cleared and, of course, to collect new rents on it. In either case, the assart was usually enclosed, kept distinct from the open fields, and used—like the farmyard around the house—for whatever purposes a family might choose. Bringing new lands into cultivation was an important strategy for medieval peasants everywhere. Between 1000 and 1300, peasants across Europe brought thousands of acres of previously untilled land—marshes, wasteland, moors, forests, and unpopulated territories—into cultivation. Often this was small scale, as with assarts. But sometimes, it was large scale, as in the case of the founding of Stanion by settlers from Brigstock.

Running through the fields and assarts of Brigstock was another important resource for Cecilia and her family. Harper's Brook, which created the small valley in which Brigstock lay, yielded fish available to everyone. It was also a useful spot for washing clothes, rinsing tools, and playing. But Harper's Brook offered danger as well. Few people in Brigstock could swim well, so if a young girl lost her footing or a man tumbled down the bank, she or he was likely to drown.

Beyond the fields and assarts of Brigstock lay a place just as dangerous and productive as Harper's Brook: the forest. Some parts of the forest were heavily wooded, but other sections lay open for pasture or other uses. To Cecilia and her family, the wooded parts of the forest were places where outlaws, fairies, and other unknowns might be encountered. Perhaps they told stories, as did later generations, of a disastrous visit by the forest outlaw Robin Hood to Brigstock. The tale relates how Robin and his men, attacked while in Brigstock church, made a bold escape, but left behind a dead priest, inadvertently struck by an arrow while celebrating Mass. Despite the many dangers—human and supernatural—of the woodland, it was a place of industry too. More than six hundred medieval sites for burning charcoal have been found in Rockingham Forest, some of the charcoal used to fuel nearby iron-producing furnaces. We do not know whether any of the Penifaders were charcoal-makers or iron-smelters, but they surely went often into all parts of Rockingham Forest. It was as essential to their economy of makeshifts as their arable strips or their farmyard. With her mother and siblings, young Cecilia gathered fallen wood in the forest; helped in the digging of peat; checked on the Penifader pigs feeding wild in the underbrush; and collected nuts, berries, honey, and herbs. Whenever her father or brothers had the nerve, they also trapped hare and shot deer in the forest. If caught by foresters, they faced prosecution for poaching (animals on royal preserves were to be hunted only by the king or his friends), and if convicted, they faced fines or imprisonment.

So when Cecilia ventured outside her parents' house and farmyard, she walked through a tight cluster of homes in Stanion, crowded on a few streets. She found the same whenever she wandered down Harper's Brook to Brigstock village. Surrounding these twinned clusters of houses and outbuildings, lay arable fields, meadows, pastures, and forest, and in all of these, Cecilia worked and played as a young child. She went into the fields often to help with weeding, breaking clods of earth, tying bundles at harvest, or perhaps even moving ever so slightly the boundary stones that separated Penifader and Everard land; in the pastures around Brigstock, she watched animals or drove them to and from various fields; she played and fished in Harper's Brook; and she accompanied her mother into the forest to forage for nuts, berries, fallen wood, and other necessities. This was the Brigstock and Stanion that Cecilia knew: within about 7,600 acres lay two nucleated settlements of about nine hundred adults total, several arable fields, extensive pasture and meadow, numerous small assarts, a stream full of fish, and a forest beyond.

The Wider World

Cecilia's world did not end at the boundaries of Brigstock and Stanion. As a child, she would often have run into the road to stare at people passing through—pilgrims on their way to holy shrines; knights and ladies riding out for pleasure or hunting; peddlers offering goods for sale; carpenters and thatchers looking for work; beggars seeking alms; migrant laborers following the harvest; local folk walking to weekly markets in nearby villages and towns. Some of these people stopped for a while in Brigstock, to visit with kin and friends, or to take advantage of some occasional employment. Some even ended up settling in the community. Over the course of Cecilia's life, about one-third of the people living on Brigstock manor moved there from elsewhere. Whether staying for a long or short time, these newcomers brought news and gossip of other places, new ideas, new fashions, new songs. From them, Cecilia learned early that there were villages, towns, and people far beyond what she saw with her own eyes.

Moreover, as she grew older, Cecilia saw many more people and places. Most peasants moved readily and often within a fifteen-mile radius of the villages in which they lived and worked. Brigstock was especially well situated, surrounded by nearby towns or villages, all within ten miles or less, that hosted markets on one day of every week. On any day, except Sunday, the Penifaders could easily reach a market—Rothwell on Monday, Thrapston on Tuesday, Geddington on Wednesday, Corby on Thursday, Kettering on Friday, and Oundle on Saturday (see Map 2). At these markets, the Penifaders bought and sold goods; hired workers and offered themselves for hire; gossiped about local news; and heard stories from other places. They traveled by foot, walking with an ease and speed that many hikers today might envy. At a pace of about four miles an hour, Cecilia's mother could reach Corby in two hours, sell her eggs and cheese, and get back home well before dark. At the same pace, her father

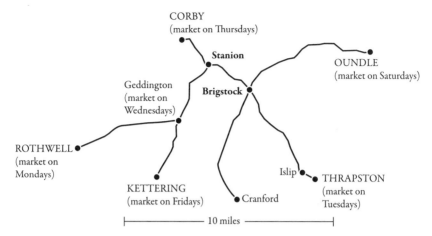

Map 2. Brigstock and Its Region. On every day of the week except Sunday, Cecilia Penifader could easily walk to a market and back.

could get to Kettering market on a Friday, collect a new plowshare, and return within one day, and her sister Christina could walk to the village of Cranford, spend an afternoon with the man she eventually married, and be home for supper. By the time Cecilia reached the age of eight, she was probably accompanying her parents and older siblings on trips such as these. From then on, she was well aware of the world beyond the village of her birth. She talked with itinerant peddlers and laborers, she sold and bought goods at local markets, and she visited her married sister in Cranford.

Cecilia never left Brigstock for an extended period, but one of her brothers did; to get an education, William Penifader left his home for almost a decade, and when he returned to Brigstock, he had the sophistication of a man who had walked the streets of such towns as Oxford, Cambridge, Lincoln, and, possibly, London. Perhaps Cecilia also traveled a bit too, and if so, she most likely undertook a pilgrimage to Lincoln, about sixty miles to the north. There, pilgrims prayed at the shrine of Little St. Hugh, a boy supposedly martyred by the Jews in 1255. When Hugh's body was discovered in a well, hysterical townspeople accused eighteen Jews of his murder and hanged them; such hysterical accusations, known today as *blood libel*, first developed in twelfth-century Europe, but they soon became a common and dangerous expression of Christian anti-Semitism. At York in 1190, for example, 150 Jews—men, women, and children— were massacred after another spurious charge of child murder. For Cecilia, however, Hugh of Lincoln was not an unfortunate child whose death was explained away by false charges against Jews; he was a holy martyr whose cult attracted attention far and wide. If she did journey to Lincoln to pray at his shrine, her pilgrimage combined piety and pleasure. Like the pilgrims of Chaucer's *Canterbury Tales*, she would have met new people, seen new places, and learned new customs and ideas.

Cecilia was further integrated into a wider world by the bureaucracy of the English realm. By the late thirteenth century, English kings offered justice to their subjects in a variety of forums including hundred courts ("hundreds" were subsections of counties), county courts, courts in Westminster, and most importantly, courts convened by itinerant justices who moved through the realm, bringing the king's justice with them. Most of the crimes and quarrels of Brigstock were easily resolved in its three-weekly manorial court, but some crimes could only be adjudicated in royal courts. Any untimely death, for example, had to be investigated by the king's coroner, and any accused murderers could only be tried before the king's justices. The exchequer, the heart of the royal finances, also reached into the lives of Cecilia and other people in Brigstock. When the king's officers arrived to collect taxes, they expected cooperation from local deputies and prompt payment by local taxpayers. And the military demands of England's kings also touched the lives of ordinary peasants who were expected to contribute men and supplies to the army. As a woman, Cecilia never had to testify on a royal jury or serve in the king's army, but she knew well the power of the king's courts, his exchequer, and his army.

Cecilia met few foreigners. Living as she did in the heart of the English midlands, she seldom encountered anyone from Wales, Scotland, France, or even farther afield. She almost certainly never met a non-Christian, for few Muslims traveled into rural England and Jews had been expelled from England in 1290. Yet Cecilia lived in a multilingual culture. Lords and ladies spoke French; all clerics and clerks knew some Latin; and everyone was familiar with the Latin Mass, celebrated every Sunday and on other holy days, too. Cecilia's mother tongue was English, but she possibly understood a few words or phrases in French and Latin. All in all, Cecilia's horizons might not have been as broad as those of most modern people, but her world was not confined to the fields of Brigstock and Stanion.

Suggestions for Further Reading

For material culture, see Roberta Gilchrist, *Medieval Life: Archaeology and the Life Course* (2018); and Nat Alcock and Dan Miles, *The Medieval Peasant House in Midland England* (2014). For excavations of one village, see Maurice Beresford and John Hurst, *Wharram Percy: Deserted Medieval Village* (1990). For essays on a range of rural topics, see Christopher Dyer, *Everyday Life in Medieval England* (1994). For open fields, see his essay "Open Fields in Their Social and Economic Context: The West Midlands of England," in Christopher Dyer et al., eds., *Peasants and Their Fields: The Rationale of Open-Field Agriculture, c. 700–1800* (2018), pp. 29–48 (this volume includes essays on open fields in Scandinavia and the Low Countries). For more on European expansion and the cultivation of new lands, see Robert Bartlett, *The Making of Europe: Conquest, Colonization, and Cultural Change, 950–1350* (1993).

Brigstock during Cecilia's day is more fully described in my *Women in the Medieval English Countryside: Gender and Household in Brigstock Before the Plague* (1987).

CHAPTER 3

Lords, Ladies, and Peasants

December 1290, Geddington: On a chilly December evening, a grieving Edward I—escorting the body of his queen, Eleanor of Castile, from Lincoln to London—stopped in Geddington, about three miles from Brigstock, for the night. He left there a permanent reminder of his sad visit, ordering that crosses be erected at each of the twelve sites where Eleanor's body had rested for a night. Cecilia Penifader was not born when this grim procession moved so close to her home, but as a child, she might have played at the foot of this "Eleanor Cross" whenever her parents took her to Geddington for the Wednesday market. Children do the same today. Most of the Eleanor Crosses are gone, and the one in Geddington is the best preserved of those that remain (see Figure 6).

When Edward I passed through Geddington in 1290, Robert and Alice Penifader got as close as they ever would to a king or queen of England. Like all peasants, they were taught to revere royalty, and Edward I, an especially strong and bellicose king, inspired special respect. He had faced baronial revolt in his youth, but in 1290, such threats were in the past. Ruling by the fact of his birth, the power of his wealth, the influence of his bureaucracy, the force of his personality, and the success of his military campaigns, Edward I was a formidable figure. For Robert and Alice Penifader, however, Edward I was even more than an awesome king, far richer and more powerful than anyone else in their world. He was also their manorial lord.

Brigstock was a royal manor. Sometimes kings took the profits of the manor for themselves, but usually they granted it to their queens as *dower* (that

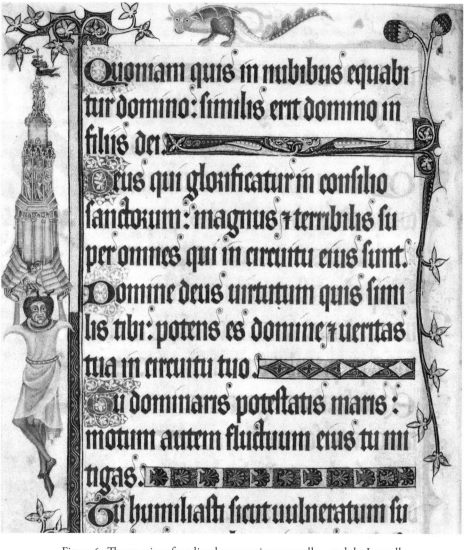

Quomam quis in nubibus equabi
tur domino: similis erit domino in
filiis dei. Deus qui glorificatur in consilio
sanctorum: magnus et terribilis su
per omnes qui in circuitu eius sunt.
Domine deus uirtutum quis simi
lis tibi: potens es domine et ueritas
tua in circuitu tuo. Tu dominaris potestatis maris:
motum autem fluctuum eius tu mi
tigas. Tu humiliasti sicut uulneratum su

Figure 6. The margins of medieval manuscripts generally—and the Luttrell
Psalter especially—are filled with whimsical and beautiful marginalia. In the
left margin here, the monument balanced on the man's head might be one of
the Eleanor Crosses, built wherever Queen Eleanor's body rested overnight on
its journey from Lincoln to Westminster Abbey in 1290. Some art historians
suggest that the man is the mason who supervised construction and that he
appears again as the smaller man who seems to be putting final touches on the
steps of the monument. (British Library, Luttrell Psalter, folio 159v.)

is, as part of the lands designated for support in widowhood). (**Dower** and **dowry** are different but often confused. Both were arranged at marriage to ensure that the bride would have sufficient support in widowhood, but they came from different sources—dower was a portion, usually one-third, of a husband's lands, and dowry consisted of property from the bride's family. By Cecilia's day, dower was more common in England and northern Europe, and dowry was more common in southern Europe.) In 1262, Brigstock had been assigned to the mother of Edward I, Eleanor of Provence; after her death in 1292, the manor passed to Edward I; then to his second wife Margaret of France; then to Edward II; and finally to his wife Isabella of France (who died in 1358). As these transfers suggest, royal revenues were a complex business, and Brigstock manor was just a tiny piece of the pie (in 1262, for example, it accounted for only 1 percent of Eleanor of Provence's dower). No royal lord or lady of Brigstock seems to have ever visited the manor, and, indeed, they usually leased it out to someone who managed the manor, paid an agreed-upon annual rent, and took any extra income as profit. For the Penifaders, the seignorial power of the manor's royal owners was a distant power.

Of the three institutions that structured life in Brigstock—village, parish, and manor—the last was the most removed from the day-to-day life of Cecilia Penifader. Every day she chatted with some neighbors, worked with others, and fed her sheep on the fields and pastures that were open, by general agreement and custom, to common use. She sometimes argued with her neighbors and sometimes stole from them too, but for her, the "community of the vill" was a real community. The parish also wielded a strong presence in Cecilia's life. The churches of St. Andrew and St. Peter were the most imposing buildings around; the priests, one of whom was likely Cecilia's brother, would have impressed everyone with their education, religious authority, and perhaps also, sanctity; and the Masses said by these priests attracted Cecilia to church not only on Sundays but also on many holy days throughout the year.

The manor of Brigstock was also important to Cecilia, for she paid her rents to the manor and brought her business before its court. But the manor was a more extraneous entity. Devised as a profit-making mechanism for its owners, Brigstock manor was part of a grid for the management of land and people that had been superimposed, many centuries before Cecilia's day, on the already settled villages of the English midlands. In the case of Brigstock, as we have seen, this grid had settled messily on the village, for Brigstock manor excluded a few small holdings in the village of Brigstock and took in much of nearby Stanion as well as small bits of two other nearby villages. Brigstock manor made its modest contribution to the revenues of its lord or lady in typical ways: the produce from the demesne, the rents of the tenants, and the income generated by court fines and administrative fees. In Eleanor of Provence's day, she and her clerks knew precisely how much money they could expect to get from Brigstock each year: £41 and 10 shillings. (The symbol £ designates a **pound sterling**. In the monetary system then used, a penny was the basic coin, a **shilling** consisted of 12 **pence**, and there were 20 shillings to the pound sterling.) Small as this was in the context of royal finances, £41 and 10 shillings was a lot of money to the peasants of Brigstock, amounting to more than sixty-five days of work for one hundred men. A lot of labor and a lot of wealth flowed out of the cottages of Brigstock and into the system of estates through which the landed elite profited from "those who work."

Seignorial Powers

Compared to most medieval peasants, Cecilia Penifader and the other tenants of Brigstock were remarkably unencumbered by manorialism; they did not suffer from over-zealous administrators; they enjoyed an especially privileged legal status; and they were even able, for most of Cecilia's life, to lease Brigstock manor and manage it directly on their own. Cecilia grew up, reached maturity, aged, sickened, and died without ever bowing before any lord or lady of Brigstock.

Yet most peasants lived in much closer proximity to their lords or ladies, especially if their manors were held by baronial or knightly families. Holding only a few manors or even just one, these knights and ladies often lived on their manors for at least part of the year. Sometimes they traveled from manor to manor, consuming the produce of each demesne before they moved on. Resident lords and ladies exerted a powerful and continuing presence over the lives of tenants. They required deference at all times—a bowed head when met in the street, a special place in the parish church, an immediate response to any request or command. They proffered hospitality, especially at Christmas, when it was customary to open the hall of the manor house to feasting by the tenants. And they sometimes directly managed the manor, supervising the tenancies, presiding over the manorial court, and taking its profitable rents, fines, and fees. Resident lords and ladies knew their tenants well, and their tenants probably knew them even better. This sort of intimate seignorial relationship was far from the experience of the people of Brigstock. William I and Henry I each

visited Brigstock briefly, but when the newly widowed Edward I stopped in
Geddington on that cold evening in December 1290, he got as close to Brigstock as would any of the kings of the thirteenth or fourteenth centuries.

Many medieval peasants also endured much closer administrative supervision than did the tenants of Brigstock, especially if their manors were part of
an ecclesiastical estate. Manors could be held by institutions as well as by people,
and many monasteries, colleges, and bishoprics developed highly sophisticated
mechanisms for administering their various lands and tenants. The abbey of
Ramsey, for example, held twenty-three manors in the region to the east and
south of Brigstock, and its officers were constantly moving between these
manors—keeping accounts, checking on reeves (the men responsible for most
of the day-to-day work of the manor), convening courts, and generally making
sure that everything was managed as efficiently and as profitably as possible.
Armed with ink and parchment, these clerks kept such careful records that they
could trace persons, lands, and money owed across many generations. Rather
than being kinder and gentler, religious institutions like Ramsey Abbey were
especially tenacious landlords.

Perhaps most important, many medieval peasants were personally unfree
in ways that the Penifaders and other tenants of Brigstock were not. A free peasant was able to emigrate, work, marry, and take grievances to the king's court; a
serf was restricted in all these respects. There were many intermediate categories
between freedom and serfdom, and to complicate matters even more, these distinctions were applied to land as well as people (so that a free woman could hold
land for which the labor services of serfdom were due). By Cecilia's time, serfdom meant less than it once had, but it was still onerous enough that peasants
sought to evade or escape it whenever possible.

Serfs differed from free peasants in three important ways. First, serfs were
"tied to the land," and if they wished to marry someone on another manor or
move elsewhere, they had to get permission to do so. Many serfs never moved
away from the manors of their birth. Of those who did, some left surreptitiously,
but most paid a small annual fee (called **chevage**) to live legally off the manor.
They paid the fee, doubtless grudgingly, because it assured not only that they
could return for visits but also that no one else, especially their parents, would
suffer for their unauthorized absence. This was a heavy enough burden, but the
second burden was worse: serfs had to pay some of their rent in labor. Many had
to do **week-work** on demesne lands, usually a day or two each week spent plowing, sowing, weeding, or doing whatever the reeve said needed to be done; almost all had to do **boon-works** during harvest, undertaking special work

Figure 7. Carting. The carting service required of serfs was dangerous work.
If the driver lost his balance, the cart might tip him under the horses'
hooves. If the men at the back failed to push hard enough, the wheels (notice
their metal spikes!) might crush them. Even the fellow using a stick to keep
the load intact is at risk of tumbling cargo. Notice the skillful composition
of the scene: the artist has depicted the cart moving from the bottom of the
page up into the left-side margin. (British Library, Luttrell Psalter, folio 173v.)

harvesting crops on the demesne (in compensation for their extra work during
harvest, serfs often got food and ale); and some others were also obliged to perform other petty services, such as carting or carrying goods at certain times to
certain places (see Figure 7).

Third, serfs often had to pay a variety of small fines and fees, which were
expensive, irritating, and, in some cases, humiliating. Many manors required
serfs to use manorial services—mills, winepresses, ovens—whose profits
went, of course, into the hands of the lord or lady. Often peasants tried to
avoid these expenses (for example, by using hand-mills to grind their own
grain or seeking out millers who charged cheap prices), but many lords and
ladies obstructed these money-saving strategies by insisting that *their* serfs
had to patronize *their* mills, winepresses, and ovens. Another small fee was
the **leyrwite**, due from any unfree women, and rarely men, who were sexually
active before marriage. Marriage itself could be costly; unfree women (and,
again, occasionally men) had to pay **merchet** for permission to marry. Most
manors also required that a **heriot** be paid whenever an unfree tenant died.

Traditionally, the heriot was the most valuable animal of the dead tenant, but this was often converted to a cash amount. Finally, on many manors, lords and ladies enjoyed the right of **tallage**, the right to levy an arbitrary tax on serfs. Heriot and tallage sprang from the same fundamental principle: the notion that all of a serf's property, movable goods as well as tenancies, ultimately belonged to the lord or lady. Everything a serf possessed—cash, furniture, clothing, pots, bedding, sheep, pigs, goats, and land—was held "at the will of" the manorial lord or lady.

These obligations of serfdom were costly and demeaning. Of them all, serfs especially resented obligatory work, for days spent laboring on the demesne were days lost from work on their own tenancies. They also strongly resented the uncertainty of their obligations. A lord or lady could levy tallage in one year and not the next, or could convert labor services into cash payments in one year and insist on their performance in the next. These legitimate but arbitrary actions introduced a maddening instability into peasant budgets. Whenever they could, serfs aggressively and persistently sought freedom. They tried to avoid paying servile fees such as merchet or tallage; they purchased their freedom; they went to court to claim free descent; and especially in the decades that followed the Black Death of 1347–1349, they rebelled against the manorial regime.

Distinctions between free and unfree readily capture modern imaginations, and it would certainly be a mistake to underestimate serfdom. But it would also be a mistake to make too much of distinctions between free peasants and serfs. After all, free peasants had obligations too. They had to pay their rents, render deference to their "social betters," answer charges in manorial courts, and sometimes even take business to manorial mills or other facilities. Moreover, although distinctions between free and unfree were important, they did not mean as much by 1300 as they had in the past. It helped a bit that some obligations of serfs were set by *custom* and could not be changed for the worse. Whatever a serf's parents had done, he or she also had to do—but no more.

In fact, custom sometimes protected serfs from market forces. In the late thirteenth century, as population pressure made land scarce and more valuable, rents on free lands were readily raised to new heights, but rents on serf lands stayed at their old, customary levels. Serfs were similarly protected by rules, found on many manors, against the subdivision of unfree tenements. Free tenants so often divided their lands between sons that after a few generations, many free tenants held small, even tiny, properties. Serfs, sometimes required to keep tenancies intact by lords or ladies who wanted easy-to-collect rents, had to provide for noninheriting children in other ways. As a result, some serfs numbered among the prosperous few who held thirty acres or more, while many free tenants possessed holdings that were too small to support their households. In other words, serfdom was an undesirable state, but it would be wrong to equate serfdom with poverty and degradation. By Cecilia's time, free and unfree peasants regularly intermarried, held each other's lands, and otherwise intermingled. Although freedom and serfdom still determined various rents and obligations, the lines were so blurred and confused that they had fairly weak social meaning. In most villages by 1300, it mattered more whether you held thirty acres or five acres than whether you were free or unfree.

In any case, distinctions of free and unfree were even less relevant to the people of Brigstock. Like many other manors in royal forests, Brigstock was part of the **ancient demesne**, defined as the manors held directly by William the Conqueror at the time of the Domesday Survey in 1086. Long before Cecilia's birth, tenants of the ancient demesne had come to enjoy a special legal status, different from either free peasants or serfs: lawyers called them "privileged villeins of the ancient demesne." Cecilia and her fellow tenants had to tolerate a few vestigial remnants of serfdom: they had to pay various small annual fees; they had to provide minimal labor services (especially boon-works at harvest); their tenancies had to pass through the bailiff's hands whenever sold, transferred, or inherited; and they had, in a few restricted instances, to pay merchet and heriot. But the tenants of Brigstock and other ancient demesne manors had privileges unknown to other peasants, either free or serf: they did not have to pay tolls or customs anywhere in England; they could not be obliged to attend county courts; and they were able to use royal writs to bring their cases to court (this meant that they could use the power of the king to resolve disputes, especially property disputes, in their favor). Cecilia's status, then, exemplifies the blurring between free and unfree that was so common by her time. Neither a freewoman nor a serf, she tolerated a few servile obligations but also enjoyed other exceptional privileges.

The most startling manifestation of Brigstock's unusual manorial status was the leasing of the manor by its tenants. Under this arrangement, the people of Brigstock managed their own manor. They took profits off the demesne by cultivating it or renting it out; they convened the court and made sure that its fines were paid; they collected all rents and fees. From these profits, they paid the lease of the manor, and as long as they paid the lease on time, they were left

HOW DO WE KNOW ABOUT EVERYDAY LIFE?

"From a distance"—this is how historians see medieval peasants. We have no firsthand accounts of their lives—no diaries, no letters, no farmers' notes, no family keepsakes, no accounts of household spending. We find pots and locks and knives when we excavate peasant homes, but no peasant writings at all—and until the very end of the Middle Ages, it is fair to assume that all peasants, save those who propelled themselves out of the peasantry by pursuing church careers, were illiterate. As a result, most of our information about peasants is filtered through people who were not themselves working the land: manorial clerks who recorded proceedings of courts or toted up annual accounts; monastic artists who drew pictures of peasants in the margins of their books; writers who described peasants, but did not live among them (William Langland, author of the deeply sympathetic *Piers Plowman,* spent most of his adult life in London); clerks and students who scribbled out songs, ballads, and proverbs that might, we can hope, have deep origins in the oral culture of the medieval countryside. It is as if we tried to reconstruct the lives of twenty-first-century students by examining what their professors and parents wrote about them. The picture is not wrong but it is certainly incomplete and partial.

For medieval peasants, one source offers precious snippets of everyday life, and it is, ironically enough, a source that tells us about everyday death. Whenever a person died by accident or violence, English law required that a royal officer called a *coroner* had to investigate, ideally within a day or two. He viewed the body and looked at its wounds; he interviewed the person who found the body and other witnesses; he assembled a jury of local men to determine cause of death; and he (or his clerk) then wrote up a report for the king. Sound familiar? It should. In many modern jurisdictions and in many crime dramas, coroners have much the same duties today. Unlike today, however, coroners in the Middle Ages were not chosen for their medical expertise.

Medieval coroners reported on some spectacular murders, but we best see daily life in their reports on accidental deaths. Here are some examples from the county of Bedfordshire in the later thirteenth century:

> On 12 August 1267 in Great Barford, William and Muriel Blaunche were working in the fields while their daughters Muriel, aged six years, and her sister Beatrice, almost three years, were at home. A fire broke out in the house, and Beatrice died.

> At dawn on 31 December 1268 in Goldington, the brothers Henry and William Carpenter quarreled in their father's house over a loan of a halfpenny which one had made to the other. As they walked out the door, William whacked Henry with a crab-apple staff so hard that he fell down. Henry died just after nightfall.

> On the afternoon of 2 October 1270 in the hamlet of Staploe, Amice Belamy and Sibyl Bonchevaler were in a brewhouse, carrying a tub full of herbs which they intended to empty into a vat of boiling water. Amice slipped and fell into the vat and then the tub fell on top of her. Sibyl dragged Amice out and called for help, but Amice was mortally scalded and died the next day.

On the afternoon of 23 June 1271 in Eaton Socon, William Witside, aged fifteen, took a boat onto the river Ouse to search for a second boat that had floated away. When he reached the missing boat, he stretched out his hand to grab it, lost his balance, fell into the water, and drowned.

Rather like fifteen-second TikTok videos, these case stories allow us to glimpse medieval peasants for a few fleeting moments. These stories are tragic, but their matter-of-factness lets us feel almost as if we were right there, on the scene, watching two brothers quarrel as they grumpily head out for the day's work or two young women awkwardly slip-sliding beside a heavy vat.

But not quite so fast. All historical sources require careful study. In the case of coroners' rolls, two rules of historical research especially apply.

1. Know your source. We need to know why and how a document was created in order to assess its utility. In the case of coroners' rolls, it matters that the coroner was mainly interested in pursuing murderers and confiscating property for the king. Homicide was a felony reserved for the king's courts, so the king relied on coroners to tell him what deaths were murders, who the perpetrators were, where they could be found, and what goods they had (so the king could confiscate them). These were serious matters, and it is likely that coroners, who were busy men, pursued homicides with special vigor. In responding to accidental deaths, their attention was strongly skewed toward men, for they investigated about four male deaths for every one female death. This seems not to be because more men died by accident, for this 4:1 ratio applies even in cases that should have affected both sexes equally (such as night-time deaths caused by fires or collapsed roofs). And of course, we must always consider the possibility that coroners and their juries did not report deaths honestly—perhaps they wanted to protect a well-liked neighbor; or to prevent the confiscation of some goods; or simply to close a case as quickly as possible.

2. Remember context. Coroners' rolls are great for counting, and these counts can show, for example, that many men died by falling off carts and getting kicked by animals, while many women died by falling into wells and vats. On the face of it, these numbers could lead us to conclude that men worked mostly outside in the fields and women mostly around the house—an expected and traditional division of labor. Not so. These numbers actually tell us what were the most dangerous tasks of men (carting) and women (water-carrying), not what each sex spent most of their time doing. We know from wage records, for example, that women often worked in the fields, but their work there—weeding, harrowing, reaping, binding—was relatively risk-free. Numbers are useful, but only in context.

Coroners' rolls offer us rare peeks into everyday life, but they are not as straight-forward as they seem on first glance. They are, like videos of adorable dogs or cats, mere snippets—and heavily edited snippets at that.

To learn more, see the edition from which my examples are taken: R. F. Hunnisett, ed., *Bedfordshire Coroners' Rolls*, Publications of the Bedfordshire Historical Record Society, vol. 41 (1961); and Barbara A. Hanawalt, *The Ties That Bound: Peasant Families in Medieval England* (1986), which is based largely on coroners' rolls. For other interesting artifacts of everyday life, see Matthew Champion, *Medieval Graffiti: The Lost Voices of England's Churches* (2015), and Roberta Gilchrist, *Medieval Life: Archaeology and the Life Course* (2012).

alone until the lease expired. The privilege of leasing their manor did not come cheap. In 1270, the tenants of Brigstock purchased a ten-year lease at a one-time cost of more than £13, promising further that they would pay an extra 30 shillings per year beyond the manor's set value. In 1318, they offered the king £50 each year to lease directly from him, but he refused and instead, probably as a favor, offered the lease to Margery de Farendraght for about £13 a year. The tenants then promised to pay £46 annually to sublease the manor from her. Dearly bought, the privilege of managing their own manorial regime must have been much valued by the people of Brigstock.

Why was this privilege so highly valued? After all, when the tenants held the lease or sublease of Brigstock manor, they were not free of rents, fines, fees, and services. These obligations were as necessary as ever, for they generated the income needed to pay the lease. Yet, as the tenants of Brigstock charged themselves to raise the money for their lease, they gained two tangible benefits. First, they gained some dignity. Like townspeople who were often fiercely proud of the charters whereby they acquired some rights of self-government, the people of Brigstock valued the opportunity to manage their manor themselves. Cecilia and her neighbors still had to defer to their "social betters," but they ensured, for the duration of the lease, that no lord or lady could try to revive old obligations or impose new ones. Second and perhaps more important, they gained some economic relief and some stability of obligation. Since the tenants managed the profit-making capabilities of Brigstock manor with the sole purpose of paying the lease, they were not interested in profit for profit's sake. Once the lease was paid, there was no need to milk manorial perquisites for every possible penny. Whenever the manor lay in the hands of the tenants themselves, in other words, the people of Brigstock could rest easier about their tenancies and goods. They paid what they had to pay to cover the lease, but no more.

As the leasing of Brigstock manor to its tenants shows, profit-taking was at the heart of the manorial enterprise. Yes, seignorial rights spoke to the inferiority of tenants and the deference expected from them; thus, a merchet symbolized the dependency of serfs who could not marry without permission. Yes, the dominating power of the feudal elite ensured that peasants did what they were supposed to do; thus, peasants paid merchets because they would incur fines, punishments, and other unpleasantness if they did not respect their "social betters." Dependency and domination were critical to manorialism, but they were supporting actors to the main manorial role: profit. For many peasants, the people of Brigstock among them, seignorial power was expressed more often through clerks, officers, and administrators than through the imposing presence of a resident lord or lady.

Peasants and Their "Social Betters"

During the harvest of 1304, two of Cecilia's sisters, Emma and Alice, failed to appear for boon-works on the demesne, and that September they were cited in court because they had "refused to do the boon-work of our lord the king." How should we understand their absence? It is possible that the Penifaders forgot to bring everyone to the boon-work, leaving behind their least fit children (both girls seem to have died at early ages). But it is also possible that the absence of Emma and Alice from this servile labor was deliberate, a small but telling way in which the Penifaders resisted the seignorial power of Brigstock's lady, Queen Margaret, second wife of Edward I. Just as we cannot know whether the absence of Emma and Alice was accident or deliberate design, so we cannot know about the many other instances in which tenants fell foul of their servile obligations. Was a missed week-work a matter of forgetfulness or resistance? Were unpaid rents a matter of poverty or truculence? Was a marriage concluded without merchet a clever dodge to save money or a deliberate assertion of the right to marry without seignorial permission?

While we cannot always know how to interpret instances in which peasants failed to fulfill manorial obligations, we can be certain of several things about relations between peasants, on the one hand, and the lords or ladies of manors, on the other. First, tenants often came up short in meeting their obligations. Work was left unfinished; rents and fines were unpaid; and other things got done only after repeated reminders and even harassment. Second, tenants sometimes fulfilled their duties in sullen and minimal ways. For example, reeves complained long and hard about the unenthusiastic efforts of serfs forced to work on the demesne: they came late to work; they paid poor attention to instructions; they worked slowly. Third, tenants occasionally resisted seignorial demands outright (see Figure 8). Some serfs on a Ramsey Abbey manor to the southeast of Brigstock got so angry about the poor quality of food provided at their boon-works that they walked off and refused to work. One young man on another Ramsey manor resisted forced boon-works in a surprisingly modern way—he lay down in the field, obstructing with his body further work on the harvest. Other tenants argued with their lords or ladies over more substantial matters such as new increases in labor services, and, in some cases, these disputes

Figure 8. Peasant Complaints? This vignette is hard to interpret. Some think it shows a game, with the man on the left stepping up to a mark from which he will throw his ball. But it might also be a critique of the ideal of Three Orders. Placement is one clue: it sits across from another image of conflict (see Figure 1 on p. 5) and adjacent to a text that describes how God has the power to demean nobles and elevate the poor (Psalm 107:40–41). The glove waved by the man on the left is another clue, because brandishing or tossing a glove is a classic gesture of challenge. If so, he might be throwing a rock at the man in the middle (a noble? a manorial officer?) who wags his finger (in warning?) and grabs his purse. The man on the right strips off his tunic, possibly forced to give up even the shirt off his back. (British Library, Luttrell Psalter, folio 198.)

dragged on for years and even ended up before the justices of the king. One famous case pitted the tenants of Halesowen, located about sixty miles west of Brigstock, against the abbey that held the manor. It lasted for more than seventy years, and involved royal inquests, petitions to the king's council, settlements gone awry, and a great deal of animosity. In the end, the abbey won.

After the Black Death of 1347–1349, resistance to manorialism took a new turn, with peasants mounting full-scale revolts to better their circumstances. The first revolt was the French *Jacquerie* of 1358 (so called because many peasant men in France were named Jacques). In England, the Peasants' Revolt in 1381 severely frightened the landowning elite, and Jack Cade's Rebellion in 1450 did much the same. In Germany, peasants sought, in the Peasants' War of 1524–1525, to ease some of their social and economic difficulties. In all these cases, peasants were cruelly crushed by the forces of the feudal elite. Yet they often won in the long haul, for many of their demands were eventually met, albeit slowly. For example, the English peasants of 1381 sought, among other things, the abolition of serfdom. To this end, rebels burned buildings, murdered several people (including the Archbishop of Canterbury), and marched on London. There, they met on two occasions with the fourteen-year-old Richard II. The rebels revered the king and trusted him; their anger was aimed at the lords and ladies of their own manors—that is, at those who demanded their labor services, collected their rents, and gave, the rebels thought, bad advice to a good king. When the peasant leader Wat Tyler was slain in the second meeting and Richard II asked the crowds to disperse, the rebels left. From that point on, their revolt was doomed; they were hunted down, imprisoned, and hanged. Serfdom was not abolished. But within a hundred years, it had almost withered away in England—thanks in part to peasant resistance, but thanks also to new economic circumstances that changed the ways in which lords and ladies tried to profit from their manors. The rebels of 1381 lost, but their descendants eventually won.

For the people of Brigstock in the early fourteenth century, tensions over seignorial demands were less intense than elsewhere, if only because seignorial demands were relatively mild. Indeed, in their suit against the abbey, the tenants of Halesowen sought to be treated as privileged villeins of the ancient demesne, the status that Cecilia and others in Brigstock already enjoyed. On a scale that extended from the most oppressed of medieval serfs to those peasants least restricted by manorialism, Cecilia and the other tenants of Brigstock were toward the least restricted end. Yet this does not mean that Cecilia was free of seignorial demands and servile obligations; it means that she lived under a muted form of manorialism. Moreover, manorialism was just one aspect of Cecilia's subservient place. Like all medieval peasants, Cecilia lived under the ever-present shadow of superior powers, of which the power of the lord or lady of Brigstock was but one.

As a child, Cecilia learned from the clergy—her parish priest, his assistants, or the sermons of visiting friars—to see the world as divided into three mutually supporting groups or orders (as briefly discussed in Chapter 1). Developed by clerical authors in the eleventh century, this tripartite view had been popularized by Cecilia's day, and it was commonly taken to represent God's will for the ordering of human relations.

The first and most important was the clerical order, composed of "those who pray." By their prayers and holy service, bishops, priests, monks, nuns, and friars bridged the gap between ordinary people and God. Since Cecilia had been taught that the business of life was eternal salvation, it was easy to convince her that the holy efforts of "those who pray" were much more important than her own modest work on the land. Moreover, without the priests who managed the two churches of Brigstock and the friars who preached sermons when they passed through Brigstock, Cecilia's life would have been much more boring and dull. As we shall see in Chapter 4, Christianity, with its crowded calendar of festivals and rituals, created a steady rhythm of worship, celebration, and festivity that richly shaped the days and years of Cecilia's life.

Second in importance came the landed elite, "those who fight." By their military power and strong governance, kings, earls, barons, and knights ensured, according to the theory, that everyone else could go about their business in peace and security. Unlike peasants elsewhere, Cecilia did not have to seek much protection from war and invasion. If she had lived in Spain (where Christian and Muslim armies fought each other—and among themselves—from the thirteenth century) or on the eastern borders of the Holy Roman Empire (where German settlers bumped up against Slavs), she would have been especially grateful to feudal armies that protected villages from destruction and, in some cases, won new lands for settlement. Yet even Cecilia, living in the relatively stable and secure English midlands, could be grateful for strong knights and strong kings. These men brought peace to her countryside; they discouraged marauders and bandits; and they punished those guilty of murder, theft, rape, and other felonies. Cecilia readily believed that the firm hand of the king protected her, not only from Welsh and Scots invaders but also from murderers, rapists, and other felons.

Third, at the bottom of the heap came the mass of medieval peasants, "those who work." By the sweat of her hard labor, Cecilia supported, so priests and friars taught her, those who prayed for her soul and guaranteed her security.

This was a neat and coherent theory. Every order had a role to play, and if each did its part well, salvation, security, and support were assured. But this theory worked less well in practice. To begin with, some groups of people fit poorly into the theory: there was no place in this neat, tripartite world for merchants, artisans, and other townspeople, and little place for women, either. Moreover, the theory was too idealized. Clerics could sin with as much gusto as they prayed, and they were sometimes more noted for their wealth than for their holiness. The feudal elite similarly caused disorder as well as peace. Violent and proud, these men, and sometimes women, thought nothing of pursuing petty arguments through battle, cantering through ripening fields in pursuit of deer, or breaking fences and scattering herds that stood in their way. Most of all, Cecilia surely felt, when tithes, taxes, and rents were all due at once, that her role among "those who work" was the hardest and least fulfilling of the three.

Alongside this idyllic but not entirely convincing tripartite scheme of three mutually supportive orders was another world view, one that saw a straightforward division between privileged and not-privileged, empowered and disempowered. On one side stood elites; on the other side stood ordinary people. On one side stood barons, nuns, merchants, and many people even richer and more powerful; on the other side stood laborers, peasants, and the poor. This was the world view that English peasants rejected a few generations after Cecilia's death when, in the Peasants' Revolt of 1381, they asked:

When Adam delved and Eve span,
Who then was the gentleman?

What was the biblical justification, they were asking, for dividing people into "haves" and "have-nots"? This radical question, phrased in exactly this form, was raised by disgruntled peasants throughout Europe on many occasions between 1300 and 1550.

Both views of medieval society—the tripartite view, which ranked peasants last, and the bipartite view, which separated the privileged and the not-privileged—encouraged elites to see themselves as better sorts of people, almost different races. Peasants were sometimes pitied for their poverty, but neither their persons nor their labors were appreciated. Elites treated peasants with scorn and disgust, and they described peasants as dishonest, irreligious, dirty, stupid drudges. Said to be descended from Cain or Ham, peasants were seen as almost a different race made for sweated work alone. "What should a serf do," asked one monk, "but serve?"

The most startling manifestation of elite disdain for the peasantry is the ready assumption by privileged men that peasant women were theirs for the taking. Matters were not as bad as we moderns sometimes imagine, for there was no "right of first night" in the Middle Ages—that is, no lords could demand sexual intercourse with a peasant bride before she slept with her husband. This is a fiction about the Middle Ages created in the sixteenth century and still popularized today—it is, for example, critical to the plots of the opera *The Marriage of Figaro* and the movie *Braveheart*. Yet even without any right of the first night, peasant women were at special risk. Sometimes peasants were seen by their social superiors as so naturally earthy and lusty that men could easily, as one text for young scholars put it, "make free with their wives and daughters." Sometimes they were seen as natural prey for elite men. Courtly poems written in the twelfth and thirteenth centuries celebrated the rape of peasant women by young knights, and Andreas Capellanus, the twelfth-century author of *The Art of Courtly Love*, advised any knight enamored of an unyielding peasant maiden, "do not hesitate to take what you seek and to embrace her by force." Rape cases were rarely prosecuted in medieval courts, so we cannot know how often this talk about the sexual availability of peasant women was translated into action. As best we know, Cecilia never fell victim to such deluded ideas.

More mundanely but just as profoundly, the ambitions of peasant children were necessarily limited. Peasants were often pious, but they seldom found careers in the Church. Precocious boys occasionally took holy orders and served in rural parishes, but there were almost no peasant monks or nuns, few peasant bishops (Robert Grosseteste is one exception) or popes, and indeed, few peasant saints. Peasants were often clever, but most received no formal education, and even those few seldom advanced to training at universities or law courts. Peasants were sometimes wealthy, but they rarely found merchants or knights willing to deal with them as business partners, or, even more unlikely, willing to join their families in marriage. Peasants were often politically astute, but when Edward I began to call together the first parliaments of England, he gathered lords, churchmen, knights, and townsmen into Westminster Hall, but not a single peasant. Peasants far outnumbered the ecclesiastical, feudal, and mercantile elites, but the wealth and power of the Middle Ages lay beyond their reach.

Within the community of Brigstock, Cecilia was born into a well-off and well-respected family. By the standards of most medieval peasants, her lot was an enviable one indeed. Yet Cecilia's life was structured at every turn by people and institutions more powerful than she. The Church told her how she should live and worship; it stood ready to punish her if need arose; and it took a compulsory tithe from her fields and flocks. The king claimed the right to punish her for murder, theft, and other major crimes, and to collect, when he had need, taxes, food, and soldiers from Cecilia and the other tenants of Brigstock. The king and queen also sought, as lord and lady of Brigstock, to take as much profit from Brigstock manor, by lease or direct management, as they could. And any merchant, knight, or abbess who rode through Brigstock expected Cecilia to greet them with proper deference and humility. Well-off within her community, Cecilia was just another peasant to the many different sorts of people who sought to profit from her life and labor. It is easy to understand the powers of these people and to describe them, but it is impossible to answer the most intriguing question: What did Cecilia think about it? When she bowed to a passing lady, paid rent to the queen's bailiff, or bargained with a merchant, did she think that her "social betters" were truly better than she?

Suggestions for Further Reading

For elite views of peasants, see especially Paul H. Freedman, *Images of the Medieval Peasant* (1999). See also his *The Origins of Peasant Servitude in Medieval Catalonia* (1991), an outstanding study of rural subjugation. For more on modern fantasies of a medieval "right of the first night," see Alain Boureau, *The Lord's First Night: The Myth of the Droit de Cuissage* (1995). For the slow demise of serfdom in England, see Mark Bailey, *The Decline of Serfdom in Late Medieval England: From Bondage to Freedom* (2014). For the historiography of class relations, see John Hatcher and Mark Bailey, "Class Power and Property Relations," in their *Modelling the Middle Ages: The History and Theory of England's Economic Development* (2001), pp. 66–120. For the peasants' revolt, a recent study is Juliet Barker, *1381: The Year of the Peasants' Revolt in England* (2014), published in the UK as *England, Arise: The People, the King and the Great Revolt of 1381.*

CHAPTER 4

Parish, Belief, Ritual

July 1326, Brigstock Court: Cecilia's brother William arranged in this court for a young man identified as John, the son of Alice Perse of Kingsthorpe, to inherit his lands—some twenty separate properties, including his house in Stanion, located next door to Cecilia's own home. "Master William," as he was known, never married, and he was likely a local cleric, trained by the church and bound by vows of celibacy. Why did William leave his property to John Perse? We learn the answer some eighteen years later, when John, in a dispute about another inheritance (that of Cecilia herself), is identified as Cecilia's nephew. In other words, John, the son of Alice Perse of Kingsthorpe, was the bastard son of Master William Penifader.

In the center of Brigstock today stands the church of St. Andrew. Some parts of the church are very old. The western tower and parts of the nave were built by Saxons, about a century before the Norman invasion of 1066. The church of St. Peter in Stanion is much the same—not quite as ancient, but also old and centrally located in the original settlement. These church buildings were already old in Cecilia's time, but much of what we can see today would have been unknown to Cecilia. Like so many English parish churches, St. Andrew and St. Peter were greatly improved by prosperous parishioners in the late fourteenth and fifteenth centuries. Today, both churches are built of fine stone; Cecilia knew smaller churches with some parts built of wood and rubble as well as stone. The interiors are different too; instead of the pews, electrical lights, and whitened walls of today, Cecilia stood (or squatted) in a nave with no pews, relied on natural light or candlelight, and looked up at colorful walls painted with scenes from Christian history and salvation. The modern churchyards are more orderly too, sedate, quiet, and well tended; the graves in Cecilia's churchyard shared space with people gathered for markets, ball games, gambling, gossip, sexual assignations, and sometimes even meetings of the manorial court. Hens, ducks, cats, and dogs also made themselves comfortable around the graves of the human dead.

Yet the biggest differences between then and now have less to do with the two church buildings in Brigstock parish and more to do with belief and ritual. Cecilia's Christian faith differed from that of the Anglicans who worship in St. Andrew and St. Peter today. Protestant reformers of the sixteenth century (including the founders of Anglicanism, a faith known in the United States today as Episcopalianism) swept aside many of the beliefs of Cecilia's time, along with some of the oldest rituals of the medieval Church. They also introduced a diversity of Christian practice unknown to Cecilia. Although there were two main branches of Christianity in the Middle Ages—Western Christianity centered in Rome and Orthodoxy centered in Constantinople (modern-day Istanbul)—Cecilia, living on the western periphery of Europe, knew only the teachings of what she simply called "the Church." Today, Roman Catholicism is the modern faith most closely tied to the teachings and practices of medieval Christianity in Western Europe, but doctrine and practice have changed considerably. Especially important in this regard have been the two reforming councils of Trent in 1545–1562 and Vatican II in 1962–1965.

The differences between Cecilia's faith and modern Christian faiths also reflect changes rooted more in history than theology. First, Cecilia's religious world was strikingly homogeneous; she might have heard stories about Jews, Muslims, or Christian heretics, but the world in which she lived offered no alternative religious practices. Jews had been expelled from England in 1290, a few years before Cecilia was born, and although the English heresy known as Lollardy developed a generation or so after she died, no heretics tempted country folk with radical interpretations of Christianity in early fourteenth-century England. Sometimes Cecilia and her neighbors frequented holy wells, cast spells, sought help from hermits, or established informal shrines. These practices were sometimes discouraged by the Church, but they were easily absorbed into Christian holiness and Cecilia would have considered them as a seamless part of her faith. Second, Cecilia's religious life was imbued by the rhythms of the natural world around her; she would not have thought it odd that she feared fairies as well as her Christian God, or that she mingled charms with prayers, or that major Christian holy days coincided with the summer and winter solstices.

Third, her religious education was accomplished more by observation and listening than by study; Cecilia understood what it meant to be a Christian from what she *saw* in church (the ritual of the Mass, the wall paintings, the statues) and from what she *heard* in occasional sermons, pious songs, and the talk of her friends and family. Indeed, Cecilia's mother was probably her most important religious instructor. Joan of Arc, another peasant woman, born in Lorraine in the early fifteenth century, testified that she learned her prayers from her mother: "Nobody taught me my belief," she said, "if not my mother."

Peasant Piety

Some historians have suggested that peasants like Cecilia were so poorly trained in Christianity and so devoted to traditional beliefs that they were not truly Christians. After all, when peasants wore animal masks at midwinter or danced around bonfires at midsummer, they echoed the customs of ancient pagans. Yet for Cecilia and others like her, there was no worship of older deities in these practices; instead, these were age-old customs that merged easily with Christianity. For the most part, folk traditions and Christianity were complementary, not contradictory. Masking became part of Christmas revelries, and midsummer bonfires burned on the celebratory night before the feast of St. John the Baptist. The Church sometimes even encouraged these blendings of Christian practice and older custom. In the early seventh century, Gregory I had advised the missionaries he sent to the English to convert pagan temples into Christian churches since people will be "more ready to come to the places with which they are familiar." Gregory was willing to make these concessions to ordinary folk because, as he put it, "it is impossible to cut out everything at once from their stubborn minds." Seven centuries later, peasants were still stubbornly fond of folk customs, and the clergy were still accommodating Christian beliefs to rural traditions.

For Cecilia and other medieval peasants, then, Church teachings, natural phenomena, and folk traditions merged easily into their understanding of religious belief and practice. In this blended form, Christianity permeated rural life. Cecilia may have prayed to the Virgin Mary as she mingled malt, yeast, and water to brew ale, or bowed her head when she passed a crucifix roughly built alongside a footpath, or whispered the Lord's Prayer before she entered the forest to gather herbs and nuts. These practices ensured that every day and in many ways, Cecilia sought the protection, help, and comfort of her God and his saints.

As a young girl and a grown woman, Cecilia particularly focused her piety on the churches of St. Andrew and St. Peter. Two contemporary alternatives to parish-focused piety were not readily available to her because she was an illiterate peasant woman. First, private piety was common only among the wealthy. For example, before she died in 1360, the widowed Elizabeth de Burgh, Lady of Clare, enjoyed the daily support of her own private confessor and was also allowed to take a vow of chastity without entering a monastery. Many aristocrats even had their own private chapels in which they could worship, without having to resort to parish churches. No peasants had the leisure, education, or money for such pieties. At least one person in Brigstock owned a psalter, but it was rare for a peasant to be able to read such a book or to be able to afford one (before the development of printing in the fifteenth century, books were handwritten and expensive). For Cecilia and her neighbors, formal religious efforts were mostly confined to church services on Sundays and holy days. Second, a career in the Church was seldom available to peasants. Sometimes a peasant boy was accepted as a priest, friar, or monk, or **deacon**, as her brother William seems to have been. But church careers were rare for boys and nearly impossible for girls. Careers among the *secular clergy*, that is, among the clergy who ministered in the lay world (*saeculum*) to the souls of the faithful, were not available to women: there were no female deacons, priests, or bishops. Medieval people told a story about a Pope Joan, a woman who had begun to dress as a man to accompany her lover to university and who had then moved rapidly up the clerical hierarchy to become pope. Most such stories ended with Pope Joan dying in a papal procession, struck down by a difficult childbirth (or, in some versions, attacked by an angry mob after her birthing pains revealed her female identity). With its story of cross-dressing, illicit sex, and confused gender roles, the legend of Pope Joan titillated medieval listeners, but it had no basis in reality. From the pope in Rome to his bishops who oversaw **dioceses** throughout Europe to the priests who worked in parishes, the worldly work of the church was done by men.

A pious girl's main option for a professional religious life was among the *regular* clergy who lived by a monastic rule (or *regula*). To medieval Christians, monastic withdrawal was the ideal religious life. Unfortunately, most female monasteries required expensive dowries (or entry payments) from would-be nuns. This practice began in the early Middle Ages, and although popes and bishops tried hard to eradicate it, they were never successful; as a result, most

HOW DO WE KNOW ABOUT PEASANT SEXUAL MORALITY?

Moral texts are easy to find for the Middle Ages. We have the pronouncements of popes and church councils; we have many, many sermons; we have manuals that taught priests how to provide good pastoral care; we have hundreds of *exempla*, short moral tales for priests to use when their audiences "begin to get sleepy." (This chapter includes three exempla—the story of the priest's concubine and the bishop; the story of how the demon Tutivillus was overwhelmed by gossiping women; and the story of the terrible fate of dancers who skipped Christmas services.)

All of these various sources *prescribe* morality (they tell us about ideals, not what people actually did), and the ideals come from above (from the Church, not peasants themselves). Peasants sometimes marched to a different moral drummer. Premarital sex is a good example. The Church actively punished people they called "fornicators," men as well as women. Offenders were stripped of their outer clothes, shoes, and headgear, paraded through churchyards, and publicly whipped. (Some avoided this public shame by paying a fine.)

Peasants punished fornication too, but much more selectively and sporadically. In manor courts in England (not elsewhere in Europe, as best we can tell), young serf women were regularly fined for fornication, paying *leyrwite*, literally a "lying-down-fine." Sometimes the fine was called *childwite*, and it was levied not for fornication but for its result—the birth of an illegitimate child. Here are some examples from Walsham-le-Willows in the county of Suffolk, about sixty miles east of Brigstock:

> January 1329:
> Christina Patel gave birth out of wedlock and pays 32 pence as childwite.

> March 1329:
> Alice Hereward gave birth out of wedlock and pays 32 pence as childwite.
> Cecilia Pudding, 32 pence for the same.

> October 1333:
> Catherine Machon gave birth out of wedlock; and therefore pays the fixed fine of 32 pence.

Unlike Church prosecutions, men are almost never mentioned in manorial fines for leyrwite or childwite. It is as though peasants thought fornication was committed by women, all by themselves.

Manorial lords and ladies profited, of course, from leyrwite and childwite, but since manors relied on local jurors to name offenders, peasants must have agreed that these women should be punished. Several clues suggest that their objections were more practical than moral. First, well-off jurors, like the Penifader men of Brigstock, did not name their own daughters for leyrwite or childwite; they instead targeted women from the poorest village families. Second, they punished these women with exceptionally large fines. In the Walsham court, fines for most offenses were set at 2 pence, 6 pence, or 12 pence,

Figure 9. A Wayfaring Mother and Child. This woman's walking stick suggests that she is a vagrant, moving from place to place in search of work and shelter. She carries a child on her back, and since no male partner walks beside her, she was likely meant to represent the wayfaring life forced upon some mothers of illegitimate children. The rosary around her arm indicates her piety, and it might have been included to evoke sympathy for her plight. (British Library, Luttrell Psalter, folio 53.)

but childwite, as explicitly stated in the case of Catherine Machon, cost 32 pence (to earn this sum, Catherine had to save all her wages from about forty-five days' work). Third, well-off villagers discouraged poor, unwed mothers in other ways, too, especially by expulsion; in the 1280s, the good folk of Horsham in the county of Norfolk, not far from Walsham, forced out of their village four poor mothers and their six small children (see Figure 9). For village elites in the hard times c. 1300, control of the proliferating poor was a survival strategy, and leyrwite, childwite, and expulsion were its tools.

Nothing proves this more clearly that the historian's best friend: chronology. English villagers punished unwed mothers in hard times and tolerated them in good times. In 1300, villages were crowded, harvests were unpredictable, life was difficult, and leyrwite and childwite flourished. In 1400, when standards of living had risen dramatically in the wake of the Black Death, peasant juries utterly ceased to report leyrwite and childwite. By 1500, however, population pressure had begun again to undermine peasant prosperity, and villagers resumed punishment of unwed mothers (because manorialism had by then declined, they used village **by-laws** instead of manorial fines). Throughout these centuries the Church continued to prosecute fornicators, but peasants harassed unwed mothers only when they threatened to become a burden on parochial charity.

We can also see peasants' acceptance of premarital sex in one last fact: many of the women fined for premarital sex c. 1300 eventually married. They were not, in other words, somehow tainted by their sexual experience or in some cases, by their bastard children. This was the happy case for Catherine Machon who, three years after she bore her out-of-wedlock child, married a local man, John Taylor.

Morality is a slippery subject for historians, with moral precepts often imposed from above and ignored in practice. In the case of premarital sex, it seems that the Church consistently worried about the morality of sex outside marriage, and peasants worried, if they worried at all, about the charitable burden imposed by unwed mothers.

FOR LEYRWITE AND CHILDWITE, see my article on "Writing Fornication: Medieval Leyrwite and Its Historians," *Transactions of the Royal Historical Society* 13 (2003): 131–162. More generally, see Marjorie Keniston McIntosh, *Controlling Misbehavior in England, 1370–1600* (2010).

female monasteries accepted only the daughters of wealthy parents who offered lucrative dowries. Moreover, even among wealthy women, monastic life was not readily available; the monasteries of England accommodated about three or four times as many monks as nuns. In England by 1300, there were about five million people but only 3,500 nuns.

Some female monasteries allowed poor women to work as *lay sisters*. Doing the chores that allowed nuns to focus on their prayers, lay sisters pursued holy lives, hoping to benefit spiritually from their hard work and their proximity to nuns. Lay sisters were helpers of nuns, not nuns themselves. For a few poor women and even fewer men, life in an **anchorhold** offered an alternative to monastic life. An anchorhold was a sort of hermitage, a small, enclosed space that was usually built alongside a church. The *anchoress* (or if male, *anchorite*) was permanently walled into this enclosure, observing holy services through a window that looked into the church, and receiving goods and visitors at a second outside window (or sometimes, door). Anchoresses and anchorites were more common in England than elsewhere, and they were tolerated by the Church but never fully integrated into the clergy. The most famous of medieval anchoresses, Juliana of Norwich, lived about a hundred years after Cecilia in the East Anglian city from which she took her name. Her book *Revelations of Divine Love* still offers inspirational reading. Life in an anchorhold was hard and chosen by only a few. All told, only a handful of peasant women ever managed to pursue pious lives as either lay sisters or anchoresses. For a woman like Cecilia, a life devoted to religion was not an option.

The Parish and Its Clergy

The physical space of the churches of St. Andrew and St. Peter followed a pattern set long before the time of the Penifaders, a pattern used in almost all parish churches (see Figure 10). They were long buildings, composed of two main rectangles: a small **chancel** (where the priest celebrated Mass) in the east and a larger **nave** (where the parishioners gathered) in the west. The chancels of medieval churches and cathedrals were oriented to the east, that is, toward Jerusalem, the center of the medieval world. Over time, the two rectangles of nave and chancel were slowly expanded; aisles were added to the nave to accommodate more parishioners, and eventually chapels were built at the east end of aisles to accommodate the veneration of particular saints. The bell tower stood at the west end of the nave, and its bells regularly called people together, for holy ser-

Figure 10. Cecilia's Parish Church. This photograph, taken from the south, shows St. Peter's Church in Stanion as it appears today. To the left stands the bell tower, and adjacent to it is the entry porch for the south door into the nave. The nave is the large rectangle in the middle, and the chancel is on the right, located at the eastern (and holiest) end of the church.

vices, to be sure, but also for deaths, fires, court meetings, and any other events that required everyone's attention. Along the south wall was usually the door through which people entered and left. Outside, a porch protected this door from rain. At St. Peter's, more than fifty stone-carved heads of women, men, and animals ran, and still run today, above the porch and along the south wall. Cecilia would have looked at these carvings, completed just before her birth, whenever she went into St. Peter's or lingered in its churchyard. Masons often carved stone from standard patterns, but they sometimes chose models from local people. So it is possible that among the faces along the south wall, Cecilia might have recognized her parents, her grandparents, and some of her neighbors.

When Cecilia entered the church and stood in the nave, she watched the priest celebrating Mass in the chancel directly in front of her, she heard the clatter of people entering and leaving to her right, and if she turned fully around, she faced the bell tower. During services, she stood or squatted with other women and girls, as the two sexes did not mingle together in church for fear, it seems, of sexual scandal in such a holy place. All around her the walls were painted with bright and vivid scenes that inspired wonder and fear. Today, no medieval paintings can be seen in the church of St. Andrew, and the two that survive in St. Peter's were completed about 150 years after Cecilia's time. One shows a stag and a unicorn kneeling before a now-obscured figure, and the other depicts the Archangel Michael weighing souls to determine whether they are saved or damned. The walls of other churches near Brigstock still contain holy scenes that are like those Cecilia would have seen on the fourteenth-century walls of St. Peter's: the Last Judgment, the Virgin Mary, the Last Supper, the Crucifixion, St. Christopher, St. Catherine, and St. Margaret of Antioch.

By custom, the chancel was the responsibility of the parish priest. If the roof leaked or the altar wobbled, he had to fix it. The nave and the rest of the church— that is, by far its largest part—was in the care of parishioners. If the door fell off its hinges or a bell cracked, then the parishioners of St. Andrew's had to raise money to cover the work. Parishioners maintained their part of the church with money-raising festivals (the most popular were church-ales, at which ale was sold for the benefit of the church), collections, and even gifts from pious and community-minded parishioners. In April 1344, for example, Denise in the Lane gave a small piece of her land to St. Andrew's church, asking that income from it be used to pay for general maintenance. Yet as neither the parish priest nor his parishioners ever had much money to spare, sometimes the chancel roof did leak, the door did sway loosely, and the bell did ring untrue.

The appointment of a parish priest was a complicated business in the Middle Ages. To begin with, control of the appointment (that is, the **advowson**) did not always rest with the local bishop or other ecclesiastical authority. Instead, the person whose family had originally built the church often appointed its priest, generation after generation. This had a certain logic to it. Some might protest that the Church should appoint its own parish priests, but lords and ladies could justifiably respond that *they* should choose the men who worked in churches that had been originally built by *their* ancestors and were still generously supported by *their* money. In the case of Brigstock, the king once held the advowson of Brigstock parish just as he held the manor, and he had once appointed a new parish priest whenever the old one died, retired, or resigned. In 1133, however, Henry I gave the parish to Cirencester Abbey (located about one hundred miles southwest of Brigstock).

Henry's gift is an example of another complication in the staffing of parishes. Ideally, a priest was appointed to care for a parish, but by his gift, Henry made Cirencester Abbey perpetually responsible for the souls of Brigstock. In effect, he made the abbey the **rector** (or appointed parish priest) of Brigstock. By the late thirteenth century, some rectors were institutions (as Cirencester Abbey was for Brigstock), and many others were individuals; both sorts of rectors were often absentees who appointed other priests to do their work. For example, the monks of Cirencester could not travel regularly to Brigstock to care for its parishioners, so the abbey appointed a priest to do the job. This priest was known as a **vicar** (from the same Latin root as such modern words as *vicarious* or *vice president*), because he acted in the place of the rector. In most parishes with a vicar, the absentee rector took most of the income from the parish and paid the vicar a measly sum. In the case of Brigstock, William de Clive was vicar of Brigstock from 1275 to 1325, Roger de Corndale from 1325 to 1340, and John de Seymour from 1340 to 1344 (the year Cecilia died). Cirencester Abbey, as rector of Brigstock, took a hefty sum from the parish each year (more than £10), and then paid their vicar less than half of the takings (a bit over £4). As the history of the advowson, rectors, and vicars of Brigstock parish shows so clearly, appointment to a parish had become by the fourteenth century a sort of commodity that could be owned by institutions as well as individual priests, and that could be bought, sold, or even traded. It was a source of income acquired by a lucky man or institution who often then hired someone else to do the work.

Supported by only a fraction of the parish income, the vicar of Brigstock nevertheless had to find money to pay others to help him in his work. Because Brigstock had two churches, the vicar had to hire a second priest to manage the church of St. Peter in Stanion. These two priests were likely assisted by still other clergy—a deacon or two and a **parish clerk**. Deacons were the chief assistants of parish priests; they helped at Mass, read scriptures during services, and instructed parishioners. Parish clerks also assisted during holy services, but, as skilled secretaries, they especially busied themselves by reading and writing up the documents of the parish.

The priests, deacons, and clerks who assisted the vicar of Brigstock are rarely mentioned in either manorial or ecclesiastical records, but it is likely that Cecilia's brother William was among them. William left Brigstock in 1308, and after he returned in 1317, he was always identified with the unusual and respectful title of *Magister* (or "Master"). Perhaps he held a degree from Oxford or Cambridge (as did many "Masters"), but more likely he was just much better educated than anyone else in Brigstock. He might have been the parish clerk or a deacon, but he was certainly well educated enough to be the second priest in Brigstock, appointed by the vicar to care for St. Peter's church in Stanion.

As one of a handful of churchmen in Brigstock parish, Master William personifies the ambivalent status of rural clergy. On the one hand, William was an ordinary person, a local boy. Older people remembered him as a child; his friends sweated beside him in field and pasture; children played with his nephews and nieces. Most days, he got up and did exactly what his neighbors did. He went into the fields to plow, sow, or weed; he tended to the health of his sheep; he cultivated fruits and vegetables in his garden. When he attended the manorial court every three weeks, he never served as a juror, **aletaster**, or other manorial officer, but he otherwise acted like his brothers. He purchased land from his neighbors, he pledged for the good conduct of his friends, and he proffered excuses for those unable to get to court. Like everyone else in Brigstock, William was a peasant, well known to his neighbors and busied by the same tasks.

On the other hand, William, as a cleric, had special stature within Brigstock parish. First, he was better educated than most people. There were no seminaries to train priests in medieval Europe, so most would-be priests had to rely on local clergymen to teach them to read Latin and to train them in the rituals of the Mass. As a result, priests in rural parishes were often minimally trained for their duties. Some were so ignorant that they could barely mumble the first lines of the Mass, and others even unwittingly led peasants into theological error. William's title of "Master" suggests that he received a better education than most priests, and when he left Brigstock for nine years, he may have studied with some learned men. His education was exceptional for a rural cleric. Yet whether highly educated or roughly trained, rural priests had more learning than their parishioners. Many read with difficulty and understood only rudimentary Latin, but they were, at least, literate.

Second, William was special because he did not marry, at least not in a technical sense. The Church had long encouraged priests to practice celibacy, and from the eleventh century, clerical marriage was explicitly forbidden. Many priests interpreted this prohibition loosely. Some sought casual liaisons, and others, although they refrained from contracting legitimate marriages, settled down with women, fathered and raised children, and sometimes even trained sons to become clerics and take over the family business. Everyone looked the other way; it was irregular, but it was common. William, for whom no "wife" is mentioned in the courts of Brigstock, had at least one child, John Perse to whom he gave his properties in 1326. Alice Perse, the mother of this son, might have lived in Kingsthorpe, a village about eighteen miles southwest of Brigstock, or she might have moved from Kingsthorpe to live with William in Brigstock. If so, she lived like numerous other "priest's concubines" in medieval villages; much like other wives in most respects, they were always vulnerable to gossip, criticism, and even Church sanction. One medieval tale related how a priest's concubine reacted to word that the bishop was coming to inspect the parish and, among other things, order her to leave. Fixing up a basket of cakes, eggs, and other good foods, she set out to meet the bishop on the road. When he asked her where she was going and why, she replied, "I'm taking these gifts to your mistress who has lately been brought to childbed." The bishop, thus reminded of his own sexual relationship, left her and her family alone. William's family was also left alone. His son John not only inherited William's lands but also became a cleric like his father. Treated kindly by his aunt Cecilia when she was on her deathbed, John seems to have been an accepted and well-loved member of the Penifader family.

Third, William and other clerics enjoyed a special legal status: if he committed a crime, he was punished in ecclesiastical courts, not secular ones. "Criminous clerks" had been the cause of a great argument at the end of the twelfth century, an argument that had pitted Thomas Becket, then Archbishop of Canterbury, against his former friend and king, Henry II. Becket supported the Church's claim to judge clerics under the procedures of canon law; Henry II thought it outrageous that he could not punish all those who committed offenses within his realm. Becket lost his life in this argument, killed before the altar of Canterbury by four knights who thought they were carrying out the wishes of Henry II. But Becket's viewpoint finally prevailed. Arrangements differed throughout medieval Europe, but in most places, the Church successfully maintained its right to judge (or sometimes just to punish) clerics for most crimes.

Fourth, if, as is likely, William was ordained as a priest, he was also a special person in Brigstock because of his sacerdotal powers. Of all the people in Brigstock, only he and the vicar could celebrate Mass, impose penance on sinners, anoint the dying, and otherwise ensure, through their special powers, God's grace and God's salvation. As someone empowered to administer the sacraments of the Church, he stood as a critical intermediary between ordinary people and their God. A priest's words were understood to transform bread and wine into the body and blood of Christ; his absolution wiped away sins; his blessings baptized infants, confirmed marriages, and eased the dead toward salvation. If the Penifaders saw William celebrating Mass when they went to St. Peter's on Sunday, they understood little of the Latin he muttered and not much about the symbolic significance of all he did, but they knew that he, alone of all of them, had a special relationship to the bread and wine, the body and blood of Christ.

The duties of the vicar of Brigstock and his assistants were carefully specified. They were to celebrate Mass every day; they were to preach sermons at least four times each year; they were to teach their parishioners about the fourteen points of the Christian creed, the Ten Commandments, the seven sacraments, and the seven deadly sins; they were to be sure that everyone confessed their sins and took communion at least once a year; they were to baptize the young, marry the nubile, and bury the dead. Whether priests did all this or not was mostly left up to their own consciences. Although bishops visited rural districts to search for incompetent or lazy priests, their visits were neither frequent nor effective. The bishop of Lincoln and his subordinates sometimes asked the vicar of Brigstock to report his doings to them, but they seldom verified his responses by directly visiting the parish. The care of the souls of Brigstock was left almost wholly to the discretion of its vicar and his helpers. Perhaps many children learned their catechism, as did Joan of Arc, more from their mothers than from their parsons.

The clergy of Brigstock took their "living" from the parish in several ways. The vicar himself managed the *glebe*, lands in the parish assigned to his use. Like the demesne and the holdings of peasants, the glebe was usually scattered through the fields of a manor. Some priests leased out the glebe to others, but most worked it, like any other peasant, with their own muscle and sweat. In addition to the glebe, Cirencester Abbey assigned 22 shillings of rent to the vicar of Brigstock. In other words, there were a few tenants in the parish whose houses were owned by the abbey and whose rent supported the vicar. Aside from the glebe and any rents that might accrue to the parish, most of a priest's living came directly from parishioners. Everyone paid **oblations;** that is, they paid (in cash or kind) for the services rendered by the priest. When the Penifader children were baptized, Robert and Alice paid for the priest's labor; when their children Emma and Alice died, they paid for their burials; and when Christina and Agnes were married, they paid the priest to officiate. In theory, these payments were voluntary, but in practice they were expected and required. Everyone in the parish was also required to tithe by contributing one-tenth of their yearly gains to the parish—every tenth sheaf at harvest, every tenth lamb born each spring, every tenth bucket of nuts from the forest, every tenth egg, every tenth of every sort of produce. Some Christians today tithe voluntarily, but in the Middle Ages it was compulsory, and it was also resented.

In addition, in Brigstock and many other parishes, a **mortuary** was customarily due on the death of every head of a household. Based on the assumption that a dead person left behind unpaid tithes, the mortuary gave to the Church the second-best animal of the deceased. More than likely, profits from tithes and mortuaries went directly to Cirencester Abbey, for their agreement with the vicar stipulated that he would keep only his glebe, his 22 shillings of rent, and his profits from oblations.

The vicar's assistants patched together their livings as best they could. Usually the vicar paid each assistant a small sum from his own income, and assistants also took oblations from parishioners. Master William, of course, had his own lands and house, so in addition to the money he got from the vicar and parishioners, he lived off properties he inherited or purchased. Other clerics made do as best they could. Absolon, the fictional cleric in the *Canterbury Tales*, made extra money by writing charters and other documents for his neighbors, but he also practiced medicine, barbered, and perhaps earned some money by singing and playing his guitar.

The churches of St. Andrew and St. Peter were familiar and comfortable places for Cecilia. She visited them often, she contributed to their upkeep, and she knew one of their clerics very well indeed. For her, as for most medieval peasants, parish churches were much more than sacred places visited on Sundays and other holy days. As the most substantial building in a village, the parish church was readily used for many purposes that some might label profane. People sometimes stored grain, cloth, or animals in the parish church, and they gathered in it to debate local issues as well as to worship their God. After all, the building was strong, and it was maintained by local funds. As long as its use as a storehouse, meeting place, or even indoor market was confined to the nave (away from the sacred space of the chancel), no harm was done.

As a familiar gathering spot, the parish church sometimes inspired more chatter than prayer. A perennial complaint of parsons was that their parishioners did everything during Mass *except* pay attention to the sacred business at hand. Priests even gave sermons about a special demon, Tutivillus, who took notes on women's chatter in church; since he had so much gossip to write down, Tutivillus had to stretch his parchment by grasping it with teeth and feet, and in so doing, he lost his balance and cracked his head. The lesson was a funny one, intended to teach that talk in church, particularly the talk of women, was the devil' s delight. This was a much-ignored lesson. Most parishioners attended church regularly, but they did not necessarily feel compelled to pay close attention to what the priest and his assistants did at the altar. They were satisfied to have made it to church at all, instead of lingering in bed or stopping at an alehouse. So, while the Mass was celebrated in the chancel of St. Peter's, some parishioners in the nave recited prayers and pondered the miracle of the Eucharist, but others discussed spring plowing, gossiped about a stranger met on the road, or planned a trip for the next Friday to the weekly market in Kettering. In short, like the men who served as its priests, deacons, and clerks, the parish church negotiated between sacred and everyday functions. It was holy space, but it was also community space.

Beyond the Parish

By Cecilia's lifetime, parishes in England were firmly established, well regulated, and responsible for most pastoral care. They also had competition. In the early thirteenth century, new orders of religious men called *friars* were established, some by St. Dominic (thus, the Dominicans) and others by St. Francis of Assisi (the Franciscans). Friars were like monks in that they took vows of poverty, chastity, and obedience, but unlike monks in that they moved around in the world rather than withdrawing into monasteries. Franciscans became especially important in England, traveling from village to village and offering an alternative to the pastoral care of the local clergy. Friars were excellent preachers, so their arrival in Brigstock or a nearby village was exciting news—a reason to gather together, to be entertained, and to learn some theology, too.

St. Francis had relied for his daily bread on the gifts of strangers, and Franciscans were supposed to follow his example. This meant that they looked to local people for food and shelter and even money. It is not hard to imagine how much local clergy chafed against visiting friars. Friars were just passing strangers, but they offered delightful sermons, riled up parishioners with newfangled ideas, and then took gifts from them. The local parson could easily feel dull and poorer by comparison.

He might also feel stodgy, because Franciscan theology was cutting-edge and radical. St. Francis and his early followers had tried to imitate Jesus and his apostles. They threw away all their possessions and worked or begged for their daily food; they embraced humility (Francis dubbed them *friars minor* or "little brothers"); they joyously accepted the world and all people within it—peasants as much as nobles. They even embraced the poor, arguing that the rich were a scandal to God and that the poor were God's true children. These ideals were too good to last, and they were even changing by the time St. Francis died in 1226. Some aspects of early Franciscan theology were even declared heretical. By 1300, the Franciscan friars were not as radical as St. Francis had been, but they still spoke positively about poverty and the poor. From their sermons, Cecilia and her siblings might have taken good heart, understanding that although the tripartite scheme that condemned peasants to labor for the rich was God-given, peasants were, nevertheless, especially loved by God.

The Ritual Year

For the Penifaders, the year had no clear beginning or end, and its rhythms comfortably mingled sacred and profane. The modern designation of 1 January as New Year's Day was as old as Rome itself, but in the early fourteenth century, it was eclipsed as a holiday by Christmas a week earlier and the feast of Epiphany a few days later. (Epiphany commemorated the arrival of the Magi, or Wise Men, to visit the infant Jesus and his mother in the manger.) On most religious calendars, the year officially changed on 25 March, the feast celebrating the Christian feast of the Annunciation of the Blessed Virgin Mary (that is, the appearance of the Archangel Gabriel before Mary to announce that she was pregnant). The Annunciation was neatly timed exactly nine months before the birth of Jesus in the Christian calendar. For Cecilia, however, "Ladyday" passed without much notice in the gloom of Lent and the bustle of spring planting. A third annual shift coincided with the end of harvest, and was linked to Michaelmas, the feast of St. Michael the Archangel on 29 September. Clerks and accountants usually figured years from one 29 September to the next, counting acres, seed, and bushels; paying workers and creditors; and adding up their figures in preparation for audit. Live-in servants were hired either at Michaelmas or a few weeks later, usually agreeing to serve year-long contracts.

Yet if Cecilia's year had no clear beginning or end, it was punctuated by many holidays. She worked hard, but she also often rested and often played (see Figure 11). The calendar of the Church dictated a great deal of this schedule of work and leisure (which explains why our word "holiday" derives from "holy day"). By Cecilia's time, holy days and Sundays accounted for about one hundred days a year—or about one of every four days. On Sundays, work in the fields was discouraged, and while women might mend clothes and men sharpen tools, it was mostly a day of rest. An additional forty-odd days, concentrated around Christmas and Easter but otherwise scattered throughout the year, were special holy days on which no one did much work. The Church's designation of holy days ran along two primary axes. The first set commemorated the story of Jesus' life and work as understood through the New Testament, and the second celebrated notable events in the lives of various saints. In Brigstock parish, the feasts of the patron saints of the two churches—St. Peter (29 June) and St. Andrew (30 November)—would have been especially observed, and for Cecilia, the feast of St. Cecilia (22 November) would have been a special day, as important as her birthday. With all of Christendom, Cecilia and the parishioners of Brigstock also rested for two long periods each year—for the Twelve Days between Christmas and Epiphany, and for all of Easter Week.

Christmas was a time of special festivity. Like everyone else, Cecilia fasted through December, restricting her diet, perhaps no meats or tasty sauces, for the four weeks of Advent that preceded Christmas. On Christmas morning, her piety was rewarded. As people gathered in church in the cold darkness before dawn, they were met with an abundance of candles and a celebratory service. Afterward, the feasting would begin, and some people were so eager to start the fun that they skipped the holy services. One grim but popular medieval story tells of twelve people who sang and danced in front of their church at Christmas; when the priest called them to Mass and they refused to come, he cursed them; for an entire year thereafter, they were condemned to dance in an endlessly wearying frenzy; when the curse was finally lifted at the next Christmas, some died, and the rest were condemned to wander the countryside, afflicted with agitated minds and twitchy limbs. A tale like this did a great deal to encourage Cecilia and her family to attend Christmas services and to wait patiently for the feasting and dancing that was to come.

Figure 11. Holidays. Wrestling was good entertainment, and all it required was eager boys and fine weather. (British Library, Luttrell Psalter, folio 62.)

By tradition, the wealthy opened their houses at Christmas, feeding the humble and poor. On manors with resident lords or ladies, tenants could expect a feast of fine meats and strong ale in the hall of the manor house. In Brigstock, with no lord or lady to act as host, the Penifaders and other well-off peasants might have fed their poorer neighbors, or perhaps all the parishioners pooled their resources for a common feast. However it was staged, the Christmas feast signaled the beginning of twelve festive days when people put aside work to eat, dance, tell stories, wear masks and costumes, and play. In castles, monasteries, and towns, professional entertainers—harpers, minstrels, and actors—provided amusement. Their grand festivals sometimes included intentional episodes of disorder and misrule; for a few hours everyone enjoyed a "feast of fools," when a servant might be crowned king, a novice monk made abbot, or an apprentice elevated to mayor. English peasants never adopted this practice (which, in any case, served more to reinforce hierarchy than to ridicule it), and in Brigstock and other villages, the songs, dances, and stories came from local talent. For Cecilia and her family, the Twelve Days of Christmas were days of full stomachs and tipsy heads. It was a good way to get through some of the darkest and coldest days of the year when neither fields nor flocks demanded much work. The worst of winter would soon be past.

On 6 January, the Twelve Days ended with an Epiphany service commemorating the arrival of the Magi and one final feast. Then, it was back to work, and especially to plowing the fields in anticipation of spring planting. In Brigstock, as in many villages, the transition to work was a gentle one; on the Monday after Epiphany, men secured blessings for their plows in the parish church and then dragged them through streets and lanes, cajoling money out of everyone they encountered. The money raised on "Plow Monday" was then put to charitable uses—perhaps to fix a loose door or recast a bell, or perhaps to aid parish orphans and other unfortunates.

A few weeks later, work paused briefly for one of the most beautiful services in the Christian calendar: the commemoration of the Purification of the Virgin on 2 February. The Old Testament had required that new mothers be purified in a ritual bath several weeks after giving birth; medieval Christians adapted this Jewish tradition not only in their commemoration of the Virgin Mary but also in **churching** ceremonies for new mothers. Each new mother in Brigstock went to church about six weeks after childbirth to celebrate her successful delivery. The medieval service stressed thanksgiving rather than purification, but its purifying implications persisted. In some parishes, women who died in childbirth (that is, without the benefit of churching) were refused burial in holy ground. Cecilia's mother Alice celebrated eight churchings over some twenty years, each time thanking God for her safe delivery and enjoying the congratulations of the women, kin and friends, who had assisted in her perilous labor. These churchings could be so happy and festive that in some towns, authorities had to step in to control crowds and to limit the "dishes, meats, and wines" consumed afterwards. Churchings were surely joyous occasions, with the new mother thanking God for her delivery, her friends and family offering their congratulations, and everyone celebrating the mother's successful passage through the perils of childbirth.

The feast of the Purification of the Virgin, then, was especially important to the mothers of Brigstock. As they gathered with everyone else on the second day of February, Alice and the other mothers of Brigstock may have felt a particular kinship with the Virgin who, like them, had offered thanks for a successful labor. This feast also marked, as Groundhog Day now does in the United

States, the early turning of winter into spring, and it was celebrated, appropriately enough, with dramatic darkness and dramatic light. Lit with an extraordinary display of candles, the church of St. Andrew welcomed the Penifaders out of the cold dawn of a February morning. After the Mass, everyone paraded around the church with candles, and when this procession ended, other candles and tapers were blessed and then saved for later use (they were considered to be especially useful for warding off demons or other evils). The candles were so bright in the darkness of early morning that the service was familiarly known as Candlemas. Afterward feasting began, and having fasted the day before, everyone ate with enthusiasm.

Within a few weeks, parishioners began to prepare for the Easter season. As the major movable feast in the Christian calendar, Easter fell on the first Sunday after the first full moon after the vernal equinox—a date that could fall anywhere between 22 March and 25 April. Each year, the forty days before Easter were times of particular fasting and self-denial (even more so than the four weeks of Advent). Before Lent began, everyone enjoyed one last party: Shrovetide. The winter stocks of foods that would be forbidden during Lent—meat, eggs, cheese, and so on—were eaten, and then, on Ash Wednesday, the fast began. The next forty days were a somber time. Everyone ate a restricted diet; no festivities eased work; and religious sculptures, paintings, or other images in the churches of St. Andrew and St. Peter were veiled from human view. These were also critical weeks in the agricultural year. Fields were plowed, sown, and harrowed; ewes were brought through lambing; and houses were swept out and spruced up in spring cleaning. With half-empty stomachs and a shrouded church, Cecilia and her family thought much about sin and redemption during Lent, but they also worked hard. Fortunately, they also relished the warming weather, increasing daylight, new flowers, migrating birds, and newborn lambs of spring.

The final week of Lent was Holy Week. On the last Sunday before Easter, the Penifaders brought branches to be blessed, a celebration of spring growth that also remembered the palms strewn before Jesus as he entered Jerusalem. Solemn services followed all week, and then, on Friday, the crucifixion was commemorated. Later generations of English peasants built Easter sepulchers—miniature tombs surrounded by candles and watched by the faithful between Friday and Sunday—for this part of Holy Week, and although we cannot be sure, the custom might date as far back as Cecilia's time. Easter sepulcher or no, Cecilia and her family gathered in church on Saturday night, extinguished all candles and flames, and then lit them anew, brightening the church with the largest candle of the ritual year, the Paschal Candle. Early Sunday morning, after forty days of moderate fast and a week of intensifying observances, the Penifaders celebrated the Resurrection in a church joyously returned to its old state—candles lit, statues unveiled, and paintings revealed. They brought with them eggs to be blessed, for even in the early fourteenth century, eggs were already a dual symbol of Easter and spring. After the Easter Mass, everyone in Brigstock enjoyed several days of feasts and games. The celebrations were not as long or as intense as those of the Twelve Days of Christmas, but they were more likely to be outside. The Penifaders watched and participated in archery contests, ball games, wrestling, tumbling, dancing, and singing in the aftermath of Holy Week.

After Easter, a variety of lesser holidays relieved the work of late spring and early summer. On May Day, Cecilia and her sisters rose before dawn and gathered flowers to decorate themselves and their house. Later, they danced with local boys around the maypole, a custom that possibly dated from before 1066. May Day was a holiday of particular importance to the young, but everyone joined in the predawn walks, the selection of the maypole, the dancing, and the feasting. Ascension (celebrating the Christian feast of the ascent of the resurrected Christ into heaven) was the next important holiday, following Easter by six weeks. On the Monday, Tuesday, and Wednesday before Ascension (known as Rogation Days), Cecilia and her sisters might have watched as their father and brothers walked the boundaries of the parish, a practice designed to ensure that each generation of men remembered the trees, ditches, and hedges that marked off the jurisdiction of Brigstock. In many parishes, boys were beaten at critical junctures, to ensure that boundary markers were forever impressed on their minds. Less than two weeks later, everyone commemorated the feast of Whitsun or Pentecost when, according to Christian tradition, the Holy Spirit had descended on the apostles. Whitsun usually fell during the fine weather of June, and it was often observed with parades, dances, games, and feasting. Many parishes took advantage of the weather to hold church-ales, using the festivities to raise money for parochial projects. Throughout May and June, the Penifaders and their neighbors continued to work hard—plowing fallow fields, weeding sown acres, fixing drainage ditches, checking flocks, and making hay.

Then, as haymaking ended at midsummer, work stopped for the bonfires of St. John's Eve, the night before the feast that commemorated the birth of St. John the Baptist on 24 June. Today, we celebrate the solstice on 21 June; medieval people considered that midsummer coincided with St. John's Eve, a small shift that neatly accommodated nature to the religious calendar. On St. John's Eve, the people of Brigstock gathered on a nearby hill, built huge piles of twigs, wood, and straw; and then, when the sun finally set on the longest day of the year, chased away the dark with fire. As she stood sweating from the blaze and panting from the dancing, Cecilia may have felt protected by the fire. Medieval children were taught that the fires of St. John's Eve guarded them from summer infections and saved the ripening crops from blight.

The time between midsummer and Advent was the busiest time in Brigstock. In late June and July, fields needed to be weeded and plowed; in August and September, harvest ruled the day; and in October and November, the Penifaders were busy slaughtering pigs, collecting fruits and nuts, and otherwise preparing for winter. In these months, only a few dates loomed large. On 29 June, the church of St. Peter in Stanion celebrated the feast day of its saint, and the church of St. Andrew in Brigstock did the same on 30 November. Some churches mounted large church-ales on such days and used the occasion to collect money for church repairs or charitable uses, but in Brigstock parish, neither saint's day fell at a convenient time. The celebration of the feast of St. Peter was likely eclipsed by the still smoldering fires of St. John's Eve, and the combination of cold weather and Advent ensured a modest feast in commemoration of St. Andrew. Aside from these two saints' days special in the parish of Brigstock, only two other holy days were particularly important to Christians in these months: the feast of All Saints on 1 November followed the next day by the feast of All Souls together marked the beginning of winter. At the moment that nature itself seemed to be dying or preparing for death, Cecilia and others remembered the human dead. In the dark afternoon, with dead leaves underfoot, and an uncertain supply of food put aside for winter, they began to ring the bells of St. Andrew and St. Peter—to comfort the dead, as they had been taught—and they continued their somber task well into the night. Less than a month later, Advent began.

Today, many things can seem familiar about the ritual year that set the pace of Cecilia's life. We can link Plow Monday with the ritual of blessing tractors in some parts of modern Germany; the Purification of the Virgin with the custom of Groundhog Day in the United States; the feasting of Shrovetide with Pancake Day in Britain as well as Mardi Gras in New Orleans; the branches blessed before Easter with modern Palm Sunday; the feast of St. John the Baptist with Québec's National Day; the remembrances of All Saints with Halloween; even the complementary rhythms of farming and schooling (for many academic calendars still offer their longest breaks during the work-heavy months of the agricultural year).

Yet Cecilia's year was different from our own. For us, May Day, midsummer, and Halloween are pleasant interruptions in modern schedules far removed from the dictates of nature. For Cecilia, the natural cycles of the year—light and dark, warm and cold, work and leisure—were strongly echoed in the ritual calendar. For many of us, religious rituals are comforting but somewhat distant from our everyday lives. For Cecilia, they often spoke not only about holy events and holy persons but also about her own life and her own experiences: about the churching of her mother on the feast of the Purification of the Virgin; about the coming work of harvest on St. John's Eve; about the deaths of her sisters Emma and Alice on the feast of All Souls. For most of us, food and fire are controllable things, available when we need them and easily put aside when we do not. Yet Cecilia would have thought it foolish to count so confidently on food and light. She saw people sicken and die from inadequate diets, and she accommodated her work to the light of the sun and the dark of a night lit only by the moon. For her, these rituals—which so often asked her to fast and then feast, to feel darkness and then see light—spoke powerfully about things that she could not fully control. So in real and direct ways, the ritual year of Brigstock spoke about the life of Cecilia, about her religious faith, to be sure, but also about her natural world, her experiences, and her fears.

Suggestions for Further Reading

Although it focuses on a later period, Ronald Hutton's *The Rise and Fall of Merry England: The Ritual Year, 1400–1700* (1994) provides an excellent introduction to many rural practices, beliefs, and rituals. See also Ronald C. Finucane, *Miracles and Pilgrims: Popular Beliefs in Medieval England* (1995). For parish life, see especially Katherine L. French, *The People of the Parish: Community Life in a Late Medieval English Diocese* (2001). For pilgrimage, see Diana Webb, *Pilgrimage in Medieval England* (2000) and *Medieval European Pilgrimage* (2002). For Europe in general, see John H. Arnold, *Belief and Unbelief in Medieval Europe* (2005), and the many, varied essays in his edited *Oxford Handbook of Medieval Christianity* (2017). For sources, see John Shinners, ed., *Medieval Popular Religion* (2nd ed., 2006).

For ecclesiastical history and religious practice, see two books by R. N. Swanson, *Church and Society in Late Medieval England* (1989) and *Religion and Devotion in Europe, c. 1215–c. 1515* (1995). For medieval ideas about poverty and the poor, see Kate Crassons, *The Claims of Poverty: Literature, Culture, and Ideology in Late Medieval England* (2010), and Sharon Farmer, *Surviving Poverty in Medieval Paris: Gender, Ideology, and the Daily Lives of the Poor* (2001).

CHAPTER 5

Changing Times

September 1319, Brigstock Court: John Tulke sold two small properties—the first to Robert, son of Henry Kroyl senior, and the second to Cecilia Penifader. Cecilia promised to pay the court 6 pence for permission to hold her new land, and her brother-in-law Henry Kroyl junior stood as her pledge.

When Cecilia Penifader was approaching adulthood, her world was shattered by famine. Early in 1315, unusually strong rainstorms raged, and rain fell for months on end, drenching the fields even in summer. The harvest that August was disappointing, and thereafter, weather and harvests got even worse. The winter of 1315 was exceptionally cold, and for several years, bad weather was more common than not. Too much cold and too much rain blighted the land. For the people who lived in southern Europe, this spate of wet and cold weather was not a problem and might even have been a relief. But for the people of northern Europe, such weather was disastrous. Wet weather meant bad harvests. Bad harvests meant less food. Less food meant hunger and possibly starvation. The years from 1315 to 1322 were bad years.

The court rolls of Brigstock tell about sales of land, straying animals, and petty crimes; they do not report directly about bad harvests, diseased animals, or Penifaders weakened by hunger. Yet there are many *indirect* suggestions that people in Brigstock struggled especially hard in these years. Many more than ever before were accused of stealing sheaves, pilfering hay, or **gleaning** without permission (gleaners gathered up small bits of grain left on an already harvested field). Many more than before took on debts they could not repay. And others, like John Tulke in the case that opens this chapter, tried to make ends meet by selling small bits of land to their better-off neighbors. These developments indicate that many people in Brigstock were resorting to desperate measures to survive.

Cecilia lost her parents in these years. Robert was dead by 1318 (we know because Cecilia's brother Robert appeared in court as his father's executor); Alice never appeared in court after 1319, so she probably soon followed her husband to the grave. It is unlikely that Robert and Alice starved to death. As relatively well-off villagers, they suffered less than many of their poorer neighbors in Brigstock. But as old people, they were especially weakened by the hardships that began in 1315. In this famine, as is still the case in famines today, young children and the elderly were at high risk, and they died less often from starvation than from diseases and accidents that befell their weakened bodies. The court rolls cannot tell us how many young nieces and nephews Cecilia lost in the Great Famine, but by the time it was over, her parents were gone.

The Great Famine, 1315–1322

The Great Famine is justly named. It was the worst famine Europe had ever seen before—or has seen ever since. Climate was a major cause, for by 1300, weather in Europe was becoming scarily unpredictable, caught in a long and bumpy transition from the "Medieval Warm Period" (ninth to thirteenth centuries) to the "Little Ice Age" (sixteenth to eighteenth centuries) that eventually followed. (For more on climate research see the sidebar in Chapter 2.) Cecilia lived during this chaotic transition, and the years from 1315 to 1322 were the most chaotic of all, marked by wild swings in weather. Chroniclers began complaining in 1315 about unusually heavy rains and cold winters. They wrote about heavy downpours, frightening storms, flooded fields, and frigid air. Scientists today have confirmed what the chroniclers then observed. By checking the growth rings of ancient oaks (trees that grow quickly in rainy years), they have found exceptional development between 1315 and 1318. As the rains fell and the oaks grew, fields flooded, seed washed away, grain rotted, and flocks suffered. As one Englishman wrote about these years, "Came never a disaster into England that made men more aghast."

The weather improved slightly after 1318, but it was still unsteady. More importantly, the damage done in 1315–1318 had a rippling effect on arable and animal husbandry that lasted well beyond the hardest years of heavy rains and bitter cold. On the arable land of Brigstock, the rains took a heavy toll. They made it difficult to maneuver plows through wet, heavy soil; they damaged the productivity of the soil by leeching nitrates from it; they washed away seed; they provided an ideal environment for mildew, mold, and other crop diseases; they beat down the growing stalks before they could be harvested. Even in the better days before 1315, the Penifaders and their neighbors had plowed, sown, and harvested for crop yields that were pathetically low by modern standards; they took about four bushels of grain for every bushel sown. From this, they would eat three bushels and set the fourth aside for next year's seed. The heavy rains of 1315 lowered the 1:4 yield ratio to dangerous levels: sometimes three, sometimes two, sometimes less than one bushel harvested for every bushel sown. These yields presented the peasants of northern Europe with a devil's bargain, a choice between hunger now or hunger later. If a family harvested two bushels of wheat from land that usually yielded four bushels, they faced immediate hunger, but they also faced long-term hunger if they ate both bushels (for they needed to save one bushel for next year's seed). This was a hard choice, and it worked to extend the famine beyond the years of the most difficult weather. As the quality and quantity of seed declined, so too did the harvest.

The animals on whom the Penifaders depended so much for draft power, food, wool, skins, and fertilizer also suffered horribly in the famine (see Figure 12). Animals felt the cold as much as humans, freezing in pastures and fields. They felt hunger, too, for the pastures were not as rich as before and fodder was hard to come by. Animals also died of disease, especially sheep scab and rinderpest for oxen and cattle. These diseases left their victims so disgustingly dead, their carcasses putrefying rapidly and smelling horribly, that no meat or hides could be salvaged from them. If the Penifaders were like most peasants, they lost about half of their herd and flock, if not more. These losses were not easily replaced, especially with the weakened stock that remained. It took years—in some cases twenty years—to build herds and flocks back to their pre-1315 strength. Both parts of the mixed farming regime of Brigstock, then, were hit hard by the famine. The fields yielded less stubble and fodder for animal consumption, and as animals died, there were fewer oxen or horses to pull the plows and less manure to enrich the soil. This was a dangerous downward spiral.

The peasants of Brigstock survived these hard years better than most. Compared to townspeople, peasants were somewhat insulated from the worst effects of the famine since they could more readily search for extra food in woodland and field. Townspeople produced some of their own food (many kept pigs or chickens and tended small gardens), but they had to buy most of what

Figure 12. Healthy Livestock. Peasants took good care of their sheep. Here, a woman milks a ewe, while the person at the back (often identified as a woman, but possibly a man) checks for sheep scab. The artist has more clearly depicted the sex of the sheep—the males have horns. Notice the sheepfold, made of woven branches or *wattle*. (British Library, Luttrell Psalter, folio 163v.)

they ate. When they went to the market during the Great Famine, they found food to be highly priced and in short supply. In the autumn of 1315, the price of wheat rose by almost 50 percent in just a few weeks; by the next summer, townspeople were buying wheat, if they could find it, at almost five times its prefamine price. Those who could not pay these outrageous prices either starved within town walls or began to wander the countryside in search of food.

People could forage for food in many ways, and the peasants of Brigstock, with the resources of Rockingham Forest around them, had better foraging than most. They poached deer and hare in the royal preserve; they found plants or barks that were disagreeable but edible; they tried eating grubs, rats, and other vermin. When crops failed and animals died, these peculiar diets eased considerably the grumbling stomachs of the Penifaders and their neighbors, offering some nourishment as well as some comfort. Our best estimates suggest that about 10 percent of the population died during the famine.

Brigstock saw many more changes than just peculiar diets during these years. Neighborliness broke down. Faced with bad harvests, people turned more than before to petty crime in the open fields; they contracted more debts they could not repay; they sold off more and more land. The incidence of these problems doubled during the famine, and in every case they created grievances—stolen grain, money not repaid, and lands unwillingly sold— between neighbors. The timing of Richard Everard's suspicion in the summer of 1316 that Cecilia and her father were pilfering hay from him is not accidental, and he must have thereafter watched his Penifader neighbors with a new sharpness and resentment (his complaint is described at the opening of Chapter 2).

Neighborliness was also aggravated by lack of charity and hoarding, for hungry people deeply resented neighbors who had food they would not share or sell. In ordinary times, the poor of Brigstock were supported by charity from kin or neighbors, by the support of parish and clergy, and sometimes even by parties thrown for their benefit (at a *help-ale*, for example, everyone paid high prices for ale, so that the poor host or hostess would benefit from the profits). During the Great Famine, these charitable activities temporarily declined, and prosperous families, like the Penifaders, hoarded what little they had. Neighborly goodwill was undermined still further by the brisk market in land, as it is clear that some peasants used the misfortunes of their fellow villagers to accumulate larger holdings. Cecilia did just that. In 1319, when John Tulke was so desperate for money that he sold off some of his lands, Cecilia was ready to buy. She did the same on five other occasions during these years, so that by the time the famine ended, she controlled properties once held by John Tulke, Richard Koyk, and Ralph de la Breche. Their misfortune was her opportunity.

At the same time as the people of Brigstock were foraging with new inventiveness for food and watching their neighbors with more suspicion than before, they also had to contend with many impoverished strangers. Beggars and vagabonds had always wandered through Brigstock in search of charity and work, but their numbers swelled during the famine. Through the lanes of Brigstock came a steady stream of laborers looking for work—smallholders who had been forced to sell their lands and take to the road, servants let go by their employers, refugees searching for any food whatsoever, and beggars who could no longer rely on charity from nearby monasteries. They came singly, in gangs, and with families. To Cecilia, it must have seemed as if strangers arrived in Brigstock every day, hungry strangers who seemed pathetic and dangerous. Some might have died on the roads around Brigstock, others might have garnered a bit of work or bread from the Penifaders, and still others were doubtless chased away lest they take some food or goods not rightfully theirs.

The Wrath of God?

Between 1315 and 1322, the people of Brigstock looked with horror at rain-soaked fields, sickened cattle, unpleasant new foods, grasping neighbors, and frightening tramps. They filled the grounds around the churches of St. Andrew and St. Peter with the bodies of the young, the old, and the poor. They also prayed with new vigor, for it seemed clear that these disasters must be the work of a God who, as one contemporary put it, had sent "dearth on earth." In the summer of 1315, as the rains were ruining the first harvest of the Great Famine, the Archbishop of Canterbury ordered the clergy to respond immediately. They were to organize solemn processions of barefooted penitents accompanied by bells, relics, and prayers; they were to celebrate special Masses; and they were to urge their parishioners to fast, pray, and give alms. By these measures, everyone hoped to appease the anger of God and to halt the terrible rains.

With the hindsight of many centuries, historians now explain the Great Famine in different ways. The changing climate was bad enough, but it was aggravated by other serious problems. First, the countryside was sorely overpopulated, a result of more than two centuries of extraordinary demographic growth. There were nearly five million people in England in 1300—about three times as many people as at the Norman Conquest of 1066, and many more people than England would again support until 1700 (see Figure 13). More than nine hundred adults and probably as many children lived in Brigstock (including Stanion) in 1300; that is, almost the same number of people who live there today. Even without famine, feeding these mouths was a problem. Second, the land was yielding less food. To feed their families, peasants turned more and more wasteland into arable and pasture. Eventually, they began to colonize moors, heaths, and other lands that were not very fertile. It is startling but true that in the early fourteenth century peasants tilled lands that modern farmers, armed with chemical fertilizers and heavy machinery, now avoid. In Cecilia's time, peasants worked more land, but took less from it. The conjunction of these two problems, rising population and inadequate productivity, created what historians today call a *Malthusian crisis*: too little food for too many mouths. (The term derives from Thomas Malthus who demonstrated in 1789 that populations tend to grow faster than productive resources.)

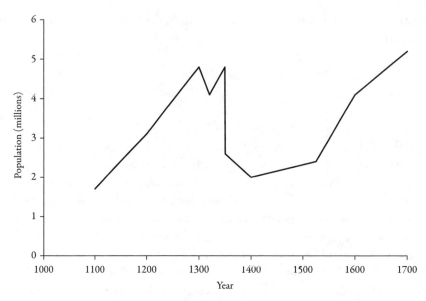

Figure 13. Population of England, c. 1086–1700.

By 1300, this crisis was adding more misery to the already difficult lives of medieval peasants. When Cecilia's older brother Henry began to seek paid work in Brigstock about 1300, he got low wages—because there were many hands eager for work at such rates. When he looked to rent some land, he had to pay higher rents—because lands were so scarce. When he purchased food, he had to pay high prices that seemed to be getting worse every year—because demand for foodstuffs was high. When he tried to bring wasteland into cultivation, he sweated over marginal lands that gave disappointing returns—because all the good land was already taken. At every turn, he found bad options and frustration. The result of these discouraging circumstances was swift and predictable: population began to level off and then decline. For historians, it is unclear whether this demographic adjustment was caused by rising mortality or falling fertility. Perhaps poorer diets hastened some people into early graves, or perhaps anxiety about hungry mouths prompted some couples—such as Henry and his wife who together produced only three grown children—to limit births. Perhaps both. Certainly, by 1300, the economy of Europe had ceased to grow and population soon followed suit.

A Malthusian crisis was a serious matter, but the landowning elite further aggravated the plight of peasants before the Great Famine. As economic expansion slowed in the late thirteenth century, landowners needed more cash, and they got it by wringing every last penny out of their manorial tenants. They raised rents and fines; they insisted that all petty fees be paid; they made the most of labor services (especially by converting them into cash rents, as was common by 1300); they sometimes even greedily claimed the fertile manure of their tenants' flocks. These demands left peasants with so little of their own time, goods, and cash that investment and innovation were hard to come by. A Marxist historian would describe this process as follows: the feudal elite extracted so much surplus from the peasantry that the rural economy stagnated. The people of Brigstock knew well what this meant. Margery de Farendraght, the wealthy widow who leased Brigstock manor from the crown for £13 a year, charged the tenants more than £46 for their sublease from her. The money that went into her coffers did not go into improving the barns, fields, and equipment of Brigstock.

Rising population, declining productivity, and grasping landowners were bad enough, but a fourth factor—the king—made things even worse. Almost from the moment Edward II succeeded his father in 1307, he faced angry and uncooperative barons, and he was eventually forced in 1327 to abdicate in favor of his son. For two long decades, his reign was one unhappy tale of baronial revolts within England, uprisings in Ireland and Wales, inconclusive war with France, and outright defeat in Scotland. To finance these wars, Edward II taxed the countryside heavily. Even minstrels complained, one bewailing in song that "every fourth penny must go to the king." To field his armies, Edward also conscripted young men out of villages and made them into foot soldiers. And to feed these armies, he took food from the countryside. Armed with the right of *purveyance*, the king's officers could ride into any village and take away grain, sheep, pigs, fruits, and other produce for the troops. They were not supposed to take so much that a family starved, and they were supposed to leave tallies promising later payment. But hasty officers often left villages bereft of adequate food and adequate compensation. Their arrival was always greeted with dread. Even in 1316, the worst harvest of the Great Famine, the king's men demanded almost one hundred thousand bushels of grain and malt from his starving subjects. With taxation, conscription, purveyance, and constant unrest, Edward II added mightily to the woes of the English peasantry.

So, when heavy rains fell in Brigstock in the winter of 1315, they fell on already troubled fields. Cecilia and her siblings long remembered the famine that began with those rains, but they had seen trouble enough before. Even when

Cecilia had played as a child on the cobbles in front of her house, times were not good. Too many people competed for too few resources; the arable seemed to be losing its productivity; lords and ladies greedily appropriated all they could; and the king took what was left. Whether God sent the rains of 1315 in wrath or not, England, and much of Europe, was ripe for famine.

The Aftermath of the Great Famine

When the worst of the famine ended in 1322, Cecilia was a grown woman, about twenty-five years old. Her parents were buried in the churchyard of St. Peter, her brother William had returned from his travels with the august title of *magister*, and her other siblings were established in various houses in the villages of Brigstock, Stanion, and Cranford. She was, by 1322, the holder of considerable lands: about twenty-five acres of meadow and three other small parcels of arable. Over the course of the next two decades, she would purchase still more land.

The years of the Great Famine, in other words, marked Cecilia's transition from the dependency of childhood to the autonomy of adulthood. When it began, she was a dependent minor in her parents' household; when it ended, she was an independent tenant in Brigstock. The Great Famine did not cause this transition, for Cecilia would have aged and grown in any case. Yet it certainly shaped her young adulthood in critical ways—after all, but for the famine, her parents might not have died when they did, and, but for the famine, she would not have so easily purchased so much land. As Cecilia tended her lands and flocks in the 1320s, 1330s, and 1340s, she worked in a world that had been deeply shaped by the Great Famine of her youth.

Uncertain weather continued through the 1320s. In the summers of 1325 and 1326, villages to the south and east of Brigstock suffered from serious drought, a hardship that must have especially embittered those who thought back to the frighteningly heavy rains of 1315 and 1316. At the same time, the rising sea encroached on arable lands near the coast, causing some communities to lose hundreds of acres to the waves. Cecilia heard about these troubles more than she suffered directly from them, for Brigstock was well protected from the sea and also escaped the worst of the drought. Yet stories of parched fields and flooded lands confirmed in her mind the wretched uncertainty of the climate. When she examined the clouds in the morning and gauged the wetness of the wind against her face, she must have worried with a special edginess about what

Figure 14. Prank or Theft? In this image, a boy has tossed off his shoes and
climbed a tree to eat cherries, while an angry man brandishes a stick below.
After the Great Famine, petty thieving of this sort caused more trouble
between neighbors. (British Library, Luttrell Psalter, folio 196v.)

the day's weather would bring. A once reasonably predictable climate was now
cruelly whimsical.

As she trusted less in the weather, Cecilia also have trusted less in her
neighbors (see Figure 14). People continued to pilfer food and grain with unpleasant regularity; indeed, the unusually high incidence of field crimes reached
in Brigstock during the famine did not decline thereafter. For the rest of her
life, Cecilia had to guard her sheaves and sheep against theft more carefully
than her parents had done. She also had to guard her house with greater care,
and perhaps she, like many others at this time, first put a lock on her door, hoping thereby to discourage thieves. Some better-off peasants even dug moats
around their houses. Brigstock—and all of rural England—was just not as reli-
ably safe as before. The incidence of bad debts and animosity between neighbors
waned after the famine years, but it grew again in the 1340s to even higher levels. Cecilia seems to have rarely either loaned or borrowed money, but she
watched as neighbors shouted at each other about misunderstood contracts,

unpaid debts, and payments gone awry. This sort of unpleasantness was not new in the fields and lanes of Brigstock, but it was now more common than before.

So too were depleted flocks and bad harvests. In 1324–1326, Cecilia saw still more sheep and oxen die from another outbreak of rinderpest. In 1331, 1339, and 1343, she faced again the troubles of a poor harvest. The economy of Brigstock after the Great Famine was fragile, and it seems to have especially faltered in the 1340s, when people again resorted to the desperate makeshifts—going into debt, selling land—that had sustained them through the hard years between 1315 and 1322. The population of the manor followed suit, falling fairly steadily. Where about nine hundred adults had lived in 1300, only seven hundred lived in 1340. (Overall, as Figure 13 shows, English population rebounded after the Great Famine, but not so in Brigstock.) The policies of the crown did not help. When Edward III launched the first campaigns of the Hundred Years War (1338–1453), he began to levy taxes that far exceeded those of his bellicose grandfather and father. He took, in other words, more resources from a countryside that had less to give. Some prosperity returned after the Great Famine, but it was a lesser and uncertain prosperity.

The Black Death

Before Cecilia died in 1344, she might have worried that the bad harvest of 1343 was the precursor of a new famine. If so, she was wrong. Yet a new danger awaited her surviving siblings, nephews, and nieces: plague. Late in 1347, Italian merchants trading with the East brought home fine silks, expensive spices, and a new disease. This contagion killed people quickly, grossly, and without any seeming logic. Some coughed blood and died; some found strange swellings in their armpits and then died; and some survived unscathed. No medicines helped, and no measures, such as appeals to God or quarantines, had any ameliorating effect. We now know that the main form of the plague, its bubonic variety, was spread by a bacillus carried on fleas and rats; most people were infected when they were bitten by a diseased flea carried by a diseased rat. Medieval people did not know this, so, instead of attempting to control the rat population, they ineffectively isolated infected people in quarantines. By 1348, the Black Death, as it came to be known, had reached England. We do not know exactly when it arrived in Brigstock, for the surviving court rolls end abruptly in September of that year. But it certainly came to Brigstock, probably in the late spring of 1349. Before it ran its course, the pathogen *Yersinia pestis* killed one of every two or three people on the manor. The plague continued to trouble Europe until the seventeenth century, but its first outbreak in 1347–1349 was the most deadly, and its effects were felt for many decades.

In the late fourteenth century, old traditions seemed less secure than before. People began to complain with new vigor about lascivious friars and greedy clerics; peasants found serfdom even more troublesome; rich and poor alike were gripped by guilt about survival, anxieties about the present, and worries about impending death. The despairing spirit of the time was captured in a poem written on the death of Edward III in 1377.

> Ah dear God, how can it be
> That all things waste and wear away?
> Friendship is but vanity,
> And barely lasts the length of day.
> When put to proof, men go astray
> Averse to loss, to gain inclined.
> So fickle is their faith, I say,
> That out of sight is out of mind.

It seems that the Black Death destroyed more than people; it also destroyed the trust and hope of those who survived.

Killing at least one-third of the population of Europe in two years, the Black Death left behind a devastated and often empty landscape. Some villages lost so many people that they were abandoned, their once-plowed fields, empty lanes, and house foundations lying today under the grasses of Europe. Other villages survived, but even they were changed in fundamental ways. The socio-economic rearrangements that followed the Black Death were complex and slow-moving. In the early decades after 1350, many peasants did well. With low population and plentiful lands, they took high wages for their work and they held lands at low rents. Eventually, serfdom began to decline as lords and ladies slowly found they could better profit from their lands without serf labor and therefore allowed serfdom to die through disuse. The revolts of French peasants in 1358 and English peasants in 1381 were cruelly crushed, but, slowly and surely, serfdom disappeared in Western Europe. High wages, low rents, waning serfdom: these were good changes for the peasantry. But by 1500, other developments boded ill. On the eve of the sixteenth century, many villages were more divided than before by a widening gulf between well-off peasants and their poorer neighbors. And a new danger threatened; lords and ladies, eager to use

WHAT CAN WE KNOW FROM MEDIEVAL DNA?

DNA is the new super-evidence of medieval history. Almost every week brings news about history-changing discoveries—that modern-day Icelanders carry DNA not only from Vikings but also from Irish women they enslaved; that the skeleton in a celebrated grave of a high-born warrior—a grave filled with expensive weapons, horses, and war games—has turned out, by DNA, to be female; and that the main settlers of early Britain were not Celts, but ancestors of modern-day Basques.

The most publicized DNA triumph thus far is a feat of genealogical as well as genetic sleuthing. In 2012, a medieval skeleton was exhumed in a car park in the English city of Leicester, just about precisely where it had been recorded that the last Plantagenet king, Richard III, was buried after his defeat on Bosworth field in 1485. The body was hastily buried, with no evidence of its identity. But the location, age, sex, and scoliosis of the skeleton were right (Richard was said to have uneven shoulders), and so, too, were skeletal injuries that suggested death by a battle-blow to the head and post-death "humiliation injuries." All these facts were suggestive, but DNA sealed the deal. Richard III took from his mother the same mitochrondrial DNA (mtDNA) as his sister Anne of York, and she passed this mtDNA to her female descendants. A genealogist traced the female-line descent of Anne through some seventeen-plus generations and located two people, one Canadian and one Australian, whose mtDNA matched each other and more importantly, matched that of the skeleton in the car park. Richard III had been found. He was duly reburied, with all royal dignities, in Leicester cathedral.

Richard III's DNA was feel-good news in 2015, and it has helped Leicester grow as a tourist destination. But although it brought closure to the story of Richard's defeat and death, it was not path-breaking history. For that, we must look at the role of ancient DNA (aDNA) in understanding the causes of the Black Death that killed so many Europeans between 1347 and 1349. Historians have long debated what disease was responsible for this mortality crisis. In 1900, we were confident that the medieval disease was plague, caused by an agent—*Yersinia pestis*—that had been carefully studied by British epidemiologists during nineteenth-century outbreaks in India and China. What they saw in nineteenth-century Asia, we applied to fourteenth-century Europe: a highly contagious disease that was primarily spread by fleas who were themselves transported via rodents.

This view held sway for most of the twentieth century, but by 2000, many historians had other ideas. They argued that modern plague and the medieval Black Death were completely different diseases, and their evidence was compelling. Compared to what we know of the Black Death, the modern plague kills too few people; it travels too slowly; its seasonality (spring and fall) is wrong; its symptoms (especially swelling buboes in the groin) match poorly with medieval medical reports; and it kills large numbers of rats (of which there is little mention in medieval sources). These new critics were not yet sure what the 1347–1349 disease was—perhaps anthrax, perhaps typhus, perhaps a filovirus like Ebola—but they were sure that it was not plague. In 2002, their view had just about won the day, with an article on the subject published in a top-notch journal proclaiming that it proved "the end of a paradigm."

They were wrong, and they were quickly proven wrong. In the last two decades, archaeologists have extracted aDNA from the teeth of skeletons found in plague cemeteries throughout Europe, and they have found, again and again, the presence of *Yersinia pestis*. It is a variant of the modern pathogen, but closely related. The Black Death and *Yesinia pestis* are one.

Skeptics might say, "So what? We knew already that huge numbers of Europeans died between 1347 and 1349. Who cares about the specific etiology of their disease?" We should all care. To begin with, we can now have greater respect for *Yersinia pestis* which, although it still withers when treated with modern antibiotics, is found today on all inhabited continents except Australia and is virulent enough for development as a biological weapon. We can also talk with greater confidence about three great plague pandemics in the past (the "Justinian" plague c. 550, the Black Death in 1347–1349, and the Third Pandemic of the nineteenth century, centered on China and India). We can even understand the evolution of *Yersinis pestis* more fully, thanks to knowing precise dates for its medieval versions; it emerged about five thousand years ago, not twenty thousand years as once thought. And by knowing that *Yersinis pestis* was the pathogenic culprit in 1347–1349, we can begin to fill in the other factors in the medieval pandemic. How much did changing climate affect the spread of medieval plague? (Fleas, after all, do not thrive in all climates.) How much did it matter that fourteenth-century Europe was overpopulated and many Europeans undernourished? What carriers other than rats—such as rabbits, goats, sheep, and camels—helped spread the disease? And although the pathogen was always present, how much was mortality affected by its different paths of entry into human bodies—flea bites (bubonic and septicemic plague), respiration (pneumonic plague), and ingestion (gastrointestinal plague)? Perhaps most of all, we are now able to see medieval *Yersinis pestis* as a global pathogen, its origins traced to the Tibetan plateau and its devastation wrought not only in Asia and Europe but also in Africa. With the help of DNA scientists, historians have solved one problem (yes, Black Death = plague), and we now happily have a host of new questions to answer.

For more on DNA and history, look at Adam Rutherford, *A Brief History of Everyone Who Ever Lived: The Stories in Our Genes* (2017). For DNA and the Black Death, see especially Monica H. Green, ed., *Pandemic Disease in the Medieval World: Rethinking the Black Death* (2015). For an example of nonhuman use of DNA, see this online essay about the aDNA of parchment and wax seals: https://www.medieval.eu /humming-bees-and-flowery-meadows-of-yesteryear/.

their properties in new ways, began enclosing lands (putting up fences around once open fields) so that they could raise sheep. To accomplish this, they terminated leases and asked long-standing tenants to leave.

Cecilia never had to endure the horrors of the Black Death or the difficult decades that followed. She never saw mass death c. 1350; plentiful land and good wages c. 1400; or the enclosures that created, by the sixteenth century, so many landless poor. But it is hard to ignore the devastation that followed so soon after her death. Did the changing times of Cecilia's life contain hints that such a disaster would soon occur? Or was the Black Death an accidental and external contagion that destroyed a vibrant Europe? If the lives of Cecilia and her neighbors in Brigstock are any measure, the first scenario is more accurate than the second. By 1300, Brigstock was overcrowded, its productive resources were stretched to dangerous limits, and its climate was newly unsteady and worsening. In 1315–1322, the Great Famine brought more hardship and devastation. Between 1322 and 1340, unsteady recovery followed the famine. Then, in the 1340s, bad harvests, royal taxation, and other woes further weakened the rural economy. The plague, in other words, did not ravage Brigstock in its prime. When the first plague-bearing rat arrived in Brigstock, perhaps swimming up Harper's Brook or perhaps catching a ride on a cart filled with grain or wood, it found a community already weakened by several decades of hard times.

Suggestions for Further Reading

For a new and breathtaking interpretation, see Bruce M. S. Campbell, *The Great Transition: Climate, Disease and Society in the Late Medieval World* (2016). See also William Chester Jordan, *The Great Famine: Northern Europe in the Early Fourteenth Century* (1996); the old, but readable and reliable, summary by Philip Ziegler, *The Black Death* (1969); the step-by-step tracing in the plague's spread in Ole Benedictow, *The Black Death, 1346–53: The Complete History* (2004); the global perspective in Monica H. Green, ed., *Pandemic Disease in the Medieval World: Rethinking the Black Death* (2015); and for primary sources, Rosemary Horrox, ed., *The Black Death* (1994). For Malthusianism and its competitors in historiography, see John Hatcher and Mark Bailey, *Modelling the Middle Ages: The History and Theory of England's Economic Development* (2001).

CHAPTER 6

Kin and Household

September 1319, Brigstock Court: Alan Koyk transferred a house to his son Richard, and Richard immediately thereafter transferred the same property to William Penifader. The house was described as nineteen-feet wide and sharing a wall, on one side, with Alan Koyk's house and, on the other side, with Cecilia Penifader's house. William received only the building itself, with no access to the farmyard around it. He paid the court 3 shillings and 4 pence for approval of his acquisition, and Gilbert son of Geoffrey stood as his pledge.

When Cecilia Penifader was a young child, the kin on whom she most relied were the people with whom she lived: her parents and her siblings. As she grew older, this straightforward situation changed. Cecilia never married, but if she had, she would have added husband, children, and in-laws to the parents and siblings of her childhood. This is what happened to her sister Christina after she married Richard Power of Cranford in 1317 and to her other sister Agnes after she married Henry Kroyl in 1319. Yet even without marriage, the meaning of kinship changed for Cecilia over time, as her parents died, several of her siblings married, and one sister moved away. By the time she was in her early twenties, Cecilia no longer lived with kin, and she had added brothers-in-law, sisters-in-law, nephews, and nieces to her pool of relatives. The nuclear kin of her childhood, the parents and siblings with whom she had eaten, worked, and slept, had been partly replaced by an extended kinship network scattered through many houses in Brigstock, Stanion, and beyond. For Cecilia, kinship was always important, but its meaning in her life was constantly changing.

Moreover, while kin were important to Cecilia, so too were the people with whom she lived, whether they were kin or not. Indeed, in Cecilia's time, the Latin word *familia* and the Middle English word *familie* meant a household, not a group of people related by blood. Three things made the *household* a central part of peasant life in the Middle Ages. First, households were a basic unit of social organization. When the king's officers arrived in Brigstock to collect food for the army or to levy taxes, they took food and taxes from households; when the vicar collected tithes, he proceeded household by household through the parish; when tenants had to agree on when and what to plant in each of the common fields, they met together as heads of households. Second, households were hierarchical places. Every household had a head (most often, a father and husband) who exercised clear authority over everyone else. This authority was recognized from without as well as within, for heads of households were often brought to public account for the actions of their dependents. Richard Everard understood this authority when he complained in 1316 about Robert Penifader and Cecilia taking hay from his fields (see the case that opens Chapter 2); he addressed his legal complaint to Robert because Cecilia, who was then a dependent in her father's household, was Robert's responsibility. Third, households were intimate places. People who lived in the same household shared many fundamental things, whether they were kin or not: they used the same bedding and ate the same food; they sweated in the same fields and worried over the same sickly lambs; they hungered together in bad times and feasted together in good; and by the time Cecilia was grown up, they also locked the door of their house against intruders. When Cecilia shared a household with someone, she shared the intimacy of day-to-day life and, at least in the short term, a common fate. Households, which often included non-kin and almost invariably excluded some kin, were as important as kinship in the daily life of the people of Brigstock.

Kin and Household in Childhood

The household of Cecilia's childhood was about twice the usual size. Her mother Alice gave birth to at least eight children and raised six to full adulthood. Most mothers had fewer children, buried more of them in early graves, and saw only three reach maturity. In another respect, however, Cecilia's household was likely to have been typical: like many other households in Brigstock, it was a *nuclear family household*, consisting primarily of parents and their children. Peasants elsewhere lived in different sorts of households. *Stem family households*—households that contained three generations (grandparents, parents, and children)—were also common among the peasants of medieval Europe. In some places, especially southern France and Italy, peasants lived in *frérèches*, households containing two or more married brothers with their wives and children. In most English villages, however, smaller households were the norm, and most were formed around a nuclear core of husband, wife, and children. Low life-expectancies partly accounted for the nuclear structure of households; since most people died in their forties, few lived long as grandparents. Housing and settlement patterns also contributed; houses could be built relatively quickly and cheaply, so it was easy to accommodate any aged grandparent in a separate house in the farmyard or village.

We do not know whether the Penifaders brought servants into their household, but it would not have been unusual if they had. (Servants, like underage children, were rarely mentioned in the Brigstock court, so we know frustratingly little about them.) Whenever the Penifaders needed an extra pair of hands, they had two options: they could hire a laborer to work by the day or task, or they could employ a servant for a year, offering room and board as well as some further reward (in cash or clothing) at the year's end. Laborers were often hired to help at harvest or other especially busy times of year; servants were hired, usually beginning in the late autumn, whenever a household needed help on a long-term basis. Servants were common in Brigstock and elsewhere; in one well-documented village not far from Brigstock, more than a third of the households contained a servant.

Most servants were adolescents, learning new skills and earning a bit of money in the hope of someday acquiring land of their own and marrying. Associated with youthfulness rather than poverty, service was not demeaning; parents at all levels of medieval society sent their growing children away to live and work in other households. Even among the richest households, teenaged children were sent to monasteries; or married young; or served in the households of family friends. The practice both encouraged independence and ameliorated parent-child conflict. Among peasants, both young men and young women worked as servants, and they worked like everyone else in the household, doing whatever needed to be done. Servants in the Penifader household would have shared its general life, sleeping and eating alongside Cecilia and her siblings, and accepting, like all the Penifader children, the authority of Robert and Alice Penifader. While living in the Penifader household, a servant had a stake in its success; a bad harvest or poor lambing meant a troubled household in which to finish the service contract. The main distinction, therefore, between servants and children came from the link between kinship and inheritance; unlike Cecilia, a servant of the Penifaders could not expect to inherit land or goods from the household. Yet, because inheritance customs favored some children over others, Cecilia could not be confident of inheritance either, and some servants did, in fact, obtain bequests from their employers. In 1339, for example, Hugh and Emma Talbot of Brigstock arranged for their servant Agnes Waleys to inherit their house and farmyard. Agnes was not related to the Talbots by either blood or marriage, but she had lived for at least five years as a valued member of their household. Even in inheritance, then, the gap between children and servants could be a small one.

The cramped and smoky house of Cecilia's childhood, then, contained her father (the head of household), her mother, her siblings, and a servant or two. More than likely, she had other kin nearby (a grandparent or some uncles, aunts, or cousins), but if so, they lived in other houses in Brigstock. Cecilia also saw her household expand in some times and shrink in others. Sometimes her parents might have earned extra cash by taking in a lodger or might have provided housing for laborers at the harvest. At other times, her siblings left home either to seek their fortunes elsewhere (as William did in 1308) or to settle in separate houses (as Christina did after she married in 1317). The size and shape of Cecilia's household varied with time, but like most households in Brigstock, its nuclear core of parents and children looks surprisingly familiar to modern eyes.

Today, it is possible to touch medieval timbers blackened by the smoky houses of peasants like the Penifaders. But there are no archaeological remains, and precious few remains of any other sort, that can reveal whether these houses were filled with love and affection as well as smoke. It is tempting to dismiss medieval parents as indifferent or even cruel. For example, medieval parents readily beat their children with sticks and boxed their ears. Robert and Alice Penifader would have thought themselves negligent if they had not disciplined Cecilia in such ways when she misbehaved, and, indeed, all adults were ready to strike any bad child. For another example, medieval parents put their children to work at young ages. By the age of four, Cecilia was expected to mingle work with play—guarding hens and geese, supervising younger children, and taking on small domestic chores (see Figure 15). By the age of eight, when she was old enough to work without supervision, she took on a wider variety of tasks. In the house and farmyard, she helped with cooking, gardening, cheese-making, or brewing. In the fields, she weeded, goaded plow-teams, and waved hungry birds away from ripening grain. In the pastures, she guarded sheep against predators,

Figure 15. Good Work for Children. This boy waves his hood and a stick to protect goslings from a hungry hawk. The goose honks and flaps to the same purpose. (British Library, Luttrell Psalter, folio 169v.)

herded them home, and made sure they did not feast in a neighbor's garden. In the woods, she picked nuts and berries, searched out herbs, and collected fallen wood. When we think of a small Cecilia, beaten by her parents and busied by work at so young an age, it is hard to imagine that there could have been much love in the Penifader household.

But the evidence suggests otherwise. To begin with, Cecilia must have been carefully tended as an infant. If her parents had neglected her, she would surely have numbered among the 20 percent of infants who never reached their first birthdays. Most of these children died from diseases that no parent's love could cure, but neglect could quickly hasten healthy infants into their graves. As a toddler, she was also closely watched by her mother or older siblings. Unwatched children tended to knock over pots of boiling water, fall into ditches, or tumble down wells. Clearly, then, medieval parents had to attend closely to their children; if they failed to do so, death or injury was a likely result. By this measure, the Penifaders, with the excellent survival rate of their offspring, seem to have been loving parents.

Moreover, neither child beatings nor child labor meant to the Penifaders what they mean today. First, although medieval children were beaten, so too were adults. Husbands beat their wives; parishioners whipped sinners around the parish church; and corporal punishment was built into the legal system. A miller or baker who cheated clients was put in the **stocks,** a wooden frame into which ankles or wrists (sometimes both) were locked. A cheating **brewster**

HOW DO WE KNOW ABOUT MEDIEVAL PUBERTY?

We have a lot of written evidence about medieval adolescence, but some of our best information comes from the bones of dead teenagers. Most have been excavated from London cemeteries, but some were buried in other cities and a few in rural parishes too. The analysis of these bones is not easy: the skeletons must be complete or nearly complete; they must show clear indications of biological sex (sex is hard to determine in skeletons of the very young and very old); they must have good dental evidence; and only after these criteria are met, can *osteoarchaeologists*—that is, archaeologists who study bones—use them to estimate when puberty began for these individuals and how long thereafter they reached full physical maturity. These requirements can quickly make a big sample much smaller. One study started with 994 skeletons aged between ten and twenty-five years at death. Of these, 645 could be assigned estimated age at death, based on their teeth. Of these, only 470 could be assigned a sex (as seems to have been common in medieval cemeteries—we are not yet sure why—the sex ratio is skewed: 283 males and 187 females). And of this precious subset of individuals whose age and sex could be determined, pubertal stage could be assessed for only 152 males and 84 females.

In forensic crime dramas, medical examiners wring amazing—and amazingly clear—results from their work with dead bodies. This makes for great fiction, but reality is messier, especially when working with the skeletons of the long dead. Determining the sex of adolescent skeletons is so hard that even the best indicators (mostly based on the pelvis and the humerus) are only accurate about 80 percent of the time. Seeing an injury in a bone is not the same as understanding its cause—so that, for example, a broken rib could be a injury sustained by work, play, or even fighting. And the dead are not always a clear reflection of the living. Because of extensive migration into towns, for example, urban cemeteries contain skeletons whose diseases and injuries might tell more about rural hazards than urban ones. And the "osteological paradox" is perhaps the biggest worry of all—namely, that a person who dies quickly of a disease will show no evidence in their bones, whereas the skeleton of someone who suffered from the same disease and survived will carry telltale lesions. In the face of these challenges, osteoarchaeologists constantly develop ever-better techniques, and they offset possible error by relying on multiple indicators drawn from large samples.

Back to puberty. In the human species, puberty proceeds in three main stages. First, both girls and boys grow taller, very quickly, and this growth spurt is indicated skeletally by, among other measures, the early development of the wonderfully named "hamate hook," a tiny bone in the palm of the hand. Second, just after the peak of this growth spurt (PHV or "peak height velocity"), girls begin to menstruate and boys' voices change. This stage can also be tracked in the hamate hook, which reaches full development just a few months before PHV. Third, growth slows, puberty ends, and individuals reach full biological maturation. Since the hamate hook is by then fully formed, some of our best evidence comes from elsewhere in the hand—from the fusion of bones that make up the fingers (the phalangeal epiphyses).

Using the hamate hook, the presence of phalangeal epiphyses, and a variety of other measures, osteoarchaeologists have determined that most medieval skeletons indicate a growth spurt beginning around ten to twelve years of age; PHV was reached at about fifteen years; and full maturity by sixteen to nineteen years. Compared to modern teenagers, medieval adolescents began puberty at about the same time, but took longer to mature. Medieval girls began menstruating at about fifteen years, roughly two years later than modern girls, on average. Interestingly enough, Londoners—both females and males—seem to have matured especially slowly, perhaps because medieval cities had poor sanitation and many diseases.

Bones also tell us that medieval adolescents worked very hard: many individuals, for example, had lesions in their spines (called Schmorl's nodes) that were caused by carrying heavy loads. Girls had more respiratory diseases and more injuries to their legs and backs; these suggest that they spent a lot of time indoors (near fires) and doing domestic work. Boys had more fractures, perhaps caused by outdoor labor, and more traumas to noses, teeth, and ribs, perhaps caused by fighting.

Want to know more? See particularly the research of Mary Lewis: "Work and the Adolescent in Medieval England AD 900–1500: The Osteological Evidence," *Medieval Archaeology* 60 (2016): 138–70; *Paleopathology of Children: Identifications of Pathological Conditions in the Human Skeletal Remains of Non-Adults* (2018); and with Fiona Shapland and Rebecca Watts, "On the Threshold of Adulthood: A New Approach to the Use of Maturation Indicators to Assess Puberty in Adolescents from Medieval England," *American Journal of Human Biology* 28 (2016): 48–56.

(that is, a female brewer) faced the dire prospect of the **cuckingstool**, an instrument reserved for the punishment of women; it consisted of a chair set at the end of a pivoting bar from which a brewster would be exhibited to her neighbors and ducked in a pond or ditch. Every manor was supposed to have stocks and cuckingstool, and most people seemed to enjoy throwing rotten food, stones, and clods of earth at those whose misdeeds merited such punishments. Second, although Cecilia worked at a young age, neither she nor her parents would have equated child labor with child abuse. After all, Cecilia's work was different from the child labor we now associate with factories in developing countries and sweatshops everywhere. Cecilia worked alongside her parents and siblings, and as she worked, she also played. For Cecilia and her parents (but less so for many modern workers), the boundaries between work and leisure were underdeveloped and fluid. As the Penifaders worked, they sang, told stories, exchanged gossip, and paused for meals and naps. As the Penifaders relaxed, they also spun wool, fixed tools, and otherwise finished small tasks. In a world that so mingled work and leisure, Cecilia worked as soon as she was able because everyone worked, and because working was, quite simply, living.

The love that Robert and Alice Penifader felt for their children can be seen most clearly in something practical: their attempts to provide for the future well-being of each child. All medieval villages had customs of inheritance. When a man died, his widow took some of the family lands as her *free bench* or dower, and the rest went immediately to his heirs. Most villages practiced either *male primogeniture*, whereby the first-born son inherited the entire family property, or *male partible inheritance*, whereby the family property was divided among all sons. Brigstock had its own rather unusual custom that divided the deceased's lands between two sons: the youngest son inherited the lands his father had himself inherited, and the eldest son inherited the lands his father had purchased during his life. All three customs—male primogeniture, male partible inheritance, and what was locally called the "custom of Brigstock"—preferred sons to daughters. Women inherited only if they had no brothers, and in such cases, *all* sisters shared in the inheritance. Each of these customs of inheritance could leave some children without portions, and in such cases, parents often took great care to ensure the well-being of non-inheriting children.

This was certainly true of Robert and Alice Penifader. They began to provide for their sons early; in 1292, when Robert and William were just boys, they already held lands for which their parents were primarily responsible. In

1297, the Penifaders purchased still more land for Robert and William; in 1314, they gave some property to Henry; between 1312 and 1316, they gave lands to Christina on three separate occasions; and in 1317, they probably helped Cecilia acquire her first small properties. We do not know about provisions made for three other children: Emma, Alice, and Agnes. Emma and Alice seem to have died young. Agnes, the youngest child, seems to have received movable goods such as animals, furnishings, cash, or other commodities at the time of her marriage to Henry Kroyl in 1319. (As a rule, daughters were more likely than sons to receive portions that involved goods or cash as distinct from land; unfortunately, such gifts were rarely noted in the court records now available to historians.) When Robert died in 1318, two of his sons, probably Robert and Henry, were his primary heirs, but he had provided something for all of his living children, except for Agnes, the youngest. By the time Alice died a few years later, she had settled Agnes in a marriage to Henry Kroyl. The generosity of Robert and Alice Penifader toward their children reflected, in part, their relative wealth; poorer peasants gave their children goods instead of land, and still others could offer their children nothing. Yet the Penifaders' generosity also reflects, it is fair to conclude, their careful and loving concern for their children.

Kin and Household in Adulthood

As Cecilia grew up, her household slowly changed in size and shape. By the time she reached her tenth birthday, her siblings were beginning to leave home. William went away to get an education, and Robert and Henry probably moved out once they acquired sufficient lands of their own. In these same years her sisters Emma and Alice seem to have died. Then her sister Christina married, a result of long and careful planning by their parents. In 1312, 1314, and 1316, Robert Penifader had gone into court and transferred properties to Christina—first a small plot, then thirty-six acres of meadow, and finally, four small bits of arable land. The next year, Richard Power of Cranford (a village located about seven miles to the south of Brigstock) married Christina. They lived briefly in Brigstock and then moved back to Cranford. Cecilia, just reaching her twentieth birthday, was left at home with her father, her mother, and her sister Agnes.

Then Robert Penifader died during the Great Famine, sometime before July 1318. Robert's death left his widow Alice as head of a household that contained herself and her two youngest daughters. She reacted to this new situation in two clear ways. First, she married off one of their remaining daughters; within a year of Robert's death, Agnes was married to Henry Kroyl. Second, she withdrew as much as she could from the usual obligations of a householder; for example, she regularly avoided going to court. Some widows assertively assumed the headship responsibilities vacated by their husbands, but Alice Penifader was not one of these. She settled one daughter in marriage and otherwise sought to be left alone. Cecilia might have stayed with her, perhaps in the house in which she had grown up or perhaps (if Robert or Henry had wanted to move into the old familial home) in another house nearby. In any case, this situation was temporary. Alice apparently lived only a year or so after Robert's death.

For the next twenty-five years, Cecilia lived in Brigstock and Stanion as a **singlewoman** (*singlewoman* is a medieval term; for Cecilia, *spinster* meant "a woman who spins for a living"). She was well off, as her parents had left her with some properties, and she later acquired more. Before he died, Robert Penifader had stood pledge for Cecilia when she acquired a small plot and a **rod** of arable from Richard Koyk (a rod was one-quarter of an acre). Before she died, Alice Penifader watched as Cecilia acquired another half-rod, this time from John Tulke. Robert and Alice might have silently financed these acquisitions, and in any case, they left Cecilia with sufficient wealth to purchase still more property. By 1322, she held another rod purchased from Richard Koyk, as well as thirty-six acres of meadow bought from Ralph de la Breche. She acquired still more land in later years.

Cecilia's parents, then, provided her with enough land and capital to sustain herself. They also left her with a supportive network of kin. For example, when Cecilia bought land, she often acquired properties that abutted those of her brothers or otherwise complemented their own acquisitions. When Richard and Alan Koyk were forced to sell land during the famine years, Cecilia and her brother William bought up several of their properties. In 1317, Cecilia purchased a plot from the Koyks that likely was adjacent to a property bought two months earlier by William; in 1319, in the transaction described at the beginning of this chapter, William bought a small house that lay between the houses of Cecilia and Alan Koyk (this purchase passed through the hands of Richard Koyk in order to guarantee that he, as his father's heir, would not later challenge the sale); and in 1322, Cecilia and William each separately purchased Koyk land in what likely was an orchard (the field was called *appletrees*). In 1328, Cecilia and William together acquired one-eighth of an acre from Richard Everard, and Cecilia, William, and their brother Robert also each acquired land from

John Tulke. Within a few years of her parents' deaths, Cecilia managed properties that lay throughout the fields and meadows of Stanion and Brigstock, but these lands were not randomly scattered. With properties that often lay near those of her brothers, Cecilia could work the land with them—plowing, weeding, harvesting, tending sheep, and the like. She was better able not only to help them but also to seek their help in return.

Kin were also important to Cecilia when she had to go to court, which as an independent tenant, she did every three weeks. Each time she purchased land or transacted other business in the Brigstock court, she needed a man to serve as a pledge that she would do as she promised. Most men in Brigstock and Stanion could have done this favor for her, but she usually turned to the same person: her sister's husband Henry Kroyl. Her brother Henry also pledged for her, as did John Kroyl, brother of Cecilia's brother-in-law; all her other pledges were friends of her brothers. In other words, when Cecilia needed help in the court of Brigstock, she relied exclusively either on her brothers or on men well known to them.

Yet although kin were important to Cecilia, she was able to pick and choose among them. Cecilia reckoned kinship, as we do today, bilaterally through both male and female lines. She was an aunt, therefore, to the children of all her sisters and brothers. But she did not treat these children equally, for she seems to have paid special attention to the least advantaged of her siblings' children— her two nieces (Matilda Kroyl and Alice, the bastard daughter of Robert) and John, the bastard son of William. She treated her siblings with similar discretion. She seems to have spent much more time with her brothers William and Robert than with her brother Henry, and although she dealt often with her brother-in-law Henry Kroyl and his brother John Kroyl, she seems to have had no dealings at all with the other Kroyl brothers. For Cecilia, kinship created a *potential* of relationship; in some cases, she developed the relationship fully, in others she maintained minimal contact, and in still other cases, she so ignored a tie of kinship that it did not matter. Kinship was a gentle web with some strong strands and others weak or broken.

In her life as a singlewoman in Brigstock, Cecilia must often have appreciated the support of this gentle web. She worked her lands in concert with her brothers; they assisted her in legal business, as did her Kroyl in-laws; and in the small ways that were so important but so little reported in court rolls, her brothers, sisters, in-laws, nephews, nieces, and other kin enriched Cecilia's world. When she went to church on Sunday, she stood with female kin in the nave; when she sat in front of her house on warm evenings, she bounced nieces and nephews on her knees; when she walked about Brigstock and Stanion during the day, she shared food, chores, and gossip with her sister Agnes and her sister-in-law Isabella (wife of Henry Penifader); when she drank a pot of ale on May Day, she told old family stories.

For much of Cecilia's adult life, however, the web of kinship that enfolded her so gently did not extend into joint residence. Many singlewomen, like many widows, lived alone in small houses, and perhaps Cecilia did the same. If so, she might have stayed alone in the house she had shared for a year or so after 1318 with her widowed mother. Since many other singlewomen lived together in twos or threes, it is also possible that Cecilia was able to live with women in circumstances similar to her own. Most probably, however, Cecilia lived by herself, possibly with a servant or two. If so, she was never far from kin. As described in the entry that opens this chapter, Cecilia's unmarried brother William bought a house that shared a wall with her own home in September 1319. For the next ten years, he lived next door, perhaps even sharing a farmyard with her.

However she lived before, Cecilia's living arrangements seem to have changed dramatically in 1336. In June of that year, she and her brother Robert combined their resources and their households. Robert gave Cecilia his lands; Cecilia gave Robert her lands; they agreed to hold all properties together and undivided. This arrangement suited them well. Robert, like Cecilia, never married, and they were approaching the last years of life. By combining their resources, they supported each other better as they aged, and they also provided more amply for whoever lived longer. According to the agreement, the survivor (it ended up to be Cecilia) was to enjoy the use of the combined properties. Just before Robert died, however, the agreement of 1336 was superseded by a new one. In 1340, he transferred his lands in Brigstock to Cecilia and his lands in Stanion to his illegitimate daughter, Alice daughter of Joan de Lowyk. Cecilia must have acquiesced in this new arrangement. In any case, for several years in the late 1330s, Cecilia and Robert, a singlewoman and a bachelor, combined their resources and created their own household.

Of the six Penifader children who grew to adulthood, William, Robert, and Cecilia did not marry. They were by no means chaste (William and Robert fathered bastards), but they never formed marital households with spouses and children. Although it was unusual for three children in one family to eschew marriage, neither singlewomen nor bachelors were uncommon. Some people did not marry for religious reasons, as was doubtless the case for William. Others were too poor or too mobile to marry; landless men and women who wandered the countryside in search of work often formed informal unions, but they were unlikely to have either the means or the need to marry (see Figure 16). Still others were deemed unsuitable for marriage, due to physical or cognitive disabilities. And others could have married but did not for reasons about which we can only speculate. (Sexual preference was likely only a minor cause of non-marriage. We know much less than we would like about LGBTQ life in the Middle Ages, but it is clear that being attracted to one's own sex did not preclude heterosexual marriage, which was as much about forming a functional economic unit as about sex or love.) Cecilia and Robert fall into this last group of people who had the means to marry but did not. They came from a settled family, they possessed ample lands, they were fully competent adults, but somehow—from choice, procrastination, or disappointment in love—they never took wedding vows.

During the Middle Ages, marriage united a man and a woman. The Christian Church had a few liturgies for uniting two men, but these created more a brotherhood than a marriage, and, to date, no such unions have been found for England. If Cecilia had cast her fate with marriage and a husband, her adult life would have developed differently, in terms of both household and kinship. Her sister Agnes provides a good contrast. When Agnes married Henry Kroyl in 1319, she moved from a household headed by her father into a household headed by her husband. In the first, she was a daughter; in the second, a wife; and in both, she was a dependent under the authority of a man. Agnes and Henry were married for thirty years or more, and they produced two children, John and Matilda, who lived to adulthood. They probably also kept servants in their household, at least occasionally. Agnes, in other words, more or less re-created the household of her childhood in the household of her marriage. Her position changed from daughter to wife and mother, but she spent her life in small, nuclear family households. Compared to Cecilia, Agnes' domestic circumstances were much more stable and continuous.

As a married woman, Agnes also differed from Cecilia in her use of kinship. For Cecilia, her brothers William and Robert were important; for Agnes, these brothers seem to have mattered little. When Agnes went to court, the men on whom she most relied were her husband and two of his closest associates, his brother John Kroyl and his friend William Werketon. It was as if Agnes, having married, redirected her attention away from the Penifaders and toward the Kroyls. To be sure, she certainly visited with Cecilia and chatted with her brothers when she met them in the street, but when she needed help in court, she turned to Kroyls, not Penifaders. Interestingly, Agnes' husband

Figure 16. A Tinker. As he moves from village to village, this tinker carries on his back the bellows he needs to fix pots and pans. He could earn enough to support himself, but not a wife and children. Notice the unfriendly dog at his heels; peasants—and their dogs—were often wary of strangers. (British Library, Luttrell Psalter, folio 70v.)

Henry made an equivalent transition. Before marriage, he relied often on his father, but after marriage, he became much more independent of paternal influence. In different ways, Agnes and Henry achieved similar ends: at marriage, they turned away from their parents. Their actions underscore how marriage created not just a new household but also, and this is important, a household separate from the parents of the new couple.

Just as we do not know whether Cecilia chose to remain unmarried or was unable to marry, we also do not know whether Agnes and Henry were sweethearts who married for love. Perhaps they were, for they would certainly have known each other from working together in the fields and from relaxing together on feast days. Brigstock and Stanion were too small for them to have been strangers. Agnes and Henry would also not have been strangers to love, perhaps not the courtly love that was becoming so popular among their social superiors, but certainly the companionable love of husband and wife. Some marriages were terrible; Agnes Pole of the nearby village of Houghton-cum-Wyton, for example, was so unhappy in her marriage that she publicly consorted with her lover and harassed her poor husband. Yet other marriages were affectionate and strong; in Brigstock, the love that one couple bore toward each other was daily recognized in the nickname, Truelove, of one of their sons. Agnes and Henry probably hoped for such a marriage when they married in 1319.

In any case, the decision to marry was not theirs alone. The death of Agnes' father in 1318 seems to have precipitated the marriage, and a substantial land settlement by Henry's parents in 1319 made it feasible. As everyone agreed in the Middle Ages, a good marriage needed much more than the loving consent of bride and groom. First, it needed to be economically viable—the bride and groom needed to have land, a house, and sufficient goods to set up on their own (see Figure 17). Parents almost always helped out. Henry's parents arranged for the newlyweds to inherit from them a standard 15-acre landholding, and they likely also financed the purchase of a small property (a house, a farmyard, and six rods of arable land) that was given to Agnes as her dower. Agnes' widowed mother Alice Penifader likely reciprocated by giving the new couple cash and other goods (some of her neighbors, we know from another case, gave their marrying daughter an unspecified amount of cash, a cow worth 10 shillings, and clothing worth more than 13 shillings). Second, a good marriage required the acquiescence of friends and neighbors. Friends helped to arrange the Penifader-Kroyl match (Henry's friend William Werketon, for example, stood pledge for him when the Kroyls settled land on the new couple), and friends celebrated with feasting in the aftermath of the church wedding. One such feast in Brigstock cost 20 shillings, more than a year's wages for a male laborer! Third, everyone also agreed that a good marriage required the approval of the Church; in every parish, the parson was expected to publicize the intended marriage to ensure that no impediments stood in the way and, then, to bless the marriage before the altar. So, although the consent of Agnes and Henry was a legally necessary part of their marriage, its full success also required the involvement of parents, the approval of friends, and the cooperation of priests. Moreover, had the Penifaders and Kroyls been ordinary serfs instead of privileged tenants of a

Figure 17. Working Together. Husbands and wives worked together to support their households. This couple is weeding, the husband equipped with impressive gloves. (British Library, Luttrell Psalter, folio 172.)

royal manor, a fourth sort of consent would have been needed—that of their manorial lord or lady.

Agnes and Henry contracted their marriage in a proper and public way, but practice often fell short of the ideal, especially in terms of consent. On the one hand, sometimes young people were married without much regard to their own feelings and opinions. Parents at all social levels sometimes tried to force their children to marry people they scarcely knew, but this was particularly common among aristocrats. When, for example, the Duke of Aquitaine lay dying in 1137, he arranged to marry his fifteen-year-old daughter Eleanor to the heir to the French throne; she had not been consulted, but she duly obeyed. On the other hand, sometimes young people married without consulting their parents or anyone else. For her second marriage in 1152, Eleanor of Aquitaine selected her new husband herself, quickly and quietly marrying a young man who shortly thereafter became Henry II of England. Moreover, although everyone agreed on the desirability of parental approval, priestly supervision, seignorial consent, and community acknowledgment in making a marriage, the Church taught that none of these was essential. A man and a woman could contract a valid marriage by exchanging binding vows in utter privacy, especially if they followed the vows with sexual intercourse (as usually happened). Couples could be punished for contracting such unions (they came to be called *clandestine marriages*), but the bonds so forged could not be dissolved. Children could and did use clandestine marriage to contract unions of which their parents disapproved. One such case involved Margery Paston, daughter of a Norfolk gentry family, who married her parents' bailiff in 1469, much to the horror of her father, mother, and grandmother. They tried to get the bishop of Norwich to declare the marriage invalid, but after examining Margery and her new husband about the exact words with which they had exchanged vows, the bishop declared the marriage a true one.

Kinship and Inheritance

In 1344, as Cecilia lay sick in bed, she called into her house three young people: her nephew John, the bastard son of her brother William Penifader; her niece Matilda Kroyl, the daughter of her sister Agnes; and Robert Malin. As they stood around her bed, Cecilia gave them a twenty-four-year lease on her lands. In so doing, she effectively disinherited (for twenty-four years) her nearest heir, and she picked among her siblings' children, favoring some over others. Illegitimate children could make no claims of inheritance, but Cecilia chose to favor William's bastard. Girls could only claim inheritance in the absence of brothers, but Cecilia chose to favor her only legitimate niece, Matilda. The big puzzle is Robert Malin, who had settled in Brigstock eleven years earlier and whose relationship to Cecilia is unknown. He might have been a nephew born of an illegitimate liaison; he might have been the husband (or betrothed) of a niece; he might have been tied to Cecilia by friendship or service rather than blood. In any case, when these three young people gathered around her, Cecilia sought to manipulate kinship for one last time.

Her efforts failed. After her death, two juries met to discuss the proper deposition of her properties. The first jury judged conflicting claims of inheritance: one made by her sister Christina and the other made by her nephew Martin, son of Henry Penifader. Christina was declared the nearer heir; she and her husband Richard Power took the lands. They immediately transferred about half the land to the disappointed Martin, a move that suggests that an out-of-court arbitration had resolved the dispute by dividing the inheritance. A second jury then dealt with the claim of John Penifader, Robert Malin, and Matilda Kroyl to a twenty-four-year lease of these properties. The lease was declared invalid. A custom of Brigstock manor, designed to avoid disputes about deathbed bequests, required that anyone who transferred land from a sickbed had to be well enough thereafter to walk out of the house. Since Cecilia never left her house after she granted the lease, her gift to John, Robert, and Matilda was void. This second dispute had a nasty edge to it: Cecilia's proper heir (Christina) and the eventual holder of some of her properties (Martin) claimed that the lease was invalid because Cecilia had not been mentally capable at the time of the gift. The jury rejected this claim. In their view, Cecilia had been sound in mind but weak in body.

As Cecilia's kin argued over her lands, her cognitive health, and her last actions, they acted out the oldest and most enduring story in peasant communities: the story of inheritance, kinship, and land. Cecilia was free throughout her adult life to purchase and sell lands at will, without regard to the claims of any future heirs. She was also free throughout her adult life to use kinship in flexible ways, ignoring some kin, dearly loving others, and perhaps sharing a household with still others. But as she lay dying, these options ceased. The gentle web of kinship had one strand that always ran strong and true: the tie between blood and inheritance.

Suggestions for Further Reading

For a broad overview, see Peter Fleming, *Family and Household in England* (2001), as well as Barbara A. Hanawalt, *The Ties That Bound: Peasant Families in Medieval England* (1986). For marriage and sexuality, see Elisabeth van Houts, *Married Life in the Middle Ages, 900–1300* (2019); Ruth Mazo Karras, *Unmarriages: Women, Men, and Sexual Unions in the Middle Ages* (2012) and her *Sexuality in Medieval Europe* (3rd ed., 2017); John Boswell, *Same-Sex Unions in Pre-Modern Europe* (1996). For primary sources, see Jacqueline Murray, *Love, Marriage, and Family in the Middle Ages: A Reader* (2001). For customary law, see L. R. Poos and Lloyd Bonfield, eds., *Select Cases in Manorial Courts 1250–1550: Property and Family* (1998).

CHAPTER 7

An Economy of Makeshifts

March 1317, Brigstock Court: Cecilia Penifader acquired two pieces of land from Alan Koyk. One was a plot that was carefully measured by Cecilia's brother William and found to extend fifty feet along one side. The other was a quarter-acre of arable. Cecilia got these properties in a two-stage process designed to guarantee that Alan's heir—his son Richard—could never contest the sale. First, Alan transferred the properties to Richard (who paid the court 2 shillings for the transfer, using Robert Penifader as his pledge). Then, Richard promptly transferred both properties to Cecilia. She also paid 2 shillings to the court, and Bartholomew de Bekeswell stood as her pledge.

When she was about twenty years old, Cecilia Penifader acquired her first bits of land from Alan Koyk. She became a landholding tenant, a person with new standing in the community. As a tenant of Brigstock manor, she was thereafter expected to attend every meeting of the manorial court and to cooperate in her use of the common fields and pastures. At this important moment in her life, Cecilia did not act alone. Her brother William measured one of the two parcels she acquired, and her father Robert served as a pledge for the initial transfer. Indeed, her father probably helped her far more than the terse court entry reveals. Cecilia might have purchased these properties with cash she had saved from working as a casual laborer or servant, but her father was possibly a silent partner, financing her purchase. Just as the Penifaders had established their other children as landholding tenants in Brigstock, so they also provided for Cecilia.

For almost three decades, Cecilia held land in Brigstock, and by the time she died in 1344, she possessed extensive properties: a house with a farmyard, more than seventy acres of meadow, more than two acres of arable, and possibly other lands not reported in the extant court rolls. Cecilia held less arable than many of her neighbors, but her overall landholdings were more than enough to support her, provided she worked them well and managed them properly. Moreover, land was not the only resource at Cecilia's disposal. She also had her own labor on which to draw, labor that was defined by her gender, age, and abilities. And she had movable goods as well as land and labor. Some of these goods were inanimate objects such as spindles, churns, hoes, tables, and other items found in her house and farmyard. Some were animate stock: sheep, oxen, goats, pigs, chickens, and other animals that yielded meat, skins, milk, and manure. Cecilia was a relatively prosperous woman in Brigstock, but in common with all her neighbors, she had to juggle land, labor, and goods to make ends meet. She also had to be flexible and innovative, prepared to take advantage of any opportunity that chanced her way. In short, she had, like all her neighbors, to make her way in an economy of makeshifts.

The Household Economy

Cecilia had to be especially willing to adopt temporary expedients in the organization of her household because, as a singlewoman, she had to scramble to replicate what her married sisters Christina and Agnes more readily had: the supportive labor of husband and children. Cecilia lived in an economic world structured around households, not individuals. Poor singlewomen and bachelors often found places as servants or lodgers in the households of others (and in towns, women sometimes pooled resources to live together in what historians inelegantly term "spinster clusters"). But Cecilia, as a well-off singlewoman, was able to create her own household. Still, she could not do all the work of her household herself. Almost every day, she encountered more tasks than she could complete on her own, some of which were considered more appropriate work for men or children than for a grown woman.

As a productive unit, the peasant household had multiple responsibilities. First, the land required constant attention: the arable had to be plowed, sown, weeded, and harvested; meadow grasses had to be cut and dried; pastures had to be carefully watched and maintained; gardens had to be weeded and checked almost every day; fruit trees had to be trimmed and plucked. Second, the animals of the household required a lot of attention, since sheep, pigs, cows, goats, chickens, horses, and oxen needed constant feeding and tending. Third, any household that failed to make use of the common areas of Brigstock—especially the woods with its nuts, berries, herbs, and timber, and Harper's Brook with its fish-—would have been much poorer than it needed to be. Fourth, almost all foodstuffs required further processing within the household: grain had to be threshed; meat had to be preserved; milk had to be made into cheese or butter. Fifth, the domestic tasks that kept everyone clothed, fed, and healthy created never-ending work: meals had to be prepared, clothes made and mended, infants nursed, toddlers watched, and the sick nursed back to health or eased toward death.

Most peasant households divided these many tasks among their members according to several different criteria. One division was based on gender. Men worked more often in the fields, and women worked more often in the farmyards around their houses. Although some aspects of this division were determined by biology (only lactating women could feed young infants, for example), other parts were not (for example, nothing biological ordained that brewing was usually the work of women). This gender division of labor was clear but not set in stone. Women went into the fields whenever their help was needed (especially at harvest time, but also to weed, break clods, fix hedges, or even, on a few occasions, plow); men similarly helped with gardening, animal care, or other tasks around the house and farmyard. Both women and men went into the woods around the manor. Women spent much of their time there gathering nuts and herbs; men set traps and hunted.

Another division was based on age. Children were given simple tasks that matched their maturity, tasks that gave them more responsibility and took them farther from home as they grew older. At the other end of life, the elderly spun wool into yarn, mended clothes, repaired tools, watched infants, and otherwise took on work that was useful but less physically demanding. A third division was based on ability. Not everyone in Brigstock had the strength and experience to plow a straight furrow, place strong crucks for new roofs, or repair a broken plowshare. Most plowmen, carpenters, and smiths were male, and many households hired such men for their skilled help (see Figure 18). Most brewers were women (they were called *brewsters*), and most households bought ale from such women on a regular basis. But even within a household, some people had special skills—skinning animals, making cheese, repairing broken furniture, and the like—that became their own responsibilities. Sometimes these skills were divided by gender and age, but not always. When Cecilia lived with her widowed mother, for example, they most likely divided work between

Figure 18. Plowing. Plowing a straight furrow requires a lot of upper-body
strength. Men usually handled the plow, helped by children or women who
goaded the oxen forward. The greater status of the plowman is indicated
here by his hat, compared to the mere hood of his helper. (British Library,
Luttrell Psalter, folio 170.)

them according to whoever made tastier cheese, grew better vegetables, or spun
wool more quickly into yarn.

For Cecilia's married sisters, the household economy seemed to be almost
naturally constituted by marriage. If Agnes did some work, and Henry Kroyl
did other work, most of the chores could get done. One medieval song, which
tells of a quarrel between a husband and wife, describes in vivid terms the complementary work of married couples. The quarrel started when the husband
came home to find that his dinner was not ready:

> Then he began to chide and say "Damn you!
> I wish you would go all day to plow with me,
> To walk in the clods that are wet and boggy,
> Then you would know what it is to be a plowman."

For her part, the wife swore back just as vigorously, and she began to itemize the
work she did each day: rising early to milk the cows (while her husband, she
said, was still asleep); making butter and cheese; caring for hens, capons, and
ducks; tending to children; brewing ale; preparing flax; cleaning, carding, and
spinning wool (see Figure 19). The husband remained unconvinced, claiming
that his wife always excused herself "with grunts and groans." Finally, they
agreed to exchange chores to determine, by experience, whose lot was the harder.
Unfortunately, the one surviving copy of this song ends at this point, so we do
not know who won the argument, the plowman or his wife. This song seems

Figure 19. Work in the Farmyard. This woman feeds her hen and chicks
while she takes a break from spinning yarn (notice the distaff and spindle
tucked under her left arm). She is barefoot, a sign of her poverty. The hen is
tethered, and although over-large, she is otherwise precisely drawn. (British
Library, Luttrell Psalter, folio 166v.)

to anticipate some of the themes we can encounter in sitcoms today: an unpre-
pared dinner; an argument between spouses; an agreement to exchange roles.
But in one critical sense, this song is quintessentially medieval: it describes two
individuals whose work was profoundly interdependent. Because the plowman
went to the fields every day, his wife had grain with which to feed her cows and
brew her ale; because the goodwife raised animals and spun wool into yarn, her
husband had manure for his fields and clothes on his back. Working at separate
tasks most of the time, husbands and wives labored together toward a common
end—support of their household.

Whenever there were extra tasks to be done, married couples had several
alternatives. They could turn to children; they could employ servants; or they
could hire laborers, paying them by the day or task. Whenever married couples
needed goods they did not produce themselves, they could buy them from their
neighbors in Brigstock or from vendors at nearby markets. The household economy matched so well the complementary work of husbands and wives that most
men, if widowed, immediately remarried. Some remarried to assuage loneliness
or sexual desire, but the strongest motivation was economic: remarriage was the
most practical way to replace labor lost by a wife's death. For many people in
Brigstock, marriage or remarriage was the best way to constitute a fully func-
tioning household economy.

Yet it was not the only way. Some people, like Cecilia and her two brothers Robert and William, set up households without ever marrying. Moreover, although men usually quickly remarried after the death of a wife, many widows never remarried, either because they could not find husbands or because they preferred their autonomy as widowed heads of household. If singlewomen, bachelors, and widows had sufficient property, they could maintain their own households, getting the work done without the assistance of a spouse. They managed their households by resorting to two strategies in particular: they relied on kin, and they purchased the labor and services of their neighbors. As to the first, Cecilia often lived in close proximity to other relatives. In her early twenties, she probably lived for a year or two with her widowed mother; almost as soon as her mother died, her brother William moved next door to her for about ten years; and as she approached her forties, she established a household with her brother Robert. Like her sisters Agnes and Christina, then, Cecilia relied on kin for help and support, but she relied on her mother and brothers, not a husband. As to the second strategy, Cecilia, as a singlewoman, probably used the local markets in labor and commodities with special frequency. Married couples also employed servants or day laborers and also purchased goods, such as ale or bread, from others, but a single householder like Cecilia made especially frequent use of these opportunities.

The Labor Market

Some households in Brigstock had more hands than they needed, and other households had too few. The solution was simple: extra hands in one household were employed in another. This labor market operated on three levels: *unskilled laborers* usually worked by the day for a set wage; *skilled workers*, such as carpenters or thatchers, usually worked to complete a specified task (and were paid by the day or by the task); *servants* worked year-long contracts, getting shelter and food in their employer's house and also a specified payment at year's end. By employing all three sorts of workers, a well-off singlewoman like Cecilia managed the work demands of her household.

As a female householder, Cecilia faced one particular problem: many tasks, skilled and unskilled, were considered the proper work of men, not women. Men usually plowed the earth, wielded the scythe at harvest, beat the stalks with flails to separate the edible grain, and did many tasks that a woman like Cecilia usually did not do. How then did Cecilia cope? In part, she coped by doing some of the work anyway, for the gender division of labor was flexible enough that some women did plow, reap, and thresh. So far as Cecilia had the time and inclination, she could have done these and other "male" tasks herself. In part, she coped by calling on the help of her brothers—first William when he lived next door, and later Robert with whom she shared a household. Her brothers, of course, faced a problem that complemented Cecilia's dilemma. They had "female" tasks that needed doing such as gardening, dairying, or herb-gathering. So Cecilia helped them just as they helped her. Finally, she also coped, in part, by employing men to do the work for her.

Cecilia employed not only local men but also men who passed through Brigstock looking for work. In the early spring, she could hire a local man to help plow her arable land. In the summer, she could hire some boys to help with haymaking. In the autumn, she could give a few days' employment to the men and women who followed the ripening grain northward in search of harvest work. Whenever a plowshare broke or her house needed repairs, she turned to a nearby smith or carpenter. More than likely, Cecilia preferred to employ men as day laborers, not as live-in servants. Few widows and singlewomen kept male servants in their households, perhaps because neighbors gossiped about imagined (or real) sexual liaisons, or perhaps because women found it difficult to control male servants. Instead of coping with such problems, most female householders found it easier to hire men by the day or task.

Cecilia found these male workers in many ways—by using a smith or carpenter whose skills were well known; by employing neighbors who needed work; by hiring strangers who stopped at her gate; by looking for strong laborers when she went to market days at Kettering, Geddington, or elsewhere. If she was lucky, she was sometimes able to turn repeatedly to the same workers, using the same plowman for several seasons, or employing the same harvest workers year after year. If not, she did not need to worry. With about five million people in England and not enough land to go around, Cecilia could always find someone willing to work. In the first half of the fourteenth century, laborers, skilled as well as unskilled, were plentiful and cheap.

Cecilia made good use of this cheap labor, especially during labor-intensive times of the agricultural year and especially for tasks that were traditionally done by men. But she might also have needed servants to provide steadier and more flexible help. Contracting to live and work with one employer for a year, servants were usually young people who hoped to learn skills and save money. Among young adults, those from poor families were especially likely to seek out such work, and most servants did whatever general work needed doing.

Although adolescents of both genders worked as servants, Cecilia, as a single-woman, probably employed female servants only and kept only one at a time. For the duration of her employment, a servant shared with Cecilia the daily life and work of the household and lived under her authority. One medieval song tells the fate of a maidservant who dared to stay out all night. On her way home in the morning, she encountered her angry mistress who shouted at her, "Say, you strong strumpet, where have you been? Your tripping and dancing will come to a bad end!" The mistress then beat the young servant, "over and over again." Good servants could hope for kind treatment; bad servants could expect harsh punishment; and all servants knew that their fate rested largely in the hands of their employers, who could also be good or bad (court cases tell us that some employers abused their servants and cheated them of their salary). Almost every day, Cecilia awoke to more tasks than she could manage. "I have more to do than I may do," was how one woman put it in another medieval song. Servants made it possible for the work to get done. When sheep had to be moved to a new pasture, and fields weeded, and butter churned, and fish caught for dinner, and pigs brought in from the woods, Cecilia did some tasks and left others to her servant.

The day laborers and servants whom Cecilia employed were distinguished from each other by more than the terms of their work. Laborers, whether skilled or unskilled, most often came from the poorer households in Brigstock. They had little or no land, so the money they earned by laboring was critical in their economy of makeshifts. In Cecilia's household economy, insufficient labor was a major problem; in a laborer's household economy, abundant labor was a major resource. Given her own particular needs, Cecilia mostly employed male laborers, but women also worked for wages. Some laborers were married; some were not. Some were old; some were not. The major characteristic of wage laborers was not gender, marital status, or age, but instead poverty born of insufficient land. In contrast, servants were distinguished more by age than by socioeconomic status. To be sure, the poor were more likely to go into service than the well-off, but this was a slight and inconsistent pattern, especially compared to the strong connection between service and youthfulness. Most servants were young people who hoped, by working in other people's households, to build a nest egg. Service, in short, was usually a temporary expedient; wage labor was a critical resource that sustained some people over many years.

By paying for the labor of poor neighbors, poor strangers, and young people, Cecilia was able to manage her household economy without the help of husband or children. Just as hired laborers completed some of the work a husband might have done, so servants replicated the work of children. But the labor market did not serve only the singlewomen, bachelors, and widows of Brigstock. Married couples also hired laborers and employed servants, since they too sometimes needed extra help at harvest or regular live-in assistance. Cecilia likely resorted to the labor market more often than did her married sister Agnes, who had husband and children to help her. Yet both sisters, as prosperous villagers with extensive lands and many animals, welcomed at times the hired labor of others.

The Commodity Market

Cecilia and Agnes also eased the labor demands of their households by buying goods from others. They were able to purchase almost anything they needed: food, tools, pots, utensils, cloth, leather, furniture, wax, animals. They bought these goods from neighbors, from peddlers or merchants who passed through Brigstock, and from vendors at the weekly markets held in nearby communities. Sometimes Cecilia and Agnes found that it was easier or harder to buy certain goods; during the Great Famine, for example, food was expensive and in short supply, and peddlers were few and far between. But for most of their adult lives, Cecilia and Agnes readily met their household needs by purchase as well as direct production. Moreover, they sold as well as bought. By selling surplus eggs, meat, or wool, peasants like Cecilia and Agnes brought much-needed cash into their households.

Like most medieval peasants, Cecilia and Agnes produced, with the help of kin, laborers, and servants, much of what they consumed. From their fields, gardens, and woods, they gathered grain, fruits, and vegetables to feed their households. From their flocks and herds, they took skins, wool, milk, and meat for their daily use. In the kilns of Stanion, the center of a small pottery industry, they fired the pots and jugs they used at home (see Figure 20). From the quarries outside Stanion, they found stone and rubble for the foundations of their houses, barns, and sheds. Cecilia and Agnes produced these commodities not only for consumption but also for sale—to peddlers who came through Brigstock, to entrepreneurs seeking good pottery or building stone, and directly to consumers at local markets. Many of the foods and goods that peasants sold eventually found their way to urban marketplaces, where townspeople were eager to buy them. Like most medieval peasants, however, Cecilia and Agnes not only produced and sold goods

Figure 20. Stanion Pottery. These pots and jugs were found during a recent
excavation of a potter's house in Stanion. They were coil-built, finished on a
turntable, and then covered with a green glaze. They have some decorative
features (notice the edging around the lips of the jugs), but they are
primarily utilitarian pieces, as was typical of peasant pottery. The largest jug
(at the back left) is about 18 inches high; the smallest jug (front right) is
6 inches tall. Pottery made in Stanion was used locally and marketed
throughout Northamptonshire. (Photograph by Andy Chapman.)

but also purchased them. Some goods were too difficult to find or make in a
rural household. Since iron tools could be made only by skilled blacksmiths,
cloth production required looms, and salt could be found only in special locations, these were the sorts of commodities that Cecilia and Agnes sought
to buy rather than make. Sometimes, however, they paid for goods that they
could produce, but only with much inconvenience. Almost all peasant
households, for example, were able to brew their own ale and bake their own
bread (often using a communal oven), but many chose to purchase these
foodstuffs at least part of the time.

The trade in ale offers a good example of buying and selling within Brigstock. Ale was as important as bread in the medieval diet. Because Cecilia
avoided water (it was often polluted), turned milk into butter and cheese,
and could not afford wine, ale was her basic liquid refreshment. She drank
ale every day and throughout the day, not only as an adult but also as a child.

As a grown woman, she might have drunk as much as a gallon a day. This does not mean that Cecilia and other medieval peasants passed their days in drunken hilarity. Instead it means that ale had a different function in the Middle Ages than do alcoholic drinks today: ale was an essential part of the daily diet. (Cecilia and other medieval peasants did also drink ale for relaxation and inebriation. But they separated the weak ales for daily use from the strong ales they consumed for pleasure in evenings or at holidays.) The dietary importance of ale required that Cecilia to provide herself and the other members of her household with a regular and large supply. When she lived with her brother Robert, for example, they drank about fourteen gallons a week, and since they likely lived with a servant or two, they needed even more.

Producing this ale was time-consuming work. A lot of labor went into preparation: grain (usually oats or barley) had to be turned into malt, with several days of careful soaking, turning, and curing; the malt then had to be ground (either at one of the two mills of Brigstock or with a hand-mill); water had to be hauled from a well or from Harper's Brook to the brewing site; and wood had to be collected for a long and hot fire. Brewing itself was also laborious: the water was boiled; then the malt and water were run together into a kettle or vat; then the used malt was drawn off (and put aside to reuse for a second, much weaker batch of ale); then yeast or spices were added as the mixture cooled and fermented. The ale that came from this work was sweet to the taste (no bitter hops were used in English brewing until after 1400) and quick to sour. If not consumed within a few days, ale quickly became undrinkable. For Cecilia and Robert, this meant that they either had to brew ale every few days or they had to purchase ale from others. For a labor-poor household like their own, the answer was simple: expend labor on other projects and purchase ale.

Cecilia bought her ale from local women. Some women offered ale for sale only when they had extra—when their own households could not consume all they had brewed. Cecilia's mother sold ale in this casual and informal way, as did her married sister Agnes—they told a neighbor that they had extra ale, and a deal would be struck. Other sales were less casual, for some women sold ale as a business venture. These brewsters clearly relied on the trade to support their households, and Cecilia could almost always buy ale from them. In Cecilia's day, about three dozen brewsters worked in Brigstock and Stanion, but they did not all work at the same time. Indeed, some brewsters sold ale in one month and not the next, and others ceased to brew for several years but then returned to the trade. When Cecilia purchased ale, in other words, she occasionally bought it from a neighbor who happened to have extra on hand, but she usually purchased it from one of several nearby brewsters who, she knew, regularly brewed ale expressly for sale. Most of these brewsters were married women from households of middling status, women with sufficient resources of labor and capital to make commercial brewing a viable enterprise.

Ale was the commodity most frequently bought and sold within Brigstock. Some households, Cecilia's likely among them, bought most of their ale, perhaps even all. Some households, Agnes' likely among them, alternated buying ale with producing it and even sometimes selling off the excess. The poorest households never bought ale at all, either always producing their own or drinking water instead of ale. For some, the ale market was a way to avoid the laborious work of malting and brewing; for some, it provided a source of needed income; and for others it was unimportant. The market for other commodities in Brigstock worked much the same: many goods were available for those who wished to buy them and had the cash (or credit) at hand. On most days, Cecilia could find someone nearby selling bread, meat, fish, wood, or even a cooked pie. On most days, she could, in other words, supply many of the needs of her household by purchase rather than production.

Three things are particularly striking about Cecilia's ready ability to buy or sell goods. First, the commodity market worked reciprocally. When Cecilia went to Kettering market on a Friday, she went both to sell and to buy. The simple exchanges that happened on market days fed more complex regional and international markets. Cecilia's eggs, sold at Friday market in Kettering, might have eventually been eaten by a monk in Peterborough, and her wool, sold to a woolmonger each spring, might have ended up in the cloth of a Dutch weaver. She, in turn, purchased goods from far away, such as finished cloth from York or salted herrings from the Netherlands. Second, the commodity market emphasizes the importance of cash in the peasant economy. Although some goods were bartered for services or other goods, most were sold for cash (or credit) that was then used to pay rents, buy lands, hire laborers, and, of course, purchase other goods. Third, the strong commodity market of Cecilia's day shows that medieval peasants were neither self-sufficient nor isolated. Cecilia's household economy had to be flexible and adaptable, but it did not have to produce everything she needed. When Cecilia sold some of the wool from her sheep to a woolmonger and spun the rest into yarn to sell to a weaver, she was a confident participant in a complex market economy. She sold her wool and yarn because she knew she could later buy cloth without having to weave it herself.

The Land Market

Land was a critical part of every peasant's economy of makeshifts. Whether a household had much, some, or little land determined, in large part, its viability. People in land-poor households could adopt various strategies to get by—such as keeping animals on the common lands, or seeking employment as laborers, or selling ale—but none of these could entirely offset a paucity of land. A well-off household had sufficient land (thirty acres or more); a poor household made do with seven and one-half acres or less. Yet thirty acres did not automatically produce a well-housed and well-fed household. Even tenants of large properties, like Cecilia, had to manage their lands carefully to maximize their value.

Cecilia was not always a well-off tenant; over the course of nearly two decades, she purchased the more than seventy acres that she held at her death. She held land, in other words, not because it was family property that had been held by Penifaders since time immemorial, but instead because she was able to take advantage of Brigstock's active market in land. At almost every court meeting, several people in Brigstock transferred parcels of land (usually small parcels of less than an acre) to new holders. As a result, over the course of any single year, dozens of households in Brigstock altered the size and configuration of their tenancies. This does not mean that there was no family attachment to land in Brigstock, but it does mean that the attachment was a weak one. In 1391, a statement of the custom of Brigstock explained that even legitimate heirs did not always inherit family land because *if their fathers had sold the land*, there was no inheritance to be had. Any tenant in Brigstock could, in other words, sell land, even family land that he or she had inherited from parents. Although Brigstock had an exceptionally vigorous land market, peasants on other manors also bought or sold land.

Moreover, peasants could lease land as well as sell it. This market is virtually hidden from modern eyes, as leases were seldom registered in manorial documents. Leasing allowed Cecilia and other peasants to manage their holdings to best effect. Peasants sometimes let out land that they temporarily did not need or could not cultivate; older tenants, for example, found that this was a good way to keep the security of tenancy without having to work the land themselves. Occasionally, leasing turned peasants into minor landlords; in one

HOW DO WE KNOW ABOUT THE PEASANT LAND MARKET?

Historians used to think that medieval English peasants and their land were tied together in a uniquely peasant way—that most land was "family land" passed intact from one generation to the next. It could not be broken up; it could not be sold; it could only be passed at death to the heirs of the next generation. We thought this for comparative reasons (inalienable "family land" is common in peasant societies), for legal reasons (we assumed that tenants, especially serf tenants, could not sell or divide their tenancies), and for research reasons (inheritance customs were compellingly diverse and well documented). We spent so much time sorting out differences in male inheritance (a tenant's heir was sometimes his oldest son, sometimes his youngest son, sometimes all his sons, and sometimes, as in Brigstock, his oldest and youngest sons) that we did not fully appreciate other ways in which peasants, even servile ones, could convey or acquire land *inter vivos*—while they lived.

Ownership of land rested with the manor, and peasants were land*holders* (or tenants), not land*owners*. But we now know that, as long as a tenant got the landowner's permission (almost always available on payment of a fee), he or she could treat the tenancy as a sort of commodity—sell all of it or part of it, trade it, give it away, or even lease it. We know this because of historians' hard work collecting data and crunching it. The peasant land market is a classic example of quantitative history, and the database formed from the estates of the bishopric of Winchester is the best example of all. The bishop of Winchester held some sixty manors in southern England, and although the court rolls for these manors have not survived, his officers kept copious accounts that survive in an almost unbroken series from 1262 to 1415. These accounts list every court action that generated income, including payments required whenever a peasant took possession of a new property. In the 1990s, Paul Harvey, Richard Britnell, and their assistants set out to quantify these payments. They eventually tabulated 65,891 transactions involving the transfer of 58,657 properties among 65,786 named tenants. For medievalists, this is a very, very big database.

These data show us that the land market drew on all sorts of land: land of free tenants and servile ones too; demesne land of the bishopric as well as tenant holdings; and also land newly reclaimed from waste or forest. Sometimes tiny bits of land were exchanged, and sometimes whole tenancies of thirty acres or more. Sometimes the land was expensive (as during the early fourteenth century) and sometimes it was cheaper (especially after the Black Death). And although female landholders were not uncommon, land mostly moved between men: before 1349, women accounted for only 751 of 4,080 land-buyers, and daughters inherited on only 1,026 occasions, compared to 4,684 sons. Most of all, we know that instead of a firm and unyielding bond between family and land, there was a robust market in land. Yes, a lot of land moved within families, especially by inheritance (2,485 confirmed instances), but the most common form of land transfer was sale from one family to another (3,386 instances).

These sorts of numbers are exciting and beguiling, but they can be deceptive too. For example, comparing male and female inheritances, as I have just done, is not as straightforward as it sounds. Male inheritance on Winchester manors usually went to only one son, and female inheritance, which only occurred when there were no sons at all, was usually divided among all daughters. In other words, a male heir usually got much more acreage than a female one. For another example, these numbers mostly obscure a secondary—but mostly unrecorded—market in leased land. Usually, leases did not need to be recorded if they were short (for a year or less), and many peasants simply did not bother to register longer leases (we know because some were caught and fined). The Winchester accounts record only 340 leases before 1340, and these are surely the tip of a huge iceberg. Logic tells us that leases were relatively expensive (the sitting tenant would, of course, charge a premium above his own rent); that landless men were especially willing to accept such hard terms; and that leases were less common after 1348 (when land was more plentiful) than before. But because we have so little recorded information on leases, these are reasonable surmises not proven fact.

Our new and better understanding of the peasant land market, then, shows how quantitative history can reveal unknown trends but also requires, as all history does, careful thought about what the data hide as well as what they reveal. In this case, we can see one sort of land market clearly (sales) and almost nothing about another (leases).

To LEARN MORE, look at John Mullan and Richard Britnell, *Land and Family: Trends and Local Variations in the Peasant Land Market on the Winchester Bishopric Estates, 1263–1415* (2010).

Gloucestershire village, an enterprising tenant leased his lands to more than twenty different subtenants! Peasants also sometimes leased out properties as a way of delaying normal patterns of inheritance. Indeed, this was why Cecilia, on her deathbed, tried to pass her lands to John Penifader, Robert Malin, and Matilda Kroyl. If she had managed to leave her house after granting this lease, they would have held her lands for twenty-four years, after which the properties would have reverted to Cecilia (if she had enjoyed a miraculous recovery) or her heirs. Like this deathbed arrangement, some leases were long, but others were short—just a year or two.

Between sales of land and leases of land, households in Brigstock redistributed their landed properties much as they redistributed their labor. One household would sell or lease property it did not need to another land-poor household. As with the labor market, trade in land was not always a simple matter of redistribution. The well-off could and did exploit the poor. The Koyks might not have needed the land they sold to Cecilia in 1317, but it is also possible that they sold this property as a desperate attempt to raise money for rent, food, or other necessities. If so, they temporarily solved a problem by selling land to Cecilia, but they impoverished themselves in the long run. And if so, Cecilia took advantage of their distress.

Cecilia seems to have accumulated her land with a clear eye toward its effective management. She held a house and farmyard within which she could raise chickens and pigs, grow vegetables and herbs, keep fruit trees, and otherwise manage much of her day-to-day production of food. She held a few pieces of arable land, some lying so close to the properties of her brothers William or Robert that they could work them in common. Most of her land was in meadow or pasture, devoted to animal husbandry. Since animal husbandry was much less labor-intensive than arable farming, Cecilia wisely purchased land appropriate to her situation. With the help of a servant to watch her sheep and other animals, she could usually manage her lands on her own. She probably had to hire extra laborers on only three occasions during the year: to help plow her arable in late winter; to cut the hay from her meadows in June; and to help with the harvest in August and September.

To some extent, Cecilia's lands were an inflexible resource. She had to plant in the fields what her neighbors planted, and she had to pasture her animals according to similar rules. But to a surprisingly large extent, Cecilia was free to manage her lands as she saw fit. She could grow within her farmyard whatever she wanted for her household or whatever she thought would sell well at local markets. She could buy pasture and meadow in preference to arable. She could slaughter some pigs and keep others at pasture. She could lease land for long or short periods of time, and she could even sell her land whenever it suited her (although she never did, as far as we know). Land, like labor, was a critical resource for Cecilia, and, like labor, it was capable of varied and flexible use.

Rich and Poor

Cecilia was a privileged woman, holding much property and having many kin in Brigstock. Her economy of makeshifts, therefore, can seem to be more a matter of juggling resources than a matter of desperate expedients. Cecilia enjoyed a life that was, by peasant standards, unusually prosperous and well-fed. Yet even prosperous peasants were vulnerable to hard times; Cecilia's parents, after all, had died during the Great Famine when ruined crops and sickened animals seem to have hurt almost everyone in Brigstock. Cecilia bought her first bits of land during the famine, so she might have suffered less than most, but this does not mean that she did not suffer at all.

Many of the poorer households from which Cecilia purchased labor, goods, or land faced much more desperate circumstances. Most of Cecilia's neighbors, after all, were smallholding tenants, people with too little land to get by. Like Cecilia, they had to balance labor, goods, and land, but their resources were much more limited. Most had too little land and too many idle hands. For smallholders, the economy of makeshifts was an unhappy affair, and it would have included expedients—such as occasional hunger, theft, and prostitution—which Cecilia easily avoided. To some extent, smallholders lived in a complementary relationship with privileged peasants like Cecilia. By working for her or selling goods to her, smallholders made money that helped them survive. But to some extent, smallholders were also exploited by Cecilia and other well-off tenants. In the labor-rich and land-hungry world of the early fourteenth century, Cecilia was able to pay low wages to her laborers and to buy land from the hopelessly poor. In such cases, their desperate expedients were her timely opportunities.

Suggestions for Further Reading

For peasant budgets and standards of living, see particularly Christopher Dyer, *Standards of Living in the Later Middle Ages: Social Change in*

England c. 1200–1520 (1989). For work, see James Bothwell et al., eds. *The Problem of Labour in Fourteenth-Century England* (2000), and Jane Whittle, ed., *Servants in Rural Europe, 1400–1900* (2017). For brewing, see my *Ale, Beer, and Brewsters in England: Women's Work in a Changing World, 1300–1600* (1996).

CHAPTER 8

Community

July 1317, Brigstock Court: Richard Power of Cranford went to court asking for permission "to enter the estate of the lady Queen." In other words, he sought approval to live on Brigstock manor, then part of Queen Margaret's dower. His reason was simple: he was about to marry Christina Penifader. Permission was granted, payment was waived, and Robert Penifader stood as pledge for his new son-in-law. As the final part of his move, Richard was sworn into a Brigstock **tithing** headed by William Pikard—that is, he transferred from the peacekeeping system of Cranford into the peacekeeping system of Brigstock.

When Richard Power of Cranford married into the Penifader family, he could not simply wander north to Brigstock and settle in. He had to start by obtaining permission to enter the manor, and this was granted. He then had to establish himself as a law-abiding member of his new community, and he accomplished this by entering a local tithing. A tithing was a peacekeeping group that usually contained ten or more men led by a **tithingman**. All men in a tithing were responsible for the behavior of each other. This meant that if Richard had committed a theft after moving to Brigstock, William Pikard and the other men in his tithing would have brought him to court for judgment. If they had failed to produce Richard, they themselves would have been liable for punishment. The system of tithings into which Richard Power was sworn in July 1317 was a critical part of peace and harmony within Brigstock. Every year, a special court called a **View of Frankpledge** (*frankpledge* was another word for tithing) was convened; it made sure that all males were properly enrolled in tithings, and it also punished persons guilty of petty crimes and disturbances.

Figure 21. Archery Practice. Archery was an activity for males only. These
men use two targets, so they can shoot at one target, collect their arrows, and
then shoot at the other. The man on the right appears to be in charge, and he
is wearing on his left arm a decorated armguard or bracer. So, too, is the
fellow shooting behind him. (British Library, Luttrell Psalter, folio 147v.)

The presence of tithings reveals some interesting things about the community of Brigstock. First, it was a collective effort. Today, we have police officers
to track down wrong-doers. In medieval Brigstock, tithings did the job; friends
and neighbors, not officers, had to haul in troublemakers for justice. Second,
community was an idea that somewhat respected the boundaries of households.
Since every householder was responsible for his or her dependents, wives and
children were not in tithings. If children did something wrong, as Cecilia's
sisters Emma and Alice did in 1304 when they failed to show up for boon-work
(or harvesting of the demesne), their fathers or widowed mothers answered for
them. Third, the community of Brigstock was, in large part, a community of men
(see Figure 21). All males over the age of twelve were sworn into tithings, even
if they were servants or dependent sons. Yet no women entered tithings, even if
they were living, as Cecilia Penifader was by the 1320s, outside the authority of
a father or husband.

The idea of community is an abstraction, but to the people of Brigstock, it
was an important and sometimes compelling abstraction. After all, they had to
work together all the time. As manorial tenants, they had to meet the demands
of the lord or lady (or raise money to pay their annual lease of the manor). As
parishioners, they had to keep the churches of St. Andrew and St. Peter in good
repair, as well as meeting other parish expenses. As tenants of lands in the open
fields, they had to agree with each other on what to plant, when, and where, and
on how best to use fallow lands and the pastures. Within the farmyard of her

house, Cecilia could attend to her own business without much regard for others, but everywhere else, she was part of what she and her neighbors called "the community of the vill"—the people of Brigstock and Stanion, bound together by manor, parish, and village. She was expected to work with others to common ends.

Those who failed to do so were severely punished. The same court session that allowed Richard Power to enter Brigstock and join a tithing also punished three men who threatened communal peace and goodwill. William Lori, Robert Lambin, and Peter Kut had so harmed the pastures of Brigstock that their neighbors seized the houses of William and Robert until such time as they would make good on their errors and promise to behave in the future (Peter probably had no house that could be seized). Peter and William were veteran troublemakers; Peter had earlier been involved in a burglary, an assault on a woman, and a nasty confrontation with his tithing, and William was known for eavesdropping on his neighbors, picking fights, and even creating disturbances in court. It is not clear what these three men did in the fields of the manor in 1317—maybe they released their flocks on a field not yet fully harvested, or let their dogs attack the grazing sheep of others, or put more animals than allowed onto a common pasture. Yet it is clear how their neighbors responded. They told William, Robert, and Peter that they had to leave Brigstock, unless they mended their ways. To Cecilia and her neighbors, community was a powerful idea that could have real consequences.

Managing the Community

With all men over twelve years in tithings and most women and children under the responsibility of their householders, peace in Brigstock was readily maintained. To be sure, problems developed all the time. Cecilia might have illegally taken hay off the land of Richard Everard; she may have let her animals trespass onto the property of others; she argued with Alice Barker. These sorts of troubles happened not because Cecilia was an especially obnoxious woman, but because such problems were inevitable. The people of Brigstock lived in close proximity, and they bumped into each other and each other's property almost every day. Sometimes it was easy (or tempting) to overlook a boundary stone; easy (or tempting) to let sheep wander onto fresh grasses not one's own; easy (or tempting) to argue with a neighbor about new fences, wandering chickens, or ill-spoken words. When these disruptions occurred, tithingmen and

HOW DO WE KNOW ABOUT MEDIEVAL CLOTHES?

Almost no medieval clothing survives today, and most are mere scraps of belts or tunics, not full garments. Archaeologists rarely find clothes in graves, as most bodies were wrapped naked in shrouds, and in any case, textiles survive poorly in English soils. We have lots of metal fittings—like belt buckles—but the cloth has disappeared around them. Leather shoes have lasted a bit better (over 1,500 survive for medieval London alone), and buttons, too, once they began to be used in thirteenth century. Our best trove of what we sometimes call "medieval clothing" is not strictly medieval at all: when the wreck of the *Mary Rose* (1545) was raised from Portsmouth harbor in the 1980s, seventy-seven garments were recovered, most preserved in the tightly closed chests of the soldiers and sailors. (It is not uncommon for medievalists to dip into the sixteenth century for evidence we lack for earlier times. This practice is both risky and useful.) Most evidence about clothing is visual (effigies on tombs, paintings on church walls, manuscript illustrations, sculpture) , literary (poetry, religious writing), or documentary (household accounts, letters, deathbed bequests, regulations). Although we can rarely hold medieval clothes in our hands, these various sources tell us three intriguing things about medieval dress.

First, for most people, their clothing was a high-value possession. We know this, in part, because well-off people bequeathed clothing in wills, carefully specifying, for example, who got their russet gown, who their tawny gown, and who their black gown furred with mink (like academic regalia today, gowns were worn by men as well as women, although men's were often shorter in length). For a son who received a russet gown from his father, this was a valuable gift as well as a keepsake, and its value derived more from its cloth than its style. Wool cloth, from which most medieval clothing was made, cost a lot to produce: sheep had to be raised, their wool sheared and cleaned and spun into yarn; the yarn woven into fabric; the fabric cleaned, stretched, and sometimes felted too (felting made the cloth more rain-resistant), and finally dyed. Few families had the resources to do all these tasks themselves, and the markets where they purchased cloth relied on labor-intensive industries (roughly, seven spinners for every one weaver) and Europe-wide trade networks that moved wool to spinners, yarn to weavers, and finished cloth to buyers. Because woolen cloth (and linen cloth too) was so expensive, medieval people took good care of their clothes, patched and repaired them, bought and sold them secondhand, and gave them away when they died.

Second, in the fourteenth century, European clothing became more changeable and fashionable. In 1300, clothing was simply constructed by folding and stitching a rectangular piece of cloth into a loose-fitting gown or tunic. Because this required minimal cutting and stitching, these clothes were easy to make, easy to pass down, and easy also to rip apart and repurpose. By 1350, people preferred clothing that fit more closely—for example, waist-grabbing jerkins for men (forty-six were found on the *Mary*

Rose) and tight bodices for women. European tastes in clothes also changed more quickly than before, so that each generation dressed differently from those before. We are not yet sure why these new sartorial styles emerged, but we can observe it across most of Western Europe in the second quarter of the fourteenth century, and we know that men's fashions led the way. We can trace the changes in funeral effigies and other art; in descriptions of men wearing such fancy outfits as "a jaket of plonkett chamlett and a morey bonnet"—that is, a light blue jacket made of camel's hair and a mulberry-colored hat; and even in sermons that decry the pride, frivolity, and expense of new fashions.

Third, clothes helped to create a "social body"—that is, an appearance that told people who you were. Gender was signified by length of clothing (women's gowns were longer) and headgear (only men wore *liripipe* hoods that had long tails). Age was often noted by hair. Young, unmarried women wore their hair loose, sometimes covered with small, fashionable caps, whereas married women almost always covered their hair. Young men were clean-shaven, and older men wore beards. Occupation was shown by guild-issued caps or tunics and in the case of prostitutes, by required signs of their trade, such as striped hoods, badges, or tassels. Many localities required Jews and Muslims to wear special badges or hats, a rule extended, in theory, to all of Europe by the Fourth Lateran Council in 1215. And by the Later Middle Ages, cities and states throughout Europe were trying to keep lesser folk from dressing beyond their status. (We call these efforts "sumptuary laws" because they tried to regulate consumption.) In 1363, for example, English peasants were told that they should wear only rough woolen clothing; artisans could wear better cloth but no silk, no precious stones, and no fur; merchants and gentry could wear silk, silver, and miniver furs, but no gems except on headdresses; and the very wealthy "may dress as they please," but even they could put ermine and gems only on their hats.

As best we can tell, these rules were mostly ignored (the legislation of 1363 was repealed two years later), but prescriptive literature—that is, any writing that prescribes behavior—is always interesting to historians, whether the rules were effective or merely aspirational. So, for example, Christian laws that required Jews and Muslims to wear distinctive hats or badges tell us that people of the three traditions otherwise dressed in very similar ways. And sumptuary laws tell us that ruling elites, eager to order their world by social status, worried about the deceptive powers of fashion.

FOR CLOTHING GENERALLY, see Françoise Piponnier and Perrine Mane, *Dress in the Middle Ages* (1997), and Margaret Scott, *Medieval Dress and Fashion* (2009). For England, see especially Roberta Gilchrist, "Clothing the Body: Age, Sexuality, and Transitional Rites," chapter 3 in her *Medieval Life: Archaeology and the Life Course* (2012), pp. 68–114. The *Mary Rose* and her many artifacts are on permanent display in a spectacular exhibit in the Portsmouth Historic Dockyard.

householders made sure that they were quickly resolved either in or out of court. Peace was often broken, but peace was maintained.

The peacekeeping work of tithingmen and householders was not enough, however, to manage all the complexities of life in Brigstock. So Brigstock, like other medieval communities, had a host of officers who ran the manor and its court. The most important was the bailiff, the chief officer of a manor. In Brigstock manor, there were usually two bailiffs, one for Brigstock village and the other for Stanion. The bailiffs ensured that Brigstock manor ran smoothly and produced the expected profit. (Depending on who held the manor's profits, this income sometimes enriched the king or queen, sometimes enriched a lessee such as Margery de Farendraght, and sometimes paid the lease or sublease held by the tenants.) Literate men skilled in law as well as business, the bailiffs kept track of payments coming into the manor, as well as manorial expenses.

Bailiffs also embodied the manor to its tenants and to the world. For example, since all land in Brigstock ultimately belonged to the manor (peasants were land*holders* and *tenants*, not land*owners*), land had to be returned to the bailiff whenever it was sold. This is why, when Ralph de la Breche agreed to sell seventeen and one-half acres of meadow to Cecilia in 1322, he went to court, formally returned the land to the bailiff, and then watched as the bailiff granted it out to Cecilia. The bailiff's momentary possession of the property reminded everyone that the manor was its true owner, no matter how easy it was for Ralph to sell and Cecilia to buy. In much the same way, bailiffs also acted as the spokesmen for Brigstock manor in the outside world. In 1318, for example, it was doubtless a bailiff of Brigstock who had tried but failed to persuade Edward II to lease Brigstock manor directly to its tenants rather than to Margery de Farendraght. Bailiffs, like **parsons**, were sometimes local men, but they sometimes came from outside the manor, either minor gentry or prosperous peasants from elsewhere. Everyone was expected to obey them without question. In 1297, for example, when Robert Pidenton and Henry le Leche were elected as bailiffs of Brigstock by a committee of six men, they were explicitly empowered to order the affairs of the manor in any way that they thought best. Of course, Brigstock's tenants, since they often leased the manor themselves, had an atypical relationship with their bailiffs. On most manors, the manorial lord or lady selected this critical employee.

The bailiff of Brigstock was assisted by other officers, all of them local men elected by the tenants. These officers worked part-time, for they were also landholders in Brigstock, kept busy, like all tenants, by plowing, harvesting, and herding. The most important officer was the reeve, who managed much of the day-to-day business of the manor (again, in Brigstock, there were usually two reeves, one each for Brigstock and Stanion). The reeve was especially responsible for the cultivation of demesne lands, some leased out to tenants, but others cultivated for the profit of the manor. The reeve had to make sure that these lands were plowed, sown, and harvested on time; that rents of leased portions were duly paid; and that animals were turned onto the demesne in proper numbers at proper times. The reeve supervised the **haywards**, who kept track of what went on in the fields and flocks of the manor. Bailiffs, reeves, and haywards worked together to make sure that the arable fields and pastures of Brigstock were well and honestly used. Sometimes they also made mistakes. In 1306, for example, the bailiff of Brigstock accused Robert Penifader of letting his animals feed illegally on the demesne. Robert vigorously denied the accusation and found six men willing to swear to his innocence. He was acquitted. But the haywards who had originally raised the accusation with the bailiff were then charged with doing their job so poorly that an innocent man had been falsely accused.

Three other sorts of officers did their most important work when the court of Brigstock convened every three weeks. Jurors served on an ad hoc basis, selected whenever a **jury** was needed, and they had two functions: reporting wrongdoing and judging cases. The first function is less familiar today, but it was then very important. Because reeves, haywards, and other officers inevitably overlooked some misdeeds, *juries of presentment*, as they were called, reported wrongdoers who might otherwise have been missed. Hence, at the end of every View of Frankpledge in Brigstock, a jury declared whether the officers of the manor had presented all misdoings properly; if not, the jurors could add to or emend the charges.

The second function of juries, judging special cases, helped to resolve arguments within Brigstock. For example, when Cecilia's kin argued fiercely over her inheritance in 1344, the matter was settled by *trial juries* rendering firm verdicts. Christina Penifader and her nephew Martin disagreed about who was Cecilia's nearest heir, and they jointly opposed Martin's cousins who claimed that Cecilia had granted them a twenty-four-year lease. Who was Cecilia's nearest relative? Was she of sound mind and body when she granted the lease? These are the sorts of questions that could and did create enduring enmities, and, in some such cases, the process of judgment by jury helped to calm things. In the dispute between Christina and Martin, twenty-four men were selected and sworn to serve as jurors; they talked among themselves about the inheritance customs of Brigstock and how they applied to Cecilia's survivors; and they rendered a legal verdict. They probably also did more, for when they awarded the inheritance to Christina, she promptly transferred a good part of it to Martin. This suggests that the formal verdict of the jury was accompanied by informal arbitration; in other words, the jury both rendered a legally binding verdict and facilitated an equitable resolution that went beyond the strict dictates of law. Whether jurors arranged this extra-legal resolution or not, the process of judgment by jury—friends, neighbors, and coworkers who gathered together to talk through the facts—helped to resolve disputes and cool tempers.

Resolution was not, however, guaranteed. In the dispute that pitted Christina and Martin against Cecilia's lessees, the twelve men selected as jurors offered a straightforward judgment: the lease was invalid. Christina and Martin were doubtless pleased, but Martin's cousins, who thereby lost a lucrative gift, probably left court thinking that they had been cheated and blaming their loss on the men who judged against them. Whether presenting or judging, juries were composed of local men drawing on local lore. They based their determinations on custom (for example, their understanding of how nearness of kinship was figured in Brigstock) and on knowledge of local doings (for example, their information about whether Cecilia had or had not left her house during the last days of her life). Unlike modern jurors who are, ideally, uninformed and open-minded about a case, medieval jurors were expected to be informed, knowledgeable, and even opinionated about the cases before them.

Court business was completed with the help of two other officers. Aletasters supervised the brewers of Brigstock, making sure that they sold good quality ale at fair prices and in fair measure. The work of an aletaster can sound delightful, for (as the title implies) he was expected to taste each batch of ale before it was put on sale. But an aletaster had a hard job. He had to be ever-vigilant against the cheating schemes of brewers, and he also sometimes had to taste ale that was sour or even unhealthy. In many places, he also was supposed to oversee the trade in bread, checking to be sure that bakers sold bread that was good quality, proper weight, and fairly priced. Aletasters were kept very busy. Usually there were two aletasters working in Brigstock village and another in Stanion. Every three weeks, these men stood before the court of Brigstock and announced the results of their ongoing supervision, naming all brewers and specifying their misdeeds, if any.

Affeerors had a single but important function: they determined how much money had to be paid for each reported action or offense. Almost every transaction in court resulted in a payment of money—money paid to transfer land, money paid to resolve a dispute between neighbors, money paid by brewers (even honest ones) to practice their trade, and money paid as punishment by wrongdoers. Affeerors determined how much would be due from each person for each transaction. They seem to have based their judgments partly on the nature of each transaction (was the offense grievous? was a particularly valuable piece of land being sold?) and partly on the ability of people to pay. Fines for poor people were often forgiven, and fines for everyone were reduced in hard times. For example, brewers' fines fell rapidly during the Great Famine and somewhat more slowly thereafter. The most likely explanation is that the affeerors of Brigstock, well aware of how everyone was suffering, assessed lower sums.

All of the officers who helped to manage the community of Brigstock were men; no woman ever served as bailiff, reeve, juror, or even aletaster in Brigstock. For Cecilia, this aspect of community life was closed to her. This was true elsewhere too, for with a few rare exceptions, peasant women did not hold manorial offices. The officers of Brigstock were also *prosperous* men. Well-off families in Brigstock regularly produced most of the manor's officers, and poorer families usually produced none. The system was largely self-perpetuating. The Brigstock court rolls say that officers *electi sunt* ("were chosen"), but in some cases, this clearly meant that a committee of six or twelve men (usually themselves former officers) selected new officers. About one-third of the households in Brigstock boasted a man who at least occasionally held office, and the Penifaders were among them. Cecilia's father Robert served at various times as an aletaster, a juror, and an affeeror. Her brothers were less active: Robert served only twice as a juror; Henry never held office; and the same was true of William (who, as a cleric, would have been passed over for such work).

Bailiffs were usually paid directly, but reeves, haywards, jurors, aletasters, and affeerors often worked without direct compensation. Why did men serve? In part, they served because of the indirect profits of their offices. In Brigstock, as elsewhere in medieval Europe, an office was a responsibility, but it was also a source of income. Officers expected to receive gifts or fees from those they helped, to gain advantages from insider knowledge, and to profit from all sorts of special favors. In part, however, men served because they were expected to do so. In Brigstock and elsewhere, social prominence brought social responsibility: well-off men were expected to help govern their communities. Sometimes peasants sought to avoid official duties, but shirking was rare and discouraged. In 1314, for example, the affeerors of Brigstock told Cecilia's father that he would have to pay the considerable fine of 12 pence if he wished to be excused from the office he was then holding. Robert Penifader thereby avoided official duties, but he paid dearly for his exemption.

Householders and tithingmen helped to maintain the peace; bailiffs, reeves, and haywards kept the manor running in good order; jurors, aletasters, and affeerors completed much of the crucial business of the three-weekly court. They were kept busy because arguments, disagreements, and petty crimes were daily occurrences in Brigstock. At every meeting of the Brigstock court, people arrived to register complaints and resolve disputes. In January 1343, when Cecilia Penifader and Alice Barker brought their argument to court, other problems from recent weeks were also on the agenda: John, son of John Thomason, filed a complaint against John Golle; John Colbeyn entered a similar plea against Richard Chotty; Robert de Albathia was named for letting his horse wander into the west pasture; the executors of John Birdman's estate settled an argument with John dil Sik; Richard Swargere and Isabel, daughter of William Golle, agreed to end a long-standing quarrel; Hugh Golle, John Golle, and William Miller were cited for letting their pigs loose near the millpond; and Robert ad Stagnum came to court to complain of a trespass made against him by John Stratton. There was also a lot of petty crime in Brigstock. Serious crimes had to be taken before the king's justices, but petty crimes were reported at the annual View of Frankpledge. It was reported in 1343, for example, that people in Brigstock had attacked officers, robbed houses, moved boundary markers, harbored strangers, thrown dung into the street, obstructed the road with new buildings, cheated their neighbors by selling bad goods, and drawn blood in fights. Many of these crimes were first reported by the raising of a **hue and cry**. If anyone came upon the scene of a crime, they were to shout loudly (that is, raise a hue and cry), and everyone within earshot was to run to their aid. The hue and cry must have been commonly heard in the fields and lanes of Brigstock; almost every week, someone was doing something wrong.

As they took care of the administration of Brigstock—managing its manor, settling its disputes, and punishing its crimes—the officers were guided by its customs and **by-laws**. Like all peasants, the people of Brigstock had their traditional or customary ways of doing things. The best example is the "custom of Brigstock," which divided a deceased man's lands between his eldest and youngest sons. Customs guided the actions of all. When a reeve had to decide whom to call into the fields or a hayward had to determine whose sheep should be pastured where, they used custom to guide their decisions. What had been done in the past could reasonably be done again. For example, a jury in 1304 was convened to determine customs about boon-works on the demesne at harvest time; they reported that all persons living on the manor had to perform boon-works, but those few people in Brigstock and Stanion who lived on properties not part of Brigstock manor were free of this obligation. Like other peasants, the tenants of Brigstock supplemented custom by agreeing on new rules or by-laws that they would observe. In 1337, for example, the tenants agreed on new guidelines for the harvest: no one was to take sheaves off the fields; no one who was healthy enough to work as a wage-laborer was allowed to glean behind the harvesters; and no one was to leave Brigstock during the harvest to seek work elsewhere. In the gap between old customs and new by-laws, medieval peasants often "invented tradition," developing new rules that they quickly accepted as practiced "time out of mind." In any case, the numerous officers of Brigstock had heavy responsibilities, but they did not act according to whim. At every turn, they were guided by the long-standing customs and the more recent by-laws of the community.

Friends and Neighbors

Whenever Cecilia stood upright on hot August afternoons to rest her tired back from the labor of the harvest, she saw the fields around her filled with the people of Brigstock (see Figure 22). She knew them all, even if she knew some better than others. Indeed, save for itinerant laborers working in Brigstock for the harvest, Cecilia saw people she knew intimately: her family, her friends, her neighbors, and her fellow tenants. To an outsider—to a lord who might have cantered by, or even to us, if we could have stood and stretched with her—the field would have seemed full of humble peasants, all very much the same. Some were young or old, some were male and others female, some were mowing grain while others bundled and stacked it, but they were all peasants. Cecilia saw things differently. To her, the peasants of Brigstock were not all the same. Some were well-off, and others were not. Some had been born in Brigstock, and others were more recently settled in the community. These socioeconomic differences privileged Cecilia, who had been born into a prosperous local family, but they left others in more vulnerable circumstances.

Because no complete rentals or tax listings survive for Brigstock in Cecilia's day, the Penifaders' circumstances cannot be precisely estimated or even ranked within the community. Cecilia's parents, Robert and Alice, were relatively well-off, but we do not know exactly how much land they held. For only one Penifader can we confidently state the full extent of his landholdings. In 1326, a few years before he died, Cecilia's brother William transferred his properties to his bastard son John. His grant carefully specified twenty separate units, which

Figure 22. Harvest. During the harvest, neighbors cooperated to bring in the crops as quickly as possible. Here, two women reap while a man follows them, bundling the cut grain into sheaves. The sickle in his belt suggests, as does the (awkwardly placed) sickle of the woman stretching at the back, that they will soon swap places with the reapers and give them a rest. Notice the grim expressions of everyone: harvesting was back-breaking work. (British Library, Luttrell Psalter, folio 172v.)

totaled up to a house (located next to Cecilia's house), a couple of acres of arable, and almost 140 acres of meadow and pasture. Cecilia's landholdings were smaller but certainly comparable in terms of the balance between pasture and arable: over the course of her life, she acquired more than 70 acres of meadow and pasture along with at least 2 acres of arable land. By the standards of the day, William and Cecilia held a great deal of land, even if mostly pasture. The Hundred Rolls, a survey of English landholding taken in 1279, suggest that land was distributed among the peasants of England as follows:

Tenants of 30 acres or more: 26%
Tenants of 15 acres: 32%
Tenants of 7.5 acres or less: 42%

The Penifaders were among the most privileged of peasants, holding much more land than most.

How much land did a family need to survive? The answer depends on terrain, soil, and economy. In the midlands region where Brigstock lay, a husband, wife, and three children were prosperous—by peasant standards—if they had thirty acres or more of land; in a good year, they could take from thirty acres more than they needed to consume themselves. With the surplus they sold, they could repair their house, buy more animals, fix a plow, or otherwise improve their circumstances. Only one in four peasant families was this fortunate, and the Penifaders were among them. Rather more numerous were middling families who had to get by on about fifteen acres of land. With luck and some economizing, fifteen acres could just support five people, but with no room for extra expenses and no surplus. Whenever misfortune came—rains ruining a harvest, a wife breaking her leg, a cow dying from inexplicable illness—middling families fell into debt. Yet even they were more fortunate than the smallholders who predominated in most villages. Families of five could not be supported by holdings of 7.5 acres or less, so these tenants had to supplement fieldwork with non-agricultural sources of income. Some worked as thatchers, carpenters, charcoal-makers, potters, clothworkers, smiths, or brewers; others hired themselves out as general laborers to their neighbors; all took advantage of whatever they could find in their ongoing economy of makeshifts. Still, with their small bits of land, smallholders were better off than the landless. With nothing but their labor to support them, landless men, women, and their children wandered about the countryside seeking work and charity (see Figure 9 on p. 67 and Figure 16 on p. 114).

In communities like Brigstock, then, there were some families that ate well after a good harvest, some that ate more cautiously, and some that ate with hunger always at the table. Some families were well housed with shuttered windows and high roofs to draw off the smoke; some had more simple houses that nevertheless offered sturdy protection from the elements; some made do with hovels that were easily invaded by wind, rain, and damp.

These differences affected more than just housing and food. Prosperous peasants like the Penifaders essentially ran their communities as they liked. They had considerable economic power over their poorer neighbors—offering them employment, loans, and charity, and also buying up the lands of those who fell into desperate circumstances. They exercised considerable political power because they predominated among officeholders; when Robert Penifader served as a juror, aletaster, or affeeror, he was able to manage the affairs of the manor as he, and his equally prosperous colleagues, thought fit. They even enjoyed enhanced social power, for they were often among the oldest families in Brigstock and they chose their friends and spouses from others like them. And they even had a demographic edge over their lesser neighbors, enjoying not only larger families but also better odds of living longer and healthier lives. To be born a Penifader in late thirteenth-century Brigstock was to be a very fortunate peasant.

But to be born a Penifader did not guarantee a prosperous life. What one generation had, the next could soon lose, so that distinctions between well-off, middling, and poor rarely extended over many generations. Sometimes a couple produced no offspring in the next generation; sometimes children survived but did not do as well as their parents; and sometimes some siblings managed better than others. William and Cecilia did well enough to maintain the prominent place that their father and mother had enjoyed, but their brothers Robert and Henry led much more modest lives. Similarly, Agnes Penifader's husband Henry Kroyl followed in his father's footsteps as a prominent villager, but two of his brothers were much less fortunate men. It is easier to see these patterns than to explain them. Sometimes parents discriminated among children, setting some up nicely and leaving others to fend more for themselves. Yet in other cases, the distinctions that arose among siblings or between generations seem to have resulted from luck, personality, or both. Whatever the causes, there were no long-standing dynasties among peasants. In any generation, some households were better off than others, but few families were able to sustain such dominance for long. This was as true of the Penifaders as of others. Robert and Alice Penifader led prosperous lives, as did most of their children, but a hundred years later, only a few Penifaders still lived in Brigstock and Stanion, and they scraped by in more modest circumstances.

A Loss of Community Spirit?

The community of Brigstock actively governed itself and disciplined its wrong-doers, but it was not homogeneous. Compared to her many desperately poor neighbors, Cecilia enjoyed a comfortable life. She had much land, good housing, and abundant food. Cecilia also enjoyed more social and political influence than did most people in Brigstock. Many of her neighbors had little to say about how the manor was managed, but through her father Robert, her brother William, and her brother-in-law Henry Kroyl, Cecilia had access to some powerful local men. And Cecilia was rooted especially deeply in her community. Many of her neighbors had to leave family and kin behind as they migrated in search of better opportunities, but Cecilia died where she had been born, always surrounded by kin. Cecilia was, of course, just a peasant, and to an elite lady or an urban silkworker, she seemed a pathetically poor countrywoman. She also had some neighbors who were better off and more influential than she. But all in all,

Cecilia enjoyed a more secure and prosperous life than did most other people in the English countryside.

In terms of the reality of community within Brigstock, it matters a great deal that most of Cecilia's neighbors were much less fortunate than she. The people of Brigstock cooperated with each other almost every day, and they were capable of evoking with great feeling the idea of community. Yet their communal solidarity was undercut by the poverty of some and the prosperity of others. These differences caused anger, resentment, and crime; in most villages, burglaries and assaults were most frequently perpetrated by poor peasants against their well-off neighbors (see Figure 23). Hard times worsened these tensions. When petty crimes doubled in Brigstock during the Great Famine, poorer peasants desperately resorted to theft to feed their families, and those better off sought just as desperately to protect what seemed rightfully theirs. When bad debts increased, resentments built between poor debtors and unpaid lenders. When the pace of land sales quickened, well-off peasants benefited from the hopelessness of the poor. Cecilia might have often looked at her poor neighbors with feelings of pity, exasperation, and expectation; she gave them charity and help, but she also employed them, loaned them money, and bought their land. They looked at her, in turn, with envy, deference, and anger; they needed her assistance and employment, but they also resented her privilege and readily pilfered from her.

Sorting out what "community" meant across the many jurisdictions of Brigstock manor, parish, and village was also sometimes a difficult business. For example, the jury that discussed boon-works in 1304 had to distinguish among (a) tenants of Brigstock manor in the villages of Brigstock and Stanion, (b) men in the tithings of both villages, and (c) persons who lived in Stanion and Brigstock on some of the few tenements not part of Brigstock manor. Sometimes a person was part of the community (for example, in a tithing) but also outside it (for example, not a tenant of Brigstock manor).

Moreover, Brigstock was not an island, isolated from external influences. Every day, people walked out of Brigstock to visit relatives, sell goods, and seek work—and returned again by sunset. Every day, people came to Brigstock for exactly the same reasons. When Christina Penifader moved to Cranford, the original home of her husband Richard Power, a few years after their marriage, Cecilia thought little of walking a few miles for a visit and then returning the same day. Cecilia also accepted as normal the migration that brought some people to settle in Brigstock and took others away. Like Richard Power, people moved to Brigstock, married local people, bought land, and sought work. Some

Figure 23. Disturbing the Peace. Fences were not used in the open fields, but
they were built to protect farmyards and other separate properties. By
kicking down a fence, this fellow is making trouble. Perhaps he was irritated
at neighbors who have placed their fence wrongly; or perhaps he was taking
the wood to use as fuel, a common problem of rural communities. Whatever
the reason, fence-breaking disturbed the peace. (British Library, Luttrell
Psalter, folio 162v.)

moved on in a few years, as Richard did, and others stayed put. For Cecilia and
everyone else in Brigstock, daily movement and long-term migration created
communities bigger than Brigstock—a local community of day-to-day movement that embraced a circle extending about fifteen miles from Brigstock and a
regional community that covered the English Midlands. As Cecilia and her
neighbors traveled along the roads and paths that surrounded their manor, they
moved within a broader community of villages and towns that regularly exchanged goods, people, and services.

It is possible, as some historians have suggested, that the powerful ideal of
the "community of the vill" declined after the Black Death. Some communities
were utterly wiped out by the plague. Those that survived seem to have been
under particular stress in the late fourteenth and fifteenth centuries. Men in-
creasingly refused to serve in manorial offices; by-laws became more strident
and restrictive; legal forms of cooperation among peasants declined. Perhaps
such changes show a waning of community spirit, but perhaps not; it is hard to
know, for example, whether the proliferation of by-laws suggests a stronger
community (whose practices were more fully articulated) or a weaker community (whose unwritten practices had to be strengthened by written record). We
can, however, be sure of one thing: there is no reason for us to wax nostalgic
about the "community of the vill" in Cecilia's day. Some people imagine that a

sense of community was better achieved in past times—that it was free of conflict, strengthened by homogeneity, and purified by isolation. This is a fantasy. Cecilia's experience of community was much like ours: powerful and compelling in conception, fractured and partial in reality.

Suggestions for Further Reading

For historical debates about rural community, see chapter 7 in Phillipp R. Schofield, *Peasants and Historians: Debating the Medieval English Peasantry* (2016), and see also his *Peasant and Community in Medieval England, 1200–1500* (2003). For more information on by-laws and rural self-government, see Warren O. Ault, *Open-Field Husbandry and the Village Community: A Study of Agrarian By-Laws in Medieval England* (1965). For incomes and budgets of well-off, middling, and poor peasant households, see Christopher Dyer's *Standards of Living in the Later Middle Ages: Social Change in England c. 1200–1520* (1989).

CHAPTER 9

Women and Men

June 1336, Brigstock Court: Cecilia's brother Robert stood before the court and "delivered, granted, and sold" his lands to her. Robert stipulated that he would keep for himself half the proceeds from the land, and the clerk noted that Robert and Cecilia would henceforth together hold Robert's former lands undivided. Immediately afterward, Cecilia stood before the court and "delivered, granted, and sold" her properties to her brother, stipulating, like him, that she would retain half the proceeds from the land. In the frayed and torn edge of the court roll that survives today is a second note that, although fragmentary, indicates that Cecilia and Robert would also hold Cecilia's former lands undivided. With these two transfers, Cecilia and her brother merged their properties into a combined unit.

When Cecilia Penifader and her brother Robert stood before the court of Brigstock in June 1336, they acted as two equally competent adults. Both were tenants of the manor, both freely disposed of their lands, and both transferred their properties under identical terms. Cecilia was a woman and Robert a man, but it seems that, in this instance, distinctions of gender did not matter. What Cecilia and Robert did in June 1336, their married brother Henry could also do. That is, Henry too could transfer without restriction any lands that he held by right of sale, gift, or inheritance. Yet the two Penifader sisters who married, Agnes and Christina, were not capable of doing what their brothers and unmarried sister did so easily. Agnes and Christina, as married women, could not sell or give away land, unless they had the express permission of their husbands. This was because, as a Brigstock jury baldly put it in 1315, "A wife's sale is nothing in the absence of her husband." Both married Penifader sisters acquired lands in their own right, by gift (in Agnes' case) and by purchase, gift, and inheritance (in Christina's). Both later sold these lands. And in both cases, they only did so with the approval of their husbands, who stood at their sides when they came to court to register the sales.

The experiences of Agnes and Christina reveal an important fact about the status of married women in Brigstock and other medieval communities: they were not treated by their courts as full adults. A wife was a dependent of her husband, the acknowledged head of their household. In public, he answered for the household, accepting responsibility for the misdeeds of its members, managing its real or movable property, and expressing its interests whenever villagers met to discuss the open fields and common pastures. In private, he also wielded real authority, for, as head of household, he possessed the unquestioned right to manage the household economy as he saw fit and to discipline his wife, children, and servants. Henry Kroyl might have been a loving and kind husband who never raised his hand against Agnes Penifader and always listened carefully to her advice. Yet Henry was not required to be kind, loving, and attentive. If he sold land despite Agnes' protests, or wasted their money on strong ale, or beat her regularly, Henry would not have exceeded his acknowledged authority as head of their marital household.

Cecilia Penifader provides an interesting contrast to the respective roles of her sister Agnes and her brother-in-law Henry. Cecilia and Agnes shared some important disabilities that sprang from their gender. After all, as women, they could not join tithings, could not usually act as pledges in court, and could not serve as manorial officers. Yet for most of her adult years, Cecilia behaved, in some respects, more like her brother-in-law than like her married sister. Like Henry, Cecilia went to the court as a full and autonomous tenant. Like him, she made critical decisions that affected the welfare of her household and its members. Like him, she would not have hesitated to discipline her servants if she saw need. Cecilia was a woman, but she was also a head of household, and therefore, she was able to do many things her married sister could not. In Brigstock, differences of gender profoundly shaped the lives of women and men, but so too did differences between householders and dependents.

Gender Rules in Cecilia's World

At every moment of her life, Cecilia lived in a world that clearly and firmly distinguished between female and male. Even the first moments of life were a

gendered experience, for childbirth was women's work from which men were
banished. Alice Penifader labored to bring forth each of her eight children in
the main room of their house (or perhaps in a small room off to the side); she
rested on bedding, paced the packed dirt floor, and tried to speed the birth by
squatting, possibly on a birthing stool. In her labor, she was assisted by other
women, some kin, some friends, and some neighbors. One was surely a woman
locally known for her skilled assistance at births, what we would today call a
midwife. Sent into the farmyard or a nearby house, Robert Penifader and the
Penifader children had nothing to do with this mysterious and woman-
dominated business. The same was true of the churching ceremony that followed every safe delivery. Six weeks after she gave birth to Cecilia and each of
her other children, Alice went to church to give thanks. This happy occasion
was as gender-segregated as childbirth since, except for the priest and his assistants, men stayed away from churchings. Each time she went to be churched,
Alice was congratulated and praised by the women who had helped to bring her
safely through labor.

Born into a family that already boasted several brothers and sisters, Cecilia
seems to have been welcomed and loved by her parents. But sons were preferred.
After all, it was to sons that the most important household lands would someday devolve. English peasants practiced many customs of inheritance, but all of
these customs favored sons—either oldest sons, all sons, youngest sons, or, as in
Brigstock, the oldest and the youngest sons. English peasants also sought to
provide for children excluded from inheritance, but in so doing, they were not
egalitarian. Non-inheriting sons were more likely to get a bit of land from their
parents; non-inheriting daughters were more likely to get movable goods, such
as cash, animals, or other commodities. (In some English towns and also in
some European villages, daughters inherited alongside their brothers, but even
in these cases, sons more often took their portions in land and daughters in
goods and cash.) Robert and Alice Penifader loved all their children, but they
also knew that the link between family land and family name ran through
males only. Although the active land market of Brigstock made this link somewhat tenuous, it was not altogether severed.

Did such concerns affect the care with which the Penifaders nurtured their
daughters, as opposed to their sons? We do not know. But we do know that
rates of infant and child mortality were so high that any less favored child was
put at great risk. Although outright infanticide sometimes occurred, death
through illness or accident wrought of neglect was more common. To be sure,
girls were not the only children at potential risk; so too were disabled or disfig-

ured children, illegitimate children, and unwanted children born into impoverished households. In the case of the Penifader family, only two children are
known to have died young, and both were girls.

As young children, Cecilia and her siblings mimicked the gender distinctions that were important to their parents. Coroners' reports show that young
boys often died in accidents beyond the house and farmyard; girls most often
harmed themselves playing near home. Older boys were killed in mock battles
or working in fields or meadows; older girls died by falling into vats or tumbling
down wells. Cecilia, staying near the house in the company of her mother,
learned how to care for chickens, pigs, cows, and children; how to spin wool
into yarn; how to cook, brew, and bake; and how to raise the best vegetables and
fruits. Her brothers, wandering farther from home in the company of their
father, learned how to herd sheep, manage a plow, hunt small game, and cut
ripened grains. Yet, although the gender division of labor began at an early age,
it was as flexible in childhood as in adulthood (see Figure 24). Cecilia spent a lot
of time around house and farmyard, but like her mother, she also readily worked
in pastures and fields. She watched sheep in the pastures; she broke up clumps
of earth and weeded in the fields; she bundled and stacked sheaves at harvest.

When Cecilia reached adolescence, differences of gender became more
marked. In the years between childhood and adulthood, she was neither completely under the authority of her parents nor entirely free of it. She could attend court, hold land, and work for wages, but she relied strongly on her parents,
as many adolescents still do today. She also encountered a variety of new circumstances that differentiated her from her brothers. First, her brothers
entered tithings at age twelve. They thereby became part of the peacekeeping
community of Brigstock, something that Cecilia and other young women could
never do.

Second, her brothers were able to get better training and education. Of the
few peasants who learned to read and write, all (at least all we have identified so
far) were men. When Cecilia's brother William left Brigstock for school, their
parents lost his labor and also perhaps paid some of his expenses; they were willing to make such an investment for a son who could pursue a career as a clerk or
priest, but not for a daughter. The peasants who learned well-paid skills such as
blacksmithing, milling, carpentering, or thatching were also men. Women
sometimes worked as lower-paid assistants to thatchers or carpenters, but they
rarely practiced these trades on their own.

Third, Cecilia's brothers were able to get better wages than she could.
Whenever the Penifader children worked as day laborers or servants, they

Figure 24. In the Fields. A lot of field work was sheer drudgery. Here, a woman and man break up clods together, and they look none too happy about it. (British Library, Luttrell Psalter, folio 171v.)

found that a man earned much more than a woman. Cecilia earned a penny or less for a day's unskilled work; her brothers got about 1½ pence for similar work. Everyone seemed to accept that, as one contemporary author noted, a woman will work "for much less money than a man would take."

Fourth, parents often not only gave land (rather than goods) to their young sons but also, in so doing, gave them more wealth. This seems to have been true of the Penifaders. Robert and Alice directly gave land to all three of their sons but to only one of their three adult daughters (Christina, probably their eldest girl). Agnes and Cecilia received no lands directly from their parents; both probably got movable goods and cash. In Cecilia's case, her parents might have been "silent partners" in her first small purchases of land, and they almost certainly provided the cash inheritance with which she purchased other properties after their deaths. Cecilia, in other words, was not left impoverished by her parents' arrangements, but she did not get family properties and she seems to have gotten less overall than her brothers. Because daughters received less wealth from their parents and less wealth in land itself, landholding in medieval villages was largely a male affair. In Brigstock, about 80 percent of tenants were men, and this was below the norm (in most villages, men held 85–90 percent of the land).

By the time Cecilia reached her twentieth birthday, she found still further differences between herself and her brothers. Although she was by then an independent tenant in Brigstock, she was barred from a variety of activities, especially pledging and officeholding, that could have enlarged her influence in the community. Her brothers frequently assisted other people in court, standing as pledges to ensure that someone would fulfill a stipulated obligation. All men, poor as well as middling and well-off, could serve as pledges, but women usually could not. This meant that Cecilia could not help her friends in need, that she could not reciprocate when others pledged for her, and that she could not even earn the money that some pledges got in payment for their guarantees. Her brother-in-law Henry Kroyl used pledging to build up a complex network of mutual obligation that involved literally hundreds of people in Brigstock. Cecilia could not do the same.

In much the same way, Cecilia could not hold manorial offices, a privilege reserved for males from well-off families. Officeholding could certainly be troublesome, for reeves, jurors, aletasters, and other officers were sometimes fined for dereliction of duty and sometimes attacked by disgruntled neighbors. But officeholding more often than not yielded great advantages—such as the power to control others, the prestige of public authority, and even the profit from fees or gifts. Cecilia's brother Robert served as a juror on several occasions, and her brother-in-law Henry virtually built a career out of public service. Yet, again, Cecilia could not do the same.

These restrictions were born in part of an assumption, apparently little questioned at the time, that women should accept the government of men. "Let not the hen crow before the rooster," as one medieval proverb put it. They were also born of legal traditions that assumed women were less reliable than men, and therefore, unacceptable pledges, witnesses, or peacekeepers. Yet these ideas often did not make practical sense. For example, because women could not join tithings, a singlewoman like Cecilia lived outside the peacekeeping mechanisms of the community. Peace would have been better ensured by putting Cecilia in a tithing, but this could not be done. Therefore, she lived on Brigstock manor with no father, no husband, and no tithing to take responsibility for her. For another example, women were better qualified than men to supervise the brewing industry; since women brewed the ale, they knew best how to judge its quality, set its prices, and check for cheating. Yet women could not be aletasters. As a result, the ale industry was never as effectively supervised as it might otherwise have been.

Based as they were in often impractical ideas about gender roles, these restrictions affected women's day-to-day life, within the manorial court and without. The court was a center of life in Brigstock. Meeting every three weeks, it was the heart of manor and community, the place where important matters were discussed and important business done. In this central arena of "the community of the vill," women's problems were marginalized. In terms of criminal activities, male violence against women was underreported and lightly treated in medieval courts. In Brigstock, men committed four of every five violent crimes, but suspiciously few of these crimes were assaults on women. Moreover, when women complained of male assaults, their concerns were likely to be dismissed or belittled. For example, women were twice as likely as men to be charged with raising a false hue and cry, needlessly calling their neighbors for help. Some of these women misjudged situations or even raised hues and cries for malicious and inconsequential reasons. But other women found that their genuine cries for help got them into trouble. In 1302, one woman was even punished for alerting the community to a serious attack. When Matilda Coleman discovered Adam Swargere hurting her daughter Sarah, she raised a hue and cry against him, and in the View of Frankpledge that October, the incident was reported and judged. Adam was found guilty but excused from paying any fine; Matilda was forced to pay 7 pence for "unjustly" raising the hue and cry against him.

In terms of civil actions, women seem to have been similarly disadvantaged, for they used the court to resolve disputes much less often than did men. Women seem to have been less comfortable in court, less familiar with its ways, and less eager to bring problems to its attention. For every four times that a man brought business to court, a woman came once. When a man suffered a trespass on his lands, argued with a neighbor, or sought to settle a bad debt, he took the matter to court. A woman was more likely to settle such matters privately. Cecilia was typical in this regard. In her long life as a householder in Brigstock, she pursued in court only one argument with a neighbor. Her brothers were involved in many more disputes that ended up in court—three for Robert, four for William, and five for Henry.

Cecilia's inability to serve as a pledge or officer shaped her social life as well as her court life. Friendships were based on much more than what happened in the three-weekly meetings of Brigstock's court, but they were extended and strengthened by court activities. For example, thanks to his work as a pledge and an officer, Henry Kroyl was able to do many favors for many people. He was able, in other words, to strengthen dozens of friendships not only by assistance offered in fields and lanes but also by his actions in court. Compared to women (who could not serve as pledges or officers) and poor men (who seldom held office), he was a better neighbor, an important and well-connected man. Because Cecilia could not do the same, her social world was more restricted in size and scope.

Like Henry, Cecilia spent most of her time away from the business of the Brigstock court, and she built relationships with people by working with them in the fields, worshiping with them in church, hiring them for a few days' work, walking to markets with them, talking with them over a pot of ale, and otherwise encountering them as she went about her daily business. Like Henry, she also had some social opportunities that were open only to people of her gender. As did other women, she helped at childbirths and celebrated at churchings; as did other men, he marked out the limits of the parish each spring by beating the bounds; and every Sunday, Cecilia stood with the women in the nave, as Henry stood with the men. In many aspects of their daily lives, then, Cecilia and Henry had similar social opportunities—some precisely the same, and some different but not necessarily differently valued. Yet there was one critical difference between them: Cecilia could not use the Brigstock court to expand and enhance her social relationships. As a result, Henry was a more important person in Brigstock, and he had dozens of strong friends among the people of Stanion and Brigstock. Cecilia relied much more than Henry on a few relationships, especially those based on kin and household. The gender rules of Brigstock, in short, placed Cecilia at a disadvantage. She was born into a world where daughters were less valued than sons. She supported herself in an economy where women earned lower wages than men, got less training for skilled work, and received smaller endowments from their parents. She cooperated within a community that proscribed her from participating in its tithings, its pledging networks, and its offices. She relied on a social network that was smaller, narrower, and more focused on nearby neighbors and kin than those of many men. As the daughter of well-off parents, Cecilia forged a prosperous and comfortable life for herself, but she was, all things considered, an exceptionally lucky woman.

Gender and Household

For the Penifader children, then, opportunities were divided clearly according to gender. The Penifader sons knew that they would always enjoy familial, economic, political, and social advantages their sisters lacked. The Penifader daughters knew that they would have a harder lot in life. To be sure, all was not rosy on one side and horrible on the other. Advantage brought responsibility, as the Penifader boys learned at an early age; if they were to inherit family lands, serve in local offices, or become important figures in Brigstock, they had to

HOW DO WE KNOW ABOUT MEDIEVAL COURTSHIP?

We have a remarkable amount of evidence about heterosexual courtship in the Middle Ages. From the twelfth century on, an entire genre of "romance" literature was devoted to tales of heroic knights (for example, Lancelot), charming ladies (Guinevere), and their star-crossed love (Guinevere's husband King Arthur was their major obstacle). From these popular tales emerged ideas about romantic love that are still with us today—for example, that secrecy intensifies love, that it is painful for lovers to be apart, and that love must be tested and strong. Romances were written for and about the feudal elites, and although they were entertaining fantasies full of wizards, otherworldly creatures, and lots of adultery, their ideals of love shaped behavior, as, for example, at tournaments where men proved their bravery and women admired them.

For love and courtship among ordinary people, we mostly rely on love-gone-wrong disputes adjudicated in Church courts. Witnesses in these cases describe encounters in alehouses, taverns, streets, and barns, and their accounts tell us that marriage-making involved roughly equal doses of romance and practicality. When young women and men were courting, they were affectionate both emotionally and sexually; many exchanged love tokens (especially rings), and some produced bastards. But they also investigated one another (asking about "goods and debts," as one witness put it, and whether a man was a "good farmer" in another), and they took advice from parents and friends. A suitable marriage made everyone happy—the couple, to be sure, but also their parents, their neighbors, and their priest.

Perhaps our very best evidence of medieval courtship is a single document, a letter written in February 1477 by a gentlewoman named Margery Brews to the man she hoped to marry. Her parents and his parents were negotiating how much wealth Margery's family would contribute to her dowry. Negotiations had stalled, and Margery's father had dug in his heels, declaring he would cough up not a penny more. It is at this juncture that Margery wrote what is now considered to be the earliest Valentine greeting. Beginning and ending with romantic protestations, the letter punches with practicality in the middle. By reading this single document carefully (careful reading is the first skill of all historians), you can see that Margery lived in a world that expected marriage to be made with both sweet love and hard-headed pragmatism. Here's what she wrote:

> Most respected and honorable and my most dearly-beloved Valentine,
> I commend myself to you with all my heart, desiring to hear of your happiness,
> which I pray Almighty God to preserve according to His will and your
> heart's desire. And if it pleases you to hear how I am, I am not in good health
> in body nor in heart, nor will be until I hear from you. For no one knows
> what pain it is I suffer and even on pain of death I dare not disclose it.
>
> And my lady my mother has pursued the matter [that is, the matter of their
> marriage settlement] with my father very industriously, but she cannot get any
> more than you know of, because of which, God knows, I am very sorry.
>
> But if you love me, as I truly believe you do, you will not leave me
> because of that. Because even if you did not have half the wealth that you
> do, and I had to undertake the greatest toil that any woman alive should,
> I would not forsake you. . . .
>
> No more to you for now, but may the Holy Trinity protect you. And I
> beg you that you will not let anyone on earth see this letter, except yourself.
> And this letter was composed at Topcroft with a very heavy heart, etc.
>
> By your own, MB

If you found pained, secret, and strong love in this letter, you have read it well. So, too, did John Paston. He and Margery married that autumn.

FOR MEDIEVAL ROMANCES, see Derek Pearsall, *Arthurian Romance: A Short Introduction* (2009); for cases in Church courts, see Shannon McSheffrey, ed., *Love and Marriage in Late Medieval London* (1995); for the Pastons, see Helen Castor, *Blood and Roses: The Paston Family in the Fifteenth Century* (2004); for more Paston letters, see Diane Watt's translation (from which this example was taken), *The Paston Women: Selected Letters* (2004).

mature into dutiful and responsible men. Similarly, disadvantage could bring protection, as the Penifader girls might have early discovered. Although they got less from their parents and had less stature within Brigstock society, they could nevertheless hope that their more favored brothers (and eventually, their husbands) might watch out for their interests and protect them, if cause arose. The gender rules of medieval villages gave men some powers that women lacked, but they also expected men to use those powers well.

Moreover, the gender rules of medieval villages worked alongside another set of expectations, about householders and their dependents. Men were not just men, and women just women. In theory, each person also had a position in a household: either a head of household or a dependent. In practice, some people were neither heads nor dependents, but they were anomalies in a system that *expected* everyone either to exercise authority within a household or to accept the authority of another. The two systems of gender and household partly complemented one another. The archetypal male, for example, was a married head of household; the archetypal female was a wife. Yet these two systems also sometimes contradicted and confounded one another. For example, as a woman, Cecilia was a lesser member of the community of Brigstock, but as a householder, she took on important public responsibilities. The fault line between householders and dependents often respected distinctions of gender, but when it did not, interesting situations resulted.

The most typical arrangement was exemplified by the husband as head of household and his wife as a dependent under his authority. Legally, a wife lived under **coverture**—that is, she was "covered" in all respects by her husband's protection and authority. For Cecilia's married brother Henry, this circumstance complemented his authority as a male. For her married sisters Christina and Agnes, it complemented their lesser status as females. Women earned less than men, held less land, and had less political and social status, but if they were protected by husbands, these disadvantages could be mitigated. In other words, Agnes, married to the wealthy and powerful Henry Kroyl, enjoyed by proxy his wealth and public authority. Gender and household so complemented each other that when people married, the characteristics ascribed to their gender became, in a sense, heightened: men became more authoritative, and women became more dependent.

The marriage of Agnes Penifader and Henry Kroyl is a good example. Like all young men, Henry was slowly integrated into the public community of Brigstock before he married. He joined a tithing; he acquired land from his parents; he began to attend court and stand as a pledge for others. After he married, he expanded on these roles. He worked more and more as a pledge in court; he began to serve as an aletaster and juror; and he stood before the court as a householder, responsible for the actions of his wife, children, and servants. For Henry, his tentative steps toward adulthood were fulfilled by marriage. The experiences of his wife Agnes were similar, although different in content. She too had taken tentative steps toward adulthood as an adolescent, but like all young women, she encountered some important limitations. She could not join a tithing; she did not receive land from her parents; and she seldom, as best we can tell, went to the three-weekly meetings of the Brigstock court. After she married, some of the disadvantages that she had known as an unmarried daughter grew stronger. First, as a woman, Agnes always earned low wages, but before marriage, the money was hers to keep or save; after marriage, it belonged to her husband to use as he thought best. Second, Agnes was always less likely than her brothers to acquire land by gift, purchase, or inheritance, but before marriage, such properties (if she could get them) were hers to manage; after marriage, they became part of a conjugal economy controlled by her husband. Third, like many women, Agnes went to court only if she had to answer specific charges or pleas; after marriage her husband did even these few things for her. Agnes was a busy and hard-working wife and mother, and she was certainly not confined to her home or busied with insignificant tasks (see Figure 25), but she focused her energies more on her household than her village. For men, the authority of a married householder was the logical extension of their adolescent powers; for women, the dependency of a married woman was the logical extension of their adolescent disabilities.

Yet, as the Penifader siblings knew well, everybody did not marry, and many wives and husbands ended their lives as widows or, less frequently, widowers. The household circumstances of not-married adults confounded the neat complementarity of gender and household among married couples. Some singlewomen and bachelors stayed, in terms of their living arrangements, in a state of perpetual adolescence: they lived as servants in the houses of others, lived with parents, or lived alone in hovels. Yet other singlewomen and bachelors were well-off enough to establish their own households: they had their own houses and farmyards; they had their own holdings in fields and pastures; and although they lived without spouses and usually children, they often enjoyed the help and company of servants. Living in this fashion, Cecilia retained throughout her life the stature she had attained by her early twenties. She was an independent tenant and householder, but still a woman. She was more independent than her married sisters (who could not, for example, even sell lands

Figure 25. Hard Labor. Women did a lot of heavy carrying. Here, a woman
is carrying on her back a heavy sack of grain, either delivering it to the miller
or receiving it from him. Note also the magnificent dog. (British Library,
Luttrell Psalter, folio 158.)

they had acquired while unmarried), but not as authoritative as their husbands
(who could, for example, serve in offices). Living in this fashion, Cecilia's
brothers William and Robert also retained the stature of their early youth. They
were independent tenants and householders, but still not married men. Like
other men, they joined tithings and served as pledges, but unlike married men,
they could not advance to the most important offices in the community. Robert
served twice as a juror, but this was unusual; as a rule, only married men were
eligible to serve in manorial offices.

Singlewomen and bachelors sometimes formed atypical households. Because
William and Robert produced bastard children, they each might have lived, for
a time, with the mothers of these children. If so, their households were illicit,
but not unusual; for most purposes, William would have seemed like a husband, and Alice Perse like his wife. Only a visiting bishop might have thought
otherwise, and no bishop visited Brigstock during their time. Yet, since an informal union was less stable than a marriage, the lovers of William and Robert

were likely women from relatively poor families. These women might have truly loved William and Robert, but they also might have decided that an informal arrangement with a well-off peasant offered more security than a formal marriage to a poor one. (Love and practical self-interest were not, of course, mutually exclusive.) For poor peasant women, in other words, even an illicit union might have offered some upward mobility.

For Cecilia, only downward mobility would have resulted from bringing a male lover into her household. She would have gained no extra economic security; her family would have objected strenuously; and neighbors would have been scandalized. What could be tolerated for her brothers was not acceptable for her—unless she contracted an upwardly mobile liaison with a merchant or knight (there is no evidence to suggest that she did). Still, Cecilia did not necessarily end her life ignorant of sexual pleasures. She might have flirted with many men and even made love with some; if so, they would have been wise to restrict their sexual play to activities that would not result in pregnancy. Cecilia, however, almost certainly never brought a man to live with her. Women were another matter. Singlewomen sometimes lived together, and, in at least some of these cases, women who shared homes were sexual partners, as well as companions and friends. Arrangements such as these are revealed in censuses, letters, and diaries, sources not available for Brigstock in Cecilia's time. But it is certainly possible that Cecilia, like the women revealed in these other sources, might have lived with a female companion of some sort, especially during the years that elapsed between the death of her brother William in 1329 and her joint arrangement with Robert in 1336. If so, how did neighbors view a household of two adult women? If the second woman had been Cecilia's servant or lodger, her neighbors would have seen the household as headed by Cecilia. Otherwise, they probably viewed it as a "headless" household composed of two independent adults.

Perhaps the most interesting Penifader household was that created by Robert and Cecilia when they merged their properties in 1336. By the exchanges described in the opening to this chapter, they combined their resources and also their households. For the next four years (Robert died in 1340), brother and sister lived together in one household. Was Robert considered the head of this household? Or were Robert and Cecilia each treated as independent of the other? After this merger, the clerks of the court of Brigstock continued to refer to Robert and Cecilia as separate persons, but on a few occasions they identified Cecilia as "the sister of Robert Penifader." This practice suggests that Cecilia's identity became somewhat enfolded into the identity of her brother. But even if

Cecilia sometimes deferred to her brother and even if their neighbors thought of Robert as the head of their household, Cecilia never fell under the legal coverture of her brother. Their brother-sister household never fully replicated, in other words, the dynamics of a husband-wife household.

Whereas marriage exacerbated the inequalities of gender and not-married adulthood perpetuated them, widowhood and old age mitigated gender rules. For many men, aging brought less public authority and activity, not more. Few men formally retired, but many slowed down, as did Cecilia's own father as he grew older. In the last years of his life, Robert Penifader served less often as an officer, and he also gave more of his lands to his children. Many men remained householders throughout their lives, usually remarrying if their wives died, but as their children grew up and departed, they took on fewer responsibilities and fewer obligations. Other men, and women too, even retired from active life, ceding their tenancies to children or others in return for guaranteed support.

For many women, widowhood brought an expansion, rather than a contraction, in public responsibilities. Widows demonstrate clearly how household-status could confound gender-status, since as heads of the households left by their husbands, widows enjoyed certain rights and obligations usually reserved for men. When Cecilia's mother Alice took over the Penifader household after Robert's death, she acquired a host of public opportunities that surpassed those of singlewomen and wives. She could freely trade and sell the lands of the household; she could represent the household and its dependents in court; and, most interesting of all, she could even stand as a pledge, if the need arose (Brigstock was unusual in occasionally allowing widows to pledge, but only for their children or servants). Alice did none of these things, for her main public activities after Robert died were to marry off their daughter Agnes and to obtain excuses from attending court. But other widows did what Alice chose not to do; that is, other widows fully exercised their new options as householders. For example, after her husband Peter died in the second year of the Great Famine (1316), Alice Avice changed from a reticent wife into an active widow. She paid the rent on her holding; she purchased some lands and sold others; she answered for several offenses in court; she took six different arguments with neighbors to court; she developed a much wider social network; and she even acted on three occasions as a pledge. Some widows were too old, too withdrawn, or too poor to react to widowhood as did Alice Avice, but all widows had the legal right, as householders, to take on extensive new powers and responsibilities. Toward the end of life, as the powers of old men waned and the powers of widows waxed, differences of gender became less marked.

For the people of Brigstock, then, rules of gender varied with life changes. What it meant to be a woman was different to an adolescent, a wife, a single-woman, and a widow. What it meant to be a man was different to an adolescent, a husband, a bachelor, and an old man. Most of the rules of gender were built around the ideal of authoritative husbands and dependent wives, but these rules had to adapt to the many people and circumstances that did not fit this ideal. As a woman, Cecilia faced many restrictions on her influence and power; as a householder, she faced many opportunities to enhance her stature. She negotiated a space for herself between the full dependency of married women and the full autonomy of married men.

Complications

It would be a mistake to think that Cecilia was clever to avoid marriage and that her sisters Christina and Agnes were fools to let themselves fall into the dependent status of wives. Things were more complicated than that. Christina and Agnes gained many advantages from marriage: social approval and support; greater economic security; full independence from their parents; and the protection of husbands more publicly powerful than they. They also might have enjoyed many private satisfactions. As they bore children, worked in farmyard and field, brought in money from wage-work, and profited from selling food-stuffs, wool, yarn, and other items, Christina and Agnes knew they were doing important work. They also knew that wives were so economically essential that most husbands, if left widowed, remarried immediately. As they lived with their husbands in daily intimacy, they might have enjoyed the comfort, affection, and sexual pleasures of a happy relationship. A good marriage could bring a woman many joys and satisfactions. Yes, a wife did not control her own lands or labors, but she could be known as a goodwife, respected by her neighbors, appreciated as a wife, and much loved as a mother.

A bad marriage, however, could be very bad indeed. The gender rules of medieval villages assumed, but did not require, the beneficence of men. If her husband was indifferent or abusive, a woman could find herself a sort of servant to her husband or even cast aside altogether. Some women, such as Margaret Trippes of the diocese of Canterbury, even had to get court orders to force their husbands to provide them with basic support. Other women, such as Margaret Neffield of York whose husband broke her bones and attacked her with daggers and knives, were horribly and repeatedly beaten by their husbands. These sorts of miseries rarely prompted public action, for a husband's rights were extensive, and neighbors were hesitant to intervene. Since divorce was impossible and legal separation was rare, a bad marriage had either to be endured or ended informally (that is, either by desertion or mutual agreement to part ways). As an anonymous medieval poet put it, much of a wife's happiness in life depended on her choice of husband:

> The good and bad happenstance that some women have had
> Stands in the choice of good husband or bad.
> For she who a good and faithful husband has found
> Enjoys such a jewel as few who go around.
> She who lives with a bad husband in anger and in awe
> In yokes not evenly paired uneasily does draw.

As a singlewoman, Cecilia might have been envied by women in bad marriages but pitied by those in happy ones. She did not have to worry about an abusive husband or tolerate the restrictions of coverture, but she had to manage without the many advantages of married life. Because she did not marry, her household was poorer than it would otherwise have been, and she missed the possible pleasures of loving children and a loving husband. She was also somewhat odd. In medieval villages, most adults married—so much so that the terms *wife* and *husband* then denoted adults in general, as well as married people in particular. To be sure, there were other singlewomen, bachelors, and widows in Brigstock, some so well-off that they headed their own households and many others who got by as servants, wage-laborers, and lodgers. Rural traditions, however, largely overlooked the lives of these not-married people and praised those whose lives best matched the combined categorizations of gender and household: husbands and wives.

Some peasant women followed a third course, different from the lives of either the singlewoman Cecilia or her married sisters Christina and Agnes. They left their native villages and went to towns, seeking work, shelter, and, perhaps eventually, a good marriage. More women migrated to towns than did men, but it is unclear why. Perhaps women were pushed out of their native villages by the limitations they faced. After all, they had few opportunities for well-paid work; they were unlikely to hold much land; and some parents, favoring heirs, urged daughters (and non-inheriting sons) to move on. Or perhaps they were drawn to the attractions of towns, for towns often seemed to offer not only better employment but also better prospects for marriage. Were the peasant women who migrated to towns "voting with their feet"? Was their migration a form of protest against the difficult circumstances that faced women in the countryside? Possibly sometimes, but probably not very often. There were no organized protests by medieval women, and it is not at all clear that most women resented their lot in life. One woman, however, certainly did, for in 1405, the French author Christine de Pisan was so moved by misogynist attacks on women that she published *The Book of the City of Ladies*, a celebration of great women in history. In any case, although Cecilia and her sisters stayed close to Brigstock all their lives, they doubtless knew women who, in their late teens or early twenties, left to seek their fortunes in Northampton, Peterborough, or other towns. Wherever they settled, these women had a hard time. They found that the gender rules of medieval towns were strikingly similar to those of Brigstock. Townswomen earned lower wages than men and worked at less skilled jobs; they were usually excluded not only from town government but also from trade guilds; and they were, if married, under the coverture of their husbands. They also found that the life of a new migrant was hard. Much of the available work for women involved the least desirable and least paid of tasks, such as laundering, spinning, or doing unskilled labor. Although many women migrated in groups or went to towns where they knew a cousin or friend awaited them, they nevertheless sorely missed the broader support of family and kin. Some found themselves so impoverished that they resorted to desperate measures, especially theft and prostitution. So, although some peasant women left the countryside to seek better fortunes in towns, they were, more often than not, disappointed in what they found.

Patriarchy, Past and Present

Cecilia lived in a world where men were privileged over women—that is, in a patriarchy. *Patriarchy* is a complex and much-debated word, but it means, in essence, a social system in which men enjoy advantages that are not available to their mothers, sisters, wives, and daughters. Patriarchy is *not* a male plot; it does not need ill-will or planning. It is also *not* women versus men, because men can also be hurt by patriarchy (for example, gay men in many societies) and women can be helped by it (for example, mothers of powerful sons). Patriarchy was part of Cecilia's life, and it is part of our lives too. The Me Too movement speaks to women's ongoing struggles with sexual harassment and sexual assault. Our annual stocktaking of Equal Pay Day recognizes the wage gap between women and men (in 2018, Equal Pay Day in the UK was 10 November—this is the day in the work year when women effectively start working for free, compared to the higher wages paid to men). And although 2018 was the dubbed "Year of the Woman" in U.S. politics, women still comprise only one-fourth of the members of Congress . . . and, of course, not yet any female presidents.

Cecilia's patriarchy was not like ours. She lived in a world where social hierarchy was normal; we live in a world where social equality is expected, even if not yet achieved. She also lived in a world where so few people worked for wages that the pay gap mattered much less than it does in our time when almost all of us earn wages. Some scholars have developed from these and other differences new theories about types of patriarchies—differentiating, for example, those that rely on "public" structures (like laws and wages) from those that rely more on "private" practices (within households and families). Recognizing these differences is useful. It is also useful to see patriarchal powers as part of a "matrix of oppression": opportunities (or not) for people in Cecilia's world were shaped not just by gender but also by such factors as class (land*owner* or land*holder*), legal status (free or serf), wealth (thirty acres or five acres), and household status (unmarried Cecilia or her married sisters)—and each person's life was shaped by all these forces in ways that are hard to untangle. For us today, that matrix also includes such factors as race, ethnicity, national origin, class, sexuality, and religion.

The trick for historians and students of history is to beware of jumping to conclusions about long-term trends in patriarchal power. We moderns once thought we knew this chronology, and it was a humbling one. In 1900, historians thought that women were equal to men in the earliest human societies; that they were less equal during the Middle Ages; and that their status had plummeted in modern times. But over the course of the twentieth century, our perspective flipped, and we are now inclined to sniff haughtily at Cecilia's circumstances and congratulate ourselves on living in a more egalitarian age. Both trajectories over time—downward or upward—are speculative, and they are certainly not yet proven, simply because no one has yet figured out how to measure degrees of patriarchy across time (or place). As a result, we cannot weigh up patriarchy in Cecilia's England and compare it to England today—or even compare England today to, say, China today. Until we crack that measuring challenge, we had best be cautious about any chronology of patriarchal power, past and present.

Although it is devilishly hard to trace changing extents of patriarchal power across time, its sheer persistence is a striking fact of history. The wage gap is perhaps our best measure of patriarchy's staying power. In Cecilia's day, a female earned about 71 percent of a male wage; in 2018, female wages in the UK averaged about 80 percent of male wages. The wage gap has waxed and waned again and again over the last seven centuries of English working life, and it has hurt some women more than others, but it is a remarkably sticky phenomenon. Even in top-notch jobs—for example, women and men who work as news presenters on the BBC—pay is still lower for women. The wage gap cannot serve as a proxy measure for patriarchy writ large, but it is good for thinking about the enduring presence of gender inequality—or *patriarchal equilibrium*—from the Middle Ages to our own time. When I look at history, I see a traditional dance floor in which women and men—many sorts of women and men—are dancing to different rhythms and styles, changing partners, having fun, but *always* the men are leading, at least so far. Cecilia and her neighbors are on that dance floor. So are we.

Suggestions for Further Reading

My book on *Women in the Medieval English Countryside: Gender and Household in Brigstock Before the Plague* (1987) elaborates on most of the themes of this chapter. See also Louise J. Wilkinson, *Women in Thirteenth-Century Lincolnshire* (2007); Sandy Bardsley, *Venomous Tongues: Speech and Gender in Late Medieval England* (2006); and Marjorie Keniston McIntosh, *Working Women in English Society, 1300–1620* (2005). For a summary and bibliography of recent research, see Sharon Hubbs Wright, "Medieval English Peasant Women and Their Historians: A Historiography with a Future?" *History Compass* (2018), available online at doi.org/10.1111/hic3.12461.

For more general studies, see Mavis Mate, *Women in Medieval English Society* (1999); Elisabeth van Houts, *Married Life in the Middle Ages, 900–1300* (2019); Ruth Mazo Karras, *Sexuality in the Middle Ages* (3rd ed., 2017) and also her *From Boys to Men: Formations of Masculinity in Late Medieval Europe* (2002); and the varied essays in Judith M. Bennett and Ruth Mazo Karras, eds., *The Oxford Handbook of Women and Gender in Medieval Europe* (2016). For more on patriarchy, see my *History Matters: Patriarchy and the Challenge of Feminism* (2006). For primary sources, see Emilie Amt, *Women's Lives in Medieval Europe: A Sourcebook* (2013); P. J. P. Goldberg, *Women in England, c. 1275–1525* (1995); and Christine de Pisan, *The Book of the City of Ladies*, trans. Rosalind Brown-Grant (2000).

CHAPTER 10

Medieval Peasants, Modern People

11 June 1344, Brigstock Court: Cecilia Penifader died in late May or early June, 1344, and her kin soon gathered in court to argue about her inheritance. Her sister Christina, wife of Richard Power, came from Cranford to claim the inheritance. Her nephew Martin, son of Henry Penifader, asserted a counterclaim. After a jury found that Christina was the nearer kin of Cecilia, she and her husband took possession of the inheritance, and they promptly transferred half of it to Martin. Then a second dispute arose. John, son of William Penifader (Cecilia's nephew), Robert Malin (relation unknown), and Matilda, daughter of Henry Kroyl (her niece), claimed that before Cecilia died, she had leased her lands to them for a term of twenty-four years. Christina and Martin opposed this claim, arguing that Cecilia was mentally incompetent when she made this gift. A second jury was convened, and it determined that although Cecilia had competently arranged the lease, she had never left her house afterward and therefore the lease was invalid.

When Cecilia Penifader was in her mid-forties, she fell sick. For almost a year and a half, she lingered, with her sister, brother-in-law, nephews, and nieces wondering who would be able to claim her many acres of meadow and arable. After her death, the matter came before the Brigstock court. When the court clerk recorded the proceedings that declared Cecilia's lease invalid and designated Christina as the heir of her dead sister's lands, he also idly doodled the figure of a woman in the margins of his court roll (Figure 26). As if dissatisfied with his first effort (which produced a woman with two noses), he then redrew

Figure 26. Cecilia? The doodle in the left margin sits next to the entry that records Cecilia's death. If the clerk used Cecilia as his inspiration, he created what is today the earliest surviving portrait of a medieval peasant. Notice the cross and pointing hand (or manicule) further down the left margin; these marked noteworthy entries. Also, if you look at the text to the immediate right of the doodle's head, you might be able to make out: *Cecilia soror Roberti Penifader*. The handwriting is abbreviated but closely related to ours today. (Northamptonshire Records Office, box X365, roll 51.)

the head farther down the margin. Clerks often drew arrows, pointing hands, or other stock images to direct a reader's attention to a particular entry, but they rarely doodled. Perhaps the arguments among Cecilia's kin were so long and protracted that the poor clerk sketched to relieve his boredom. Certainly, he did not draw for love of his skill, for his sketches are rough and crude. Who was the subject of the clerk's drawing on that day in June 1344? Cecilia? Christina?

Anywoman? We cannot know, but the possibility that the woman represents Cecilia is intriguing. The clerk would have known Cecilia from her many years of attending court; she was the central figure in the disputes that he recorded in the text adjacent to the doodle; and indeed, he began his sketch immediately next to the line where he began writing, "Cecilia sister of Robert Penifader has died." If Cecilia is the woman shown in this drawing, we can surmise that she was tall, thin, curly-haired, and possibly the bearer of a prominent nose. If so, this clerk's doodle provides yet another extraordinary piece of evidence about this ordinary woman. Cecilia was just a peasant, but the Brigstock court rolls have revealed a great deal about her family, her life, and now, perhaps even her appearance.

Cecilia's story is exceptional for its documentation, but it must be interpreted with care. To begin with, Cecilia was just one of the millions of peasants who lived in the Middle Ages, and Brigstock was just one of the thousands of villages found in medieval Europe. Not all peasants were like Cecilia, nor were all villages like Brigstock in the early fourteenth century. Moreover, although we can today approach her life with an intimacy that almost seems to close a gap of seven hundred years, the links between Cecilia's past and our present are not so straightforward. Therefore, we can best put closure on Cecilia Penifader's life by considering how to understand her within the context of medieval history and also within the context of our own time.

Cecilia Penifader in the Middle Ages

Brigstock, Cecilia's home for more than forty years, was an ordinary sort of medieval community. Tight clusters of buildings formed the nucleated villages of Brigstock and Stanion; open fields surrounded these houses and farmyards; the products of forest, stream, pasture, meadow, and farmyards supplemented the crops harvested each autumn from the fields; and markets lay within easy reach on any day except Sunday. Yet many other sorts of rural communities dotted the landscape of England and Europe in the Middle Ages. In settlements made on rougher terrain with less fertile soil, peasants organized themselves into smaller hamlets or even isolated farmsteads, and they relied much more on pastoral farming, viticulture, or mining than did the peasants of Brigstock. In villages located near cities, peasants accommodated to urban customers by producing vegetables, grains, or fruits to sell in city markets. In communities near the sea, peasants combined their rural labor with fishing, smuggling, and shipping. All of these variations can be seen within the various regions of Europe; in England, for example, there were shepherds in Yorkshire, tin-miners in Cornwall, market-gardeners in Essex, and fishers on the Devon coast.

Broader patterns of European settlement, climate, soil, and trade divided medieval Europe into three general regions. Brigstock lay in the area of classic manorialism, an area that stretched across much of northwestern Europe. To the south, in regions that abutted the Mediterranean, open fields were less common, sharecropping arrangements were often important, and vineyards competed for space with fields of grain. To the east, especially in lands beyond the Elbe that were colonized after 1000, peasants enjoyed cheaper rents and more autonomy than their counterparts to the west, and cultivation of grain predominated over breeding of livestock. In short, both within Europe and within its various regions, the medieval countryside was marked by diversity of settlement, social structure, and agrarian practice.

The passage of time brought further diversity. The half-century that encompassed Cecilia's life was a transitional period in medieval history; so much so that some historians place it in the High Middle Ages (thus, c. 1000–1350) and others place it within the Later Middle Ages (thus, c. 1300–1500). Their disagreement raises important questions. Should we understand the transformation of medieval civilization as precipitated by the external force of disease, as brought by the Black Death in 1347–1349? Or should we consider that the change was internal to Europe, generated by a waning of growth and vitality that began a full fifty years before plague swept through Europe?

For many peasants, the early fourteenth century was certainly a difficult time of overpopulation, low wages, high rents, and the first widespread famine for many centuries. For many landowners, clerics, and merchants, the early fourteenth century was also a troubled era—a time of war between England and France, papal disgrace and relocation to Avignon, monetary crisis, and waning trade. Whether this half-century was the end of one medieval era or the beginning of another, it was certainly a period of trial, uncertainty, and change. As a result, Cecilia's life would have been different if she had been born a hundred years earlier or a hundred years later. In 1315, Cecilia saw people sicken from hunger during the first year of the Great Famine; in 1215, she would have enjoyed a much greater abundance of food and land; and in 1415, she would have feared plague more than famine.

As times changed, so too did distinctions among the regions of Europe. In Cecilia's day, there were many serfs in Western Europe and few to the east; a hundred years later, as serfdom was declining in the west, it was being successfully imposed on the formerly free peasants of Eastern Europe. These differences of place and time distinguish Cecilia's life as a peasant from the lives of other peasants known to historians: for example, Ermentrude, wife of the peasant Bodo, who lived on an estate outside Paris at the beginning of the ninth century; Mengarde Clergue, the matriarch of a family that dominated the village of Montaillou in southern France at about the time of Cecilia's birth; or Bertrande de Rols who married Martin Guerre in a village not far from Montaillou some two hundred years after Cecilia died. Because of the place and time in which she lived, Cecilia was freer of seignorial control than Ermentrude, less tempted by heresy than Mengarde, and not as secure in her landholding as was Bertrande.

Throughout the Middle Ages, peasants planted crops, raised sheep, tended vines, and fished streams; throughout the Middle Ages, they worked in social systems, mostly households and communities, that divided their work by age, gender, status, and ability; and throughout the Middle Ages, they owed some of the profit from their work to the Church, some to the manor, and usually some also to a king. These things were common to medieval peasants, but aside from these, the circumstances of their lives could and did vary widely.

What about Cecilia as a woman, though a woman of peasant status? What might she have shared with other medieval women, particularly those who lived in the towns, manor houses, and castles of early fourteenth-century England? To a surprising extent, gender rules ran across the status lines of medieval England. All women were proscribed from formal political office: countrywomen never worked as reeves, townswomen never served as mayors, and feudal women never sat in parliament. All women also faced similar legal disabilities: inheritance customs preferred sons over daughters whether the property was acreage, shops, or manors; and courts, whether manorial, mayoral, or royal, treated wives as dependents under the legal authority of their husbands. All women also knew that their public opportunities could wax, wane, and wax again over the life cycle. They might know some independence as adolescent daughters or adult singlewomen; they could expect to be "wholly within the power" of husbands if married; and they might face the possibility of considerable autonomy as widows. Finally, to some extent, most women did similar work: they bore and reared children; they served as helpmates to their husbands, whether at the plow, in the shop, or on the estate; they prepared food and repaired clothes. Although a knight could not plow and a plowman could not fight on horseback, their wives spun wool into yarn with equal ease (Figure 27).

Figure 27. Spinning on a Great Wheel. This lady (notice her fine dress and the purse hanging from her waist) is spinning on a *great wheel*, which she rotates with one hand while twisting yarn with the other. Women of all classes spun yarn, but peasant women used distaffs and spindles (as in Figure 19 on p. 123). Spinning wheels were a new technology in Cecilia's lifetime, and were too expensive and bulky for peasant households. (British Library, Luttrell Psalter, folio 193.)

These similarities among medieval women are striking and important, for they suggest that gender rules were strong enough to cut across sharp distinctions of rank and status. Yet these similarities must not obscure the real differences that wealth and status created for medieval women. Cecilia lived in better housing and ate better food than many of her poorer neighbors, but the English aristocrat Elizabeth de Burgh, Lady of Clare, enjoyed a standard of living unimaginable to Cecilia. More importantly, although Cecilia might have punished a wayward servant and offered work to her poorer neighbors, Elizabeth de Burgh exercised an authority over lesser folk—male as well as female—that forever eluded Cecilia. Today, people often talk about how gender is shaped by class, race, and sexuality; for the Middle Ages, it is clear that gender was shaped by birth, legal status, wealth, and, as we have seen so clearly for Brigstock, household status.

In the early fifteenth century, Christine de Pisan, writing from the comforts of the French court, recognized the poverty of peasant women but idealized their status: "Although they be fed with coarse bread, milk, lard, pottage, and

water, and although they have cares and labors enough, yet their life is surer—
yes, they have greater sufficiency—than some that be of high estate." Christine
de Pisan imagined that the arduous lives of peasant women brought them a sort
of rugged security lost to aristocratic women. This was an idyllic fantasy, facilitated by de Pisan's own distance from the hard lives of those who actually lived
in the cottages of the medieval countryside. Peasant women faced many difficult circumstances, and they did not enjoy any rough and ready equality with
their fathers, brothers, and husbands. William Langland, the fourteenth-
century English poet who lived in more humble circumstances than Christine
de Pisan, offered a much more accurate judgment. In *Piers Plowman*, he wrote
of the hunger, the cold, and the work of peasant women, and he concluded:
"Pitiable it is to read or to show in rhyme the woe of those women who live in
cottages!"

Cecilia Penifader in Our Time

Interpretation is an essential part of history. Historians spend a lot of time in
archives and museums reading old documents, looking at tattered drawings,
holding ancient tools and worn-out shoes. From these sorts of materials, historians are able to verify old facts and uncover new ones, and, in this capacity, we
undertake important and satisfying work. But facts alone do not make history.
A fact by itself often means very little. For example, what does it matter that
Richard Everard complained in the Brigstock court of August 1316 that Robert
Penifader and his daughter Cecilia had taken hay from his land? This is a minor
fact about a petty quarrel between unimportant people, and it is a fact that is
unlikely to appear in any textbook survey of English history or medieval history
anytime in the near future. But once interpreted, this fact can reveal interesting
things about how ordinary people lived during the Middle Ages—about the
tensions that arose from the easily moved boundary markers in the open fields;
about the ways in which petty theft and suspicions between neighbors increased
during the Great Famine; even about how fathers were deemed responsible for
the actions of their adolescent children.

Historians interpret at many levels and in many ways. At the microlevel, we
ask about the significance of particular facts, such as Richard Everard's complaint against the Penifaders in 1316. At a broader level, we seek to understand
past customs and past societies, such as the ways in which medieval peasants
sought to manage the lands around their villages. At the most expansive level,

historians seek to relate the past to the present. In doing this, three approaches are most common: understanding the past as an antecedent to the present; using it as a tool for understanding human society in general; and examining it as a way to see the present more clearly. These approaches are not mutually exclusive, and each is useful. Weighing changes and continuities, each tries to understand the past not only on its own terms but also in the context of the present. As a result, each can suggest, in the case of Cecilia Penifader, how modern people might better understand the medieval past.

In many respects, Cecilia's world seems radically different from our own. It was, to begin with, more circumscribed. Brigstock manor was large by medieval standards, but small by modern ones; Cecilia spent her life on a manor whose boundaries she could easily walk in one day and among several hundred people whom she knew very well. Although other people came and went all the time, Cecilia might have never traveled more than a few dozen miles from Brigstock. Cecilia's world was also much poorer than our lives today. Cecilia's house was one of the best then found in Brigstock, but it was roughly made and furnished with a few simple goods. It had no glazed windows, no chimney, no plumbing. Her diet was healthy and sufficient, but simple and dull. Her clothes were made of rough cloth and simply cut. She also lived within hierarchies that are less accepted today. In early fourteenth-century Brigstock, wives were expected to defer to husbands; peasants to their "social betters"; young to old; poor to better-off. As priests and friars had taught Cecilia, the hierarchy of three orders was God-given and good; some people had more important roles than others, but all people had duties that they should fulfill as best they could. This was, of course, an ideal that everyone did not accept all the time, but for Cecilia the modern notion that all people "are created equal" would have sounded peculiar.

Yet there are startling similarities between Brigstock today and Brigstock in the time of Cecilia Penifader. She was, like most people in Brigstock today, raised within the traditions of Christianity; she grew up, as many people do today, in a nuclear family household; she earned, like many women in modern Brigstock, lower wages than those paid to men; she paid taxes to her central government, as people do today; and although she was not a modern consumer in any sense of the term, she bought many of the goods she required. Cecilia was different from modern people in many ways, but similar in others.

Some historians will interpret Cecilia's story as a precursor to the modern day, a fourteenth-century hint of things that will only be fulfilled in the twenty-first century. In this view, the past becomes the direct ancestor of the present, with a clear and untroubled link between the two. This interpretive approach

WHAT CAN WE KNOW FROM LITERATURE AND ART?

Documentary sources—court rolls and other official written reports about people, land, and manors—have been at the heart of this retelling of the lives of Cecilia Penifader and her neighbors. Documents and history go together comfortably, for documents offer seemingly straightforward information about past times (telling us that, for example, in 1319 Alan Koyk transferred a house to his son Richard who then transferred it to William Penifader, as described at the beginning of Chapter 6). But straightforwardness is not necessarily truth, and even documents have to be interpreted. Historians are taught that before we use a document, we must *understand the document* (who wrote it? what is the basic story line?), *master its context* (what conventions, and assumptions shaped the document? why was it written?), and *assess its usefulness* for history (is the source reliable and if so, about what?). In the case of the Koyk-Penifader transaction, we need to understand how manorial courts handled land transfers (that they were "transfers," seldom "sales"); we need to know why Alan's son Richard was involved (to prevent him from later complaining that his inheritance had been sold); and we learn a very useful fact from the property's description (that after this transfer, William's new house shared a wall with his sister Cecilia's house).

Literary texts and artistic works present different challenges. Just like documents, texts and images require the historian's skills of close study, context, and assessment, but they raise additional issues about artistic genius (was Geoffrey Chaucer so brilliant that his work is timeless?) and artistic traditions (did Chaucer take so much inspiration from past authors that any story he told is also out of time?). Consider, for example, Chaucer's description of a plowman in his *Canterbury Tales*, given here as translated into modern English by Nevill Coghill:

> There was a plowman with him [the parson] there, his brother;
> Many a load of dung one time or other
> He must have carted through the morning dew.
> He was an honest worker, good and true,
> Living in peace and perfect charity,
> And, as the gospel bade him, so did he,
> Loving God best with all his heart and mind
> And then his neighbor as himself, repined
> At no misfortune, slacked for no content,
> For steadily about his work he went
> To thrash his corn, to dig or to manure
> Or make a ditch: and he would help the poor
> For love of Christ and never take a penny
> If he could help it, and, as prompt as any,
> He paid his tithes in full when they were due
> On what he owned, and on his earnings too.
> He wore a tabard smock and rode a mare.

I'm not sure Cecilia would have recognized this "worker, good and true" living in "perfect charity." In her world, peasants quarreled, sulked, cheated, and sometimes beat each other up; they did boon-works for the manor grudgingly; they exiled women and bastard children who might need their charity; they avoided what tithes and taxes they could. Chaucer has drawn on contemporary peasant life to create his plowman (hard work, poverty, charity, tithes), but he has mostly played with an old literary conceit that peasants are simple, pious, and closer to godliness. (He could have chosen to play with an opposite literary tradition—that is, that peasants are hopelessly ignorant and bestial.) Chaucer's plowman is not simple in historical terms, and he is not simple in literary terms either. He is, in fact, part of a crowd of plowmen created by English authors around Chaucer's time—of these, William Langland's *Piers Plowman* is the most famous. We cannot understand Chaucer's plowman without studying these other fictional plowmen too.

Because it has provided almost every medieval image used in this book, the *Luttrell Psalter* is an especially good example of the challenges of using creative work for historical purposes. Art historians debate many things about this psalter: when it was made (1320s–1340s), why it was made (for private use by the Luttrell family or for public readings by priests during services), how it was made (five artists or possibly more), and who told the artists what to draw (Sir Geoffrey Luttrell or his chaplain). For our purposes, some of these debates do not matter—whether made in 1320 or 1340, for example, the psalter is contemporary with Cecilia's life and appropriate for our use here.

But the Luttrell Psalter is highly selective about what it does and does not show of peasant life. It mostly shows peasants as a lord like Sir Geoffrey would have seen them—at work in fields and pastures and at play during festivals. We do not see peasant houses or farmyards, and we do not see peasants in family groups or inside their homes. With a few enigmatic exceptions (see Figures 1 on p. 5 and 8 on p. 56) we see peasants who are serious and well-behaved members of "Those Who Work." Most worrying of all for those who, like me, prize these rare depictions of peasants, the Luttrell artists dressed peasants misleadingly—their clothes are exceptionally well-made and dyed in colors that few rustics could afford.

Art historians can help us navigate these challenges because they are experts in visual cultures and signs. But they also work on interpretive levels of their own. For example, the reaping scene (Figure 22 on p. 148) in the psalter has been interpreted by Michelle Brown as symbolizing procreation: the two female reapers "raise their buttocks provocatively"; the man behind with a "curious corn-dolly resembling a phallus"; the woman in the background stretching in a way that evokes the labors of pregnancy and childbirth. I prefer to see Figure 22 as a realistic reaping scene—the reapers bent as necessary for wielding sickles; the man bundling the grain into sheaves; and the tired woman part of a team of harvesters who, as we know was common, swapped reaping and resting. My interpretation is different from Brown's but not necessarily better, and of course, both her interpretation and mine can easily coexist.

So, how should historians—and students of history—approach literature and art? *Very carefully.* Documents, the bread and butter source of historical research, are certainly not mirrors of reality, but their usual purpose is to report on reality. Literature and art are usually not intended to be mirrors of reality—they are, instead, driven largely by creative concerns. History would be poorer if we ignored these aesthetic sources, but historians must be very deliberate in using them, and we have to listen to what scholars in other disciplines have to say. Working with all these cautions, historians can and should use literature and art in our own, historical ways.

Or, to put this another way, a picture is often worth a thousand words, but it also can sometimes require (as here) a thousand words of explanation.

To READ MORE, start with Barbara A. Hanawalt and David Wallace, eds., *Bodies and Disciplines: Intersections of Literature and History in Fifteenth-Century England* (1996). For a full reproduction of the Luttrell Psalter, see Michelle P. Brown, ed., *The Luttrell Psalter, A Facsimile* (2006), where you can read her interpretation of the reaping scene on pages 13–14.

has appealed to so many historians that it has a long history of its own. In terms of medieval peasants, Alan Macfarlane has been its most ardent proponent. In *The Origins of English Individualism* (1978), Macfarlane suggested that the roots of English individualism and capitalism rest with peasants like Cecilia and villages like Brigstock. Indeed, he would argue that Cecilia was so free of familial constraints and so reliant on markets that she was not really a "peasant" at all. Macfarlane's thesis illustrates how historical interpretation can go awry; his argument is so driven by modern questions (what are the origins of individualism? where did capitalism come from?) that it misunderstands the past. To be sure, Cecilia certainly did rely on markets where she sought to buy some goods and sell others; she also came from a family that readily sold and traded land, without much regard to traditions of familial ownership; and she was able to pick and choose among her kin, favoring some at the expense of others. But Cecilia and other English peasants were not modern before their time. After all, she was a villein of the ancient demesne, subject to the jurisdiction of her manor; she passed her life firmly rooted in the land and the work of her own hands; her social world was profoundly and somewhat narrowly shaped by kinship, community, household, and parish. Cecilia was a well-off peasant who cagily managed her resources, but she was still a peasant, neither a rugged individualist nor an early entrepreneur.

It is a fool's errand to try to trace a straight line connecting us back to the fourteenth-century English countryside. First, there have been too many bumps, detours, and changes on the road between Cecilia's world and our own. For example, in the time since Cecilia contributed to the royal taxes of her day, taxation has gone in and out of fashion, its modes of assessment have changed repeatedly (sometimes goods have been taxed, sometimes income, sometimes purchases), and the weight of its burden on ordinary people has gone up and down, again and again. Cecilia paid taxes in the early fourteenth century, and people pay taxes today, but that does not mean that the taxes she paid were a small egg from which has now hatched the huge tax-collecting bureaucracies of our day. Second, no modern society descends in pristine purity from Cecilia's world. All European societies today derive in part from the traditions of medieval Europe, but they are built from many other traditions as well. There are no Penifaders in Brigstock today, but if there were, these modern Penifaders would be living in ways shaped by the many histories of people who have lived and died far from Brigstock's borders. When the people of Brigstock today talk with neighbors, dress for work, check their social media, sit down to supper, play video games, and otherwise go about their daily lives, they are part of a broader world economy, world society, and world history. Thanks particularly to modern technologies of transportation and communication, as well as the interchange promoted by the United Kingdom, the now-defunct British Empire, and Europeanism, life in Brigstock today is immeasurably enriched by the traditions, histories, and customs of many people from many lands. In other words, there are many histories—not a single one going back to Cecilia and her time—that make up the world of Brigstock today, the world of Europe today, and the "Western" world today of regions that were once settled by Europeans.

Other historians have interpreted the past not as a direct antecedent of the present but instead as a laboratory that can reveal truths about the human condition. This was the intent of George Homans in his 1941 study *English Villagers of the Thirteenth Century*. His final chapter considered how the history of medieval peasants could illuminate "the elements which societies of different kinds have in common," and, to Homans' mind, his study demonstrated three essential components of any social system (he called these: interaction, sentiment, and function). Today, historians are less willing to generalize so broadly, for we realize that generalization, while useful, can obscure variation and overlook historical context. Yet generalization is still a useful product of history, especially when carefully and hypothetically framed. For example, if women in Brigstock tried to limit their pregnancies with plants and herbs, then it is interesting to consider the possibility that birth control might be used by women of all places and times. The forms might have been cruder and less effective in the past, but perhaps women have always tried to limit their fertility by whatever means they had to hand. For another example, if people in medieval Brigstock lived, like the people of Brigstock today, in a society fractured by differences between rich and poor, powerful and powerless, then it is useful to wonder if such rankings might be an inevitable part of human life—or, alternatively, how one might break such a persistent trend. Cecilia's hierarchies were based primarily on status, wealth, and gender, whereas those today draw on the somewhat different categories of class, race, gender, sexuality, religion, and world region. But we share with her the fact of hierarchy, of ranking some people above others. For a final example, since people in Brigstock paid heavy taxes to their king, then perhaps people can always, as the saying goes, trust in two things: death and taxes.

These sorts of parallels between Cecilia's time and our own are striking, and the temptation to draw general conclusions from them is strong. But when generalizing, it is best to seek hypotheses, not conclusions. To begin with, generalizations almost always break down under the weight of numerous exceptions. After all, people in some societies, past as well as present, have not used birth control, have not lived within socioeconomic hierarchies, and have not paid taxes. Moreover, any valid generalizations must be carefully and thoroughly qualified. As we have seen, for example, it is startling that female wage-earners in Cecilia's day earned about the same proportion of a male wage (two-thirds) as do many women today. Even more startling is that this differential seems to have been roughly maintained for hundreds of years, not only in Europe but also in world regions settled by Europeans. Yet this generalization is not an invariable truth. In some circumstances, the wage gap has narrowed a bit or expanded a bit, and these changes, however small and temporary, are certainly significant. Also, in different times and places, wages have mattered more (or less) in how people earn their livings. A valid generalization can be striking and significant, but it must always be understood within the changing and different contexts of societies, past or present.

If some historians interpret the past as precursor and others use the past as a social science laboratory, still other historians see the past as a sort of foreign country. This interpretation is typified by the approach of Henry Stanley Bennett (no relation to me) in his 1937 study, *Life on the English Manor*. Bennett began with a prologue nostalgically titled "A Faire Felde Ful of Folke," evoking a countryside seen from a hilltop, a land and people that looked to him both different and familiar. From his distant perch, Bennett sometimes behaved like a stereotypical tourist. At times, he saw medieval peasants as simple folk with odd customs, and at times, he saw their world as impossibly idyllic, full of harmony and free of conflict. Bennett's particular perspective would not be adopted by many historians today, for it is too driven by nostalgia and too liable to create an exotic and idealized past. But his general approach is still much used, for it offers the critical gift of broader perspective. For modern people, travel is one popular way to gain perspective. By visiting new places and meeting new people, we learn to see ourselves on a broader canvas than before. If we are lucky, we return home from our travels with a better appreciation of who we are. In a curious twist, therefore, when we travel, we learn, by appreciating others, to appreciate ourselves as well. History is travel of a different sort, travel in time. It can offer similar rewards.

The perspectival interpretation encourages us to understand ourselves through understanding people who have lived before us. For example, it is interesting to think about our own ideas of family in light of what *familie* (the Middle English term) meant to Cecilia. Kin were important to her, but so too were household members, and for most of her life, she lived in households that included non-kin as well as kin. Moreover, households in Brigstock took on some activities that families rarely do today. Like us, Cecilia looked for love and emotional support in her household, but she also saw her household as an economic unit of collective production and consumption. To her, *familie* meant household, and the composition of her household was fluid and changeable. "Family values," if she could have understood the term, would have meant taking care of the people with whom she lived, whether they were kin, servants, or friends.

Cecilia's experience of community also provides a caution against waxing nostalgic about past communities that were, we often imagine, more unified than our own. Cecilia lived in a small community in which everyone practiced the same religion, spoke the same language, ate the same foods, and followed the same customs. Nevertheless, Cecilia's community still fell short of idyllic harmony: poor peasants resented their well-off neighbors; newcomers and strangers constantly passed through; and somebody in Brigstock was always guilty of ignoring neighbors' fences, overstocking common pastures, or taking a bit of grain not their own. Perhaps community is never complete, always fractured, and always under repair. Or consider how Cecilia was taught that the three orders of her society were divinely ordained, as was the governance of women by men. Indeed, the medieval Church taught that husbands, in order to discipline their wives, could legitimately beat them. If Cecilia ever questioned these hierarchies of status and gender (and there is no indication that she did), she had to deal with compelling teachings that they were God-given and inevitable. But we do not see things the same way today. To us, the lesson of the three orders looks like a handy justification for the power of the landed elite and wife-beating looks like spousal abuse. What seemed God-given to Cecilia, looks human-made and human-justified today. Or, to put it another way, what looked natural to Cecilia Penifader, looks unnatural to us. How will things that seem natural to us look in a hundred years?

*   *   *

In undertaking this book, I hoped that modern people, through reading about Cecilia's story, might better understand the ordinary lives of medieval peasants—their families, work, communities, beliefs, fears, and hopes. I knew a great deal about the Penifaders and Brigstock when I began, but at every stage of my work, I found myself stumbling across new facts and new possibilities. First, an exceptionally well-educated brother; then, an illegitimate nephew and niece; next, an unusual merging of lands with another brother; finally, the re-markable doodle. It has been my privilege to explore Cecilia's life, and I hope this book has given readers a chance to grasp the human stories behind the abstract structures of medieval feudalism and manorialism. Cecilia was not mere *smallfolk* nor a *halfling* with hairy feet. Her story can be known in its factual details and interpreted in its complexity. Most of all, her story enriches our lives today. We see the medieval world of traditional histories—crusaders, kings, bishops, merchants—differently when we stand in Cecilia's shoes. We see ourselves more clearly as well.

Suggestions for Further Reading

For Ermentrude, see Eileen Power, *Medieval People* (1924 and many subsequent editions); for Mengarde Clergue, see Emmanuel Le Roy Ladurie, *Montaillou: The Promised Land of Error* (1978); for Bertrande de Rols, see Natalie Zemon Davis, *The Return of Martin Guerre* (1983); for Elizabeth de Burgh, see Frances Underhill, *For Her Good Estate: The Life of Elizabeth de Burgh* (2000).

GLOSSARY

Note: I have boldfaced these words at their first use in the main text of the book, and I have italicized below words that are defined elsewhere in the glossary.

advowson The right to appoint someone to an ecclesiastical office (for example, as the *rector* of a *parish*).

affeeror An officer of the manorial court who assessed the amount of fines to be paid by offenders.

aletaster An officer of the manorial court who supervised commercial brewers and *brewsters*, ensuring that ale was well priced, properly measured, and of good quality.

anchorhold A small cell in which an anchoress or anchorite was voluntarily—and permanently—enclosed to pursue a life devoted to prayer and study.

ancient demesne Any English *manor* owned directly by William I at the time of the *Domesday Book* survey in 1086. *Villeins* of ancient demesne manors enjoyed special privileges. They did not have to pay tolls or customs anywhere in England, they did not have to attend county courts, and they could obtain legal writs from the king. Many ancient demesne manors later passed into non-royal hands, but the special status of its villeins was retained.

assart Former wasteland, forest, or marsh turned into cultivated land, either surreptitiously or with the permission of the landowner.

bailiff The chief administrative officer of a *manor*. Bailiffs were usually literate men with a working knowledge of law and business. They collected rents, tracked expenses and income, and supervised *reeves* and *haywards*.

boon-work Extra harvest labor performed by *serfs* on their manorial *demesnes*, above and beyond the ordinary *week-work* due from serfs. Manors often provided food and drink for boon-workers.

brewster A female brewer. Women made most of the ale consumed in medieval England. The term "brewer" applied to both sexes, but brewster was a woman-only term.

by-laws Community rules agreed by tenants at manorial courts. By-laws could stipulate, for example, what wages should be paid to harvest-workers or when tenants could release their animals onto *fallow* fields.

chancel The sanctuary of a church—that is, the area in which the priest celebrated Mass—always located to the east of the *nave*. By tradition, only clergy and their assistants went into the chancel.

chevage Literally, a "head tax" levied on all tenants, but usually only paid by *serfs* who needed permission to live away from their manors.

churching A religious ceremony, held about six weeks after a birth, that "purified" a new mother and celebrated her successful childbirth. By the Later Middle Ages, churching ceremonies emphasized celebration more than purification, but women were still not allowed to worship in church until after this ritual.

common lands Lands, usually unplanted fields, pastures, or meadows, on which all tenants of a *manor* could graze their animals. *By-laws* often specified how many animals each household could place on these lands.

coverture The legal state of wives in medieval England in which they were "covered" by their husbands. Wives under coverture could not on their own sell property or make contracts.

cuckingstool An instrument of punishment usually reserved for women and especially *brewsters*. It consisted of a seat at the end of a pivoting bar; placed in this seat, the offender would be displayed to her neighbors and often ducked in a pond, ditch, or river.

deacon A cleric who ranked just below a priest in the hierarchy of religious officials. Deacons assisted parish priests at their duties, helping at Mass, reading scriptures during services, and instructing parishioners. In theory, no man could be ordained a deacon before the age of nineteen.

demesne Most manorial land was rented out to long-term tenants, but the demesne was reserved for direct manorial use. The demesne was usually cultivated by *serfs* and its harvest placed in the barns of lords and ladies. But the demesne was a flexible resource, and if it was easier or more profitable, a *manor* would lease out parts of the demesne on a short-term basis.

diocese The district administered by a bishop and subject to his jurisdiction. Medieval England was divided into seventeen dioceses and medieval Wales into four. Dioceses were subdivided into other units of which the most important were *parishes*.

Domesday Book A survey of English lands, landowners, and tenants commissioned by William I and completed in 1086. Because Domesday Book recorded who owned land and under what terms, it was used throughout the Middle Ages as a record of local rights and responsibilities. For example, if Domesday Book recorded that a particular *manor* had been held by the king in 1086, that manor was regarded as part of the *ancient demesne* and its *villeins* enjoyed special privileges.

dower Lands set aside for a widow to use after her husband's death, with the rest going directly to his heirs. Dower lands usually amounted to one-third of the husband's properties. They were often identified by a husband at the time of marriage, but they were also sometimes regulated by custom or law.

dowry A payment made by a bride's family to her husband at the time of marriage. Like *dower* lands, dowries were sometimes intended to support wives if their husbands died first. Provision of dowries was most common among members of the elite, and it was more common in southern Europe than in northern Europe. Although forbidden to do so by the Church, many female monasteries required dowries from would-be nuns.

fallow Unplanted land. Because fertilizers were few and inadequate, medieval peasants let some land lie fallow each year so that it could regain its productivity. See also *three-field system* and *two-field system*.

feudalism The political, military, and social system that maintained the culture and power of the military elite ("those who fight"). The term "feudalism" refers both to the customs of the feudal elite and to the hierarchy among members of this group. Peasants were not part of the feudal hierarchy; the lowest-ranking member of the feudal elite was far superior to the highest-ranking peasant. See further discussion in chapter 2.

free peasant A peasant free of the restrictions and liabilities of *serfs*. Free peasants were allowed to emigrate, work, marry, and take grievances to the king's court. Freedom was determined by birth; if born to parents who were free, a person could claim free status.

friar A member of one of the mendicant ("begging") religious orders founded in the early thirteenth century. The most important of these were the Dominicans and Franciscans. Unlike monks and nuns who stayed within monasteries, friars often wandered the countryside, preaching and ministering to the faithful.

gleaning The practice of going over a harvested field to collect grain that the harvesters had missed. Traditionally, the right to glean was reserved for the young, the old, and the poor.

hayward Haywards were responsible for the fields of the manor. They supervised the work of *serfs* at harvest; they ensured that no one stole crops from the *demesne*; they checked that fences were maintained without gaps; and they impounded cattle or sheep that escaped from pastures. Haywards usually served under the direction of *reeves*.

heriot A payment made to the *manor* when an unfree tenant died. Traditionally, the heriot took the form of the *serf's* most valuable animal (the "best beast"), but the surviving members of the household often offered a cash payment instead. See also *mortuary*.

hue and cry A loud shout made by anyone who came upon the scene of a crime, so that others would help catch the wrongdoer. People who raised the hue and cry without good reason were fined in the manorial court, as were people who failed to respond.

jury A panel of six, twelve, or sometimes twenty-four jurors who either reported on misdoings in their community (a "jury of presentment") or judged a case put before them (a "trial jury"). Juries were used at all levels of the English court system, from manorial courts to royal courts. Except for special "juries of matrons" who assessed pregnancy, all jurors were male.

leyrwite A payment due to the *manor* from young women of *serf* status (and rarely, young men too) if they were found guilty of sex outside marriage.

manor An estate consisting of land and people. Owned by privileged people or institutions, manors were worked by peasants ("those who work") for the profit of owners. Although one person or institution might own several manors, each manor usually had its own court and own officials.

manorialism The economic system whereby *serfs* and *free peasants* (who lived on *manors*) supported the landowning elite.

merchet A payment made to the *manor* when a female *serf* (and rarely, a male serf) got married.

mortuary A payment made to the parish priest when someone died. Traditionally, the mortuary took the form of the deceased person's second most valuable animal (the best animal was given to the *manor* as a *heriot*). This payment was based on the theory that parishioners were unlikely to have paid all their tithes during their lifetimes, so the mortuary compensated for *tithes* unpaid. In some places mortuaries were charged on all deaths, wives and children included, while in other places they applied only to male householders.

nave The main area of a church, where the congregation gathered to hear services. The nave stretched between the *chancel* at the east end, where the priest celebrated Mass, and the bell tower at the west end. Through most of the Middle Ages, naves did not contain pews, so people stood or sat on the floor. The upkeep of the nave was the responsibility of the parishioners.

oblation A payment made to a priest in return for his services in baptizing, marrying, burying, or otherwise caring for a parishioner. In theory, the payment was voluntary, but it was customary and expected.

open fields Fields surrounding medieval villages in which many tenants held separate *strips* of land for growing crops. Because an open field was not divided by fences, only boundary stones or other markers separated the strips of various tenants. While open fields enabled easy plowing and planting, they were the subject of conflict in manorial courts; peasants often complained that boundary markers had been moved or that their neighbors had taken grain from the wrong strip.

parish The smallest geographical unit in the ecclesiastical system. In the early fourteenth century, England and Wales contained about nine thousand parishes, each under the religious authority of a parish priest and his assistants. For most ordinary people, parishes were the focus of worship and religious activity.

parish clerk A man hired to assist a parish priest at his duties, especially the reading and writing of documents.

parson Any priest responsible for a parish, whether a *rector* or *vicar*.

pence The plural of penny, the basic medieval coin. Twelve pence made a *shilling*; 240 pence made a *pound sterling*. In the fourteenth century, female laborers usually earned 1 penny or less for each day's work, whereas a male laborer got about 1½ pence. In documents, pence were abbreviated as d., short for the Latin word *denarius*.

pledge A person who guaranteed that another person would pay a stipulated fine or perform a specified obligation. If the fine remained unpaid or the obligation unfulfilled, the pledge was liable. Pledges were almost always men, and often they were men of high social standing on the *manor*.

pound sterling A monetary unit worth 240 *pence* or 20 *shillings*. The symbol for a pound sterling is £, which derives from the Latin word *libra*.

rector A priest or institution appointed to attend to the religious needs of members of a *parish*. Many rectors directly served their parishes as priests, but some lived away from their parishes and paid *vicars* to do their work for them. In Brigstock, the rector of the parish was an institution, the Abbey of Cirencester, and as a result, a vicar always did the day-to-day work of parochial care.

reeve After the *bailiff*, the most important officer on a *manor*. Reeves managed much of the daily business of the manor, such as making sure that the *demesne* lands were properly plowed, sown, and harvested, and that rents of leased portions of the demesne were duly paid. The reeve supervised the *hayward*.

rod A small measurement of land whose exact area varied slightly from place to place. In Brigstock, four rods made an acre.

serf An unfree peasant. Serfs were not allowed to move around from place to place; they were expected to work for the *manor* on a weekly basis (see *week-work*) and at special times of the year (see *boon-work*); and they had to pay various fines and fees to their manor on particular occasions (see *chevage, heriot, merchet, tallage*). Serfdom was determined by birth. If born to parents who were serfs, a person inherited the status of serf. In England, serfs were also called *villeins*.

shilling In the medieval monetary system, 12 pence. Twenty shillings made a *pound sterling*. In documents, a shilling was abbreviated as s., short for the Latin word *solidus*.

singlewoman The medieval term for a woman who never married. In the Middle Ages, the term "spinster" described a woman who worked at spinning wool into thread.

stocks Instruments of punishment in which the offender's feet or hands were tied or locked into a wooden frame. The offender was left on display in this position for a specified length of time. Millers and bakers who cheated their customers were particularly likely to be punished in this way.

strip A long narrow area of arable land within an *open field*. Strips were of varying widths and were demarcated by stones or other markers, not fences. Each family might hold one or more strips in several fields surrounding a village.

tallage A tax on *serfs* that could be levied at will by manorial lords or ladies. Sometimes tallage was assessed according to the amount of land or the number of animals a tenant held; on other occasions a set amount was charged per individual; and on still other occasions, tenants as a group were charged a particular amount and left to work out among themselves how to divvy up the expense.

three-field system A system of farming in which peasants rotated crops each year between three fields: the first field grew a winter crop such as wheat; the second grew a spring crop such as barley; and the third was unplanted (it lay *fallow*) to replenish the soil. The next year, the first field grew a spring crop, the second lay fallow, and the third was sown with a winter crop. The three-field system was an innovation of the High Middle Ages, an improvement on the *two-field system*.

three orders An idea, created and promoted by the medieval clergy, that society was composed of three interdependent and ranked groups: first, "those who pray" (priests, monks, nuns, bishops, and other religious professionals); second, "those who fight" (knights, ladies, and other members of the landowning classes); and last, "those who work" (peasants).

tithe An obligatory payment to the Church of 10 percent of all profits and produce. All members of society, from the wealthiest aristocrats to the poorest peasants, were expected to pay tithes.

tithing A group of men (originally, ten men) responsible for the behavior of each member. If a member of a tithing was accused of committing a crime, the other members had to ensure that he was brought before the manorial court for judgment. If they failed to produce their accused member, the entire tithing could be liable for punishment. Male peasants were sworn into tithings at the age of twelve.

tithingman The man in charge of a *tithing*. Tithingmen were elected annually and were often expected to serve on *juries* in manorial courts.

two-field system A system of farming in which peasants rotated crops each year between two fields: one field was planted with crops while the other was unplanted (it lay *fallow*) to replenish the soil. The next year, the planted field lay fallow while the fallow field was planted. In the eleventh century, many villages began to switch to the more efficient *three-field system*.

vicar A priest who stood in for an absent *rector* in doing the day-to-day work of looking after the religious needs a *parish*.

View of Frankpledge A special court convened twice a year (or sometimes once a year, as in Brigstock) to make sure that every male over the age of twelve was enrolled in a *tithing* and to punish people guilty of crimes and petty offenses.

village A cluster of peasant houses. Villages varied considerably in size, from small hamlets of only a few households to settlements of several hundred people. The boundaries of *manors* and *parishes* were not always the same as those of villages.

villein An English term for *serf.*

week-work The obligation of some *serfs* to work for a few days each week on the manorial *demesne*. Typical duties included plowing, sowing seed, mending farm buildings, carting dung, harvesting grain, and caring for animals. Serfs performing week-work were supervised by *reeves* and *haywards*.

INDEX

ACKNOWLEDGMENTS

For the reproductions from the Brigstock court rolls, I thank the archivists Matt Bazley and Crispin Powell for their assistance and the Duke of Buccleuch for his permission. For the photograph of the pots and jugs excavated at Stanion, I thank Andy Chapman.

I am very grateful to Ruth Karras and Jerry Singerman for giving me the opportunity to present this book to a new public. For their advice and encouragement, I also thank Michelle Armstrong-Partida, Lisa Bitel, Lyn Blanchfield, Kit French, Shennan Hutton, Kathleen Kamerick, Maryanne Kowaleski, Mary Lewis, Shannon McSheffrey, Kim Phillips, Miriam Shadis, Kate Staples, Blain Roberts, Merry Wiesner-Hanks, Laurel Wilson, Christopher Whittick, and Patrick Wyman. And for their extended comments on all the sections new to this edition, I especially thank Sandy Bardsley, Cynthia Herrup, and Ruth Karras.

I dedicated the earlier edition of this book to my much-loved niece Nicole Bennett, and I am happy to renew that dedication here, extending it also to her daughter and my namesake Maggie (Margaret Judith) Kocsis.